D0218248

QUALITATIVE RESEARCH IN EARLY CHILDHOOD SETTINGS

EDITED BY
J. Amos Hatch

WITHDRAWN

PRAEGER

Westport, Connecticut
London

LIBRARY-MEDIA CENTER
SOUTH PUGET SOUND COMM. COLLEGE
2011 MOTTMAN RD SW
OLYMPIA, WA 98512-6292

Library of Congress Cataloging-in-Publication Data

Qualitative research in early childhood settings / edited by J. Amos
  Hatch.
     p.   cm.
    Includes index.
    ISBN 0–275–94921–4 (alk. paper).—ISBN 0–275–95151–0 (pbk.)
     1. Child development—Research. 2. Early childhood education—
Research. 3. Child care—Research. 4. Action research in
education. I. Hatch, J. Amos.
    LB1119.Q35   1995
    372.21'072—dc20   94–32916

British Library Cataloguing in Publication Data is available.

Copyright © 1995 by J. Amos Hatch

All rights reserved. No portion of this book may be
reproduced, by any process or technique, without the
express written consent of the publisher.

Library of Congress Catalog Card Number: 94–32916
ISBN: 0–275–94921–4
     0–275–95151–0 (pbk.)

First published in 1995

Praeger Publishers, 88 Post Road West, Westport, CT 06881
An imprint of Greenwood Publishing Group, Inc.

Printed in the United States of America

The paper used in this book complies with the
Permanent Paper Standard issued by the National
Information Standards Organization (Z39.48–1984).

10 9 8 7 6 5 4 3 2

Copyright Acknowledgment

The author and publisher acknowledge the use of the following material:

Chapter 1, "The Emotional Culture of Infant-Toddler Day Care" by Robin L. Leavitt, is a
substantial revision of excerpts from a larger ethnographic study (Leavitt, 1994, *Power
and Emotion in Infant-Toddler Day Care*, Albany: State University of New York Press).

LIBRARY
SOUTH PUGET SOUND COMMUNITY COLLEGE
2011 MOTTMAN RD SW
OLYMPIA, WA 98512-6292

For Brett Alexander Hatch and Jeffrey Anson Hatch

P77806

Contents

Introduction: Qualitative Research in Early Childhood Settings

J. Amos Hatch

The purpose of this book is to collect under one cover a set of studies and essays that represent the best work being done in the area of qualitative research in early childhood settings. Early childhood takes in children from birth to about age eight, and research in this area involves studies of young children in educational contexts and a variety of day care and preschool settings. Traditionally, research in early childhood has been dominated by quantitative approaches with roots in developmental and behavioral psychology. Over the past decade, qualitative methods have been more widely used and accepted, and interest in qualitative approaches has grown rapidly. This book presents reports of research and discussions of methods, ethics, and theory building by scholars who are leading the way as new directions in early childhood research are being charted.

This project has its roots in a conference on Qualitative Studies in Early Childhood Contexts that I organized at the University of Tennessee in 1989. The conference attracted an exciting collection of scholars, and several of the papers from that conference were published in a special issue of the *International Journal of Qualitative Studies in Education* (Hatch & Wisniewski, 1990). The meetings stimulated the beginnings of an informal network of scholars interested in qualitative work in early childhood settings. That network has expanded and become associated with meetings on Reconceptualizing Research, Theory, and Practice in

Early Childhood Education that have been held annually since 1991. Many of the authors of this volume were involved in the Tennessee conference and/or are regulars at the Reconceptualizing meetings.

The audience for this book includes scholars doing early childhood research and graduate students and their instructors in general early childhood research courses, specialized early childhood qualitative research courses, and general qualitative research courses. Scholars doing qualitative work related to early childhood will see the book as a collection of cutting-edge studies and thought. In addition, practitioners and qualitative and quantitative scholars who work in early childhood as a field will have an interest in the findings reported in Part I ("Studies") of the book. Individuals working in the general area of qualitative research will be attracted to the essays in Part II ("Methods, Ethics, and Theory")

Some of the features that make the book attractive to a wide audience are that it includes: (1) research spanning the full range of early childhood settings, from infant and toddler day care to primary classrooms (making it of interest to scholars with academic homes in "education" and "human ecology" contexts); (2) papers written by authors who are respected and highly visible in the field; and (3) research topics, methods, and perspectives that are currently "hot" in early childhood and qualitative research. In addition, authors of chapters that report studies were asked to detail their methods and the contexts of their studies in an intentional effort to make the book accessible and helpful to novice qualitative researchers and researchers in training.

As I have put this volume together, I have tried to balance a complex array of factors in an effort to strengthen the contribution of the book to the literatures on early childhood and qualitative research. One set of factors was the tension between providing new scholars and others new to qualitative work with a helpful guide for getting started in the field while at the same time giving experienced scholars a stimulating and provocative collection that moves their understanding forward. Authors were asked to write for both audiences as they completed their chapters. As mentioned above, authors of studies were encouraged to include more details about how and where they did their studies than are usually found in article- or chapter-length manuscripts. At the same time, authors of methods, ethics, and theory chapters were asked to include specific examples from their own or others' work to make their cases clearer for scholars inexperienced with qualitative approaches. From my perspective as editor, this strategy has been successful. The ideas and findings discussed and reported are not reduced in complexity or depth, but enough detail and examples are included to make them accessible to more than a previously initiated few.

Another tension to be balanced was between presenting actual reports of research versus essays about doing research. Serving as the executive editor (with Richard Wisniewski) of the *International Journal of Qualitative Studies in Education* for the past three years, I have thought about this issue a great deal. On the one hand, publication priority ought to be given to reports of studies since such reports are the stuff of a research journal or a collection like this; on the other, readers are hungry to learn more about the hows and whys of doing qualitative research. A roughly equal balance has been reached in the collection. In fact, several of the chapters include enough presentation of findings and exposition of methods, ethics, and theory that they could have been included in either Part I or Part II.

A final set of tensions was between including more traditional or more avant-garde approaches to qualitative work in early childhood settings. My guess is that, for many readers, all of the chapters in this book will represent avant-garde thinking; the application of qualitative methods is just beginning to be accepted by the larger early childhood research community. I wanted this book to be helpful to those individuals just beginning their efforts to move away from the dominant quantitative paradigm. The volume includes work, however, that challenges the limits of more mainstream qualitative thinking. In Part II especially, chapters move across the spectrum from the more traditional "anthropological" approach I take in my essay, "Studying Childhood as a Cultural Invention," to a more radical "post-modern" approach Joseph Tobin uses in his "Post-Structural Research in Early Childhood Education." The balance could never be perfect on any of the dimensions discussed, but the effort makes for a book that is both challenging and accessible.

Part I of this volume presents reports of qualitative studies completed in early childhood contexts. The studies included offer examples of work undertaken from a variety of perspectives. The research examines a variety of social phenomena that impact on children and their teachers and caregivers. Five studies that span the early childhood age range and a research review are included.

Chapter 1, "The Emotional Culture of Infant-Toddler Day Care," is a powerful description and interpretive analysis of the everyday experiences of infants and toddlers in day care settings. Robin Leavitt gathered participant-observation data over a seven-year period. Her analysis of the emotional culture of infant and toddler day care reveals situations in which the management of children by caregivers often takes precedence over meeting the children's emotional needs. Children learn to manage their feelings and emotional expressions to correspond with adult expectations—that is, to deny their feelings and suppress emotional expression. The chapter exposes dimensions of emotional socialization in infant and toddler settings that are troubling and important to understand.

In Chapter 2, "Family Day Care as Mothering: A Study of Providers' Perspectives," Margaret Nelson presents her examination of the experiences of family day care providers. Using questionnaire and extensive interview data, the study shows how providers construct an ideal of good care based on mothering as an analogy. This ideal downplays training and the provision of structured programs while emphasizing love and affection. The research reveals that the emphasis on mothering leaves providers vulnerable and ill-prepared to cope with failure.

The study by Maike Philipsen and Jo Agnew, "Heart, Mind, and Soul: Head Start as a Reminder of the Powerful Function of Schools for Their Communities," is reported in Chapter 3. The study combines two analyses that were part of a larger qualitative study of a poor, rural community in North Carolina. The Philipsen and Agnew chapter compares the experiences of children who participate in a Head Start program in their community with those of older students who must attend schools in other communities. The study demonstrates the consequences for the town's African-American community when it lost its schools to consolidation and desegregation efforts.

Mary Hauser uses a narrative approach to describe the life history and teaching practices of a first grade teacher. In Chapter 4, "Life History of a First Grade Teacher: A Narrative of Culturally Sensitive Teaching Practice," she tells the story of a teacher in a multiethnic school. Interview and participant observation methods were used to construct the narrative accounts in the research. The study presents exemplary classroom practices that the teacher uses to manage the complexities of teaching children from multiple language backgrounds.

In Chapter 5, "Policy Issues in the Development of Child Care and Early Education Systems: The Need for Cross-National Comparison," Sally Lubeck presents a comparison between child care and education systems in the United States and the now former German Democratic Republic. The chapter is a model for applying cross-national policy analysis in areas involving young children and their families. The study demonstrates that the policies of nations create different developmental contexts for children and that understanding the processes through which these macro-contexts are socially constructed can improve our abilities to influence policymaking in our own nations.

Chapter 6, "Qualitative Research in Early Childhood Settings: A Review," is a review of the research literature by Pamela Browning and me. The review is organized into sections by age level: pre-kindergarten, kindergarten, and primary. Studies in each section are described in terms of methods, contexts, and the nature of their findings. Publications that discuss methods and ethics specific to qualitative studies in early childhood settings are reviewed, and an appendix listing general qualitative research texts cited in the studies reviewed is included.

Part II is a collection of essays exploring methods, ethics, and theory in early childhood qualitative research and evaluation studies. In Chapter 7, "Studying Childhood as a Cultural Invention: A Rationale and Framework," I critique contemporary early childhood research and offer a framework for studying childhood as a cultural invention. The case is made that themes that have dominated child study since the end of the nineteenth century continue to strongly influence mainstream research. An alternative research framework based on constructivism is presented and contrasted with the firmly entrenched positivist paradigm.

Chapter 8 is Elizabeth Graue's and Daniel Walsh's paper, "Children in Context: Interpreting the Here and Now of Children's Lives." The chapter is organized around the idea that studying the contexts in which children operate every day has been neglected in traditional quantitative approaches. The authors define context as a culturally and historically situated place and time, a specific here and now. They offer suggestions for using interpretive strategies to study children in context.

Chapter 9, "Learning from Classroom Ethnographies: Same Places, Different Times," is a description of an ongoing ethnographic research project at the Ohio State University laboratory school. Three of the principal researchers in the project, David Fernie, Rebecca Kantor, and Kimberlee Whaley, provide a summary of some of the findings from studies in the preschool and infant-toddler programs, and they discuss the evolution of their research program and what they have learned from collaboratively studying peer culture and socialization in these settings.

Beth Blue Swadener and Monica Miller Marsh are the authors of Chapter 10, "Toward a Stronger Teacher Voice in Research: A Collaborative Study of Antibias Early Education." In this chapter, they use their collaborative examination of the implementation of an antibias curriculum to demonstrate the evolution of their collaborative research relationship. They discuss the importance of antibias curriculum work and detail the successes and challenges of collaborations between university-based and classroom-based researchers.

Chapter 11, "Multiple Voices, Contexts, and Methods: Making Choices in Qualitative Evaluation in Early Childhood Education Settings," by Mary Jo McGee-Brown is an exploration of qualitative evaluation research in early childhood education. Based in the literature on qualitative evaluation, the chapter outlines procedures and illuminates decision points necessary for doing qualitative evaluations in early childhood education settings. The essay is a primer for understanding and initiating evaluation work from a qualitative perspective.

In Chapter 12, "Ethical Conflicts in Classroom Research: Examples from a Study of Peer Stigmatization in Kindergarten," I describe ethical conflicts related to doing classroom qualitative research with young children. Based on the ethical problematics of one study, I discuss the ethical paradox of studying, but not intervening to help, children who are experiencing difficulties in the classroom. I describe factors that keep researchers from confronting ethical issues as they go about doing their studies, concluding that more awareness of motives and assumptions on the part of researchers and more involvement of participants in research design and decision making can reduce the chances that researchers will use children and other research participants to serve their own ends.

Chapter 13 is Joseph Tobin's "Post-Structural Research in Early Childhood Education." This chapter is well-placed at the end of the volume because I believe it points to the future of qualitative scholarship and of early childhood qualitative research. Tobin presents a set of post-structuralist concepts and applies these to early childhood research, using his own studies as examples. The essay offers an interesting and energetic introduction of post-structuralist thought and concludes by inviting early childhood education researchers to consider the power of applying post-structuralist analyses to their work.

The goal in putting this book together has been to assemble a collection that represents state-of-the-art thinking and research in early childhood settings. Collecting and editing the manuscripts have reminded me of the rapidity of change in our world and our scholarly work. Ten years ago, after I completed one of the first qualitative dissertations done in my college, I was a participant in the great paradigm war between the positivists and the constructivists—the Quantoids and the Smooshes (Hatch, 1985). There were few qualitative sessions at the American Education Research Association (AERA) meetings, and the *Educational Researcher* was full of salvos fired across the paradigm lines.

It feels to some of us like we won the war. Has qualitative research taken over the high ground and become what Kuhn (1970, p. 10) called "normal science"? A quick look at the AERA program, a careful reading of recent issues of the *Educational Researcher*, or an examination of other AERA journals would indicate that qualitative research is at least holding its own. One indicator that qualitative work is closer to the mainstream is that it is now being challenged by alternative paradigms. Postmodern and post-structuralist conceptions of how the world is ordered, or not ordered, and of appropriate ways to "know" the world are challenging ontological and epistemological assumptions upon which traditional qualitative work is based.

"State-of-the-art" has a shorter and shorter shelf life in all aspects of our experience, including our own scholarship. It is hoped that this volume will move a relatively new field forward and that its readers will have a firmer foundation from which to contribute to tomorrow's state-of-the-art research in early childhood contexts.

REFERENCES

Hatch, J. A. (1985). The quantoids versus the smooshes: Struggling with methodological rapprochement. *Issues in Education, 3*, 158–167.

Hatch, J. A., & Wisniewski, R. (Eds.) (1990). Qualitative studies in early childhood contexts. Special issue, *International Journal of Qualitative Studies in Education, 3*, 209–302.

Kuhn, T. S. (1970). *The structure of scientific revolutions*. 2nd ed. Chicago: University of Chicago Press.

Part I

Studies

Chapter 1

The Emotional Culture of Infant-Toddler Day Care

Robin L. Leavitt

Day care centers are interpersonal contexts in which children feel and express their emotions and interpret their emotional experiences.[1] In these pages, I tell stories emerging from a long-term investigation of problematic emotional experience within infant-toddler day care centers. Through the presentation of field note excerpts, I describe an absence of reciprocity and empathy as emotionally alienated caregivers go through the motions of caring for children. This emotional estrangement is discussed in terms of the caregivers' emotional labor—caring activity sold for a wage. I contend that these epiphanic emotional moments profoundly and negatively affect the meanings children assign to themselves, others, and their worlds.

The growing number of infants and toddlers in day care centers and the lack of research addressing their lived experiences point to the importance of this investigation. The most dramatic growth in the child day care population has been among our youngest children—those under three years of age (Friedman, 1990; Neugebauer, 1994). The relationships these children have with their caregivers and their daily emotional *experiences* within these programs have been greatly neglected in the research to date (see Leavitt, 1994; Guttentag, 1987).

The study described in this chapter focuses on children's daily experiences. The presentation and interpretation of field notes are preceded by a brief elaboration of the theoretical and methodological perspectives guiding this investigation and the specifics of data collection. The body of the paper provides concurrent illustration and discussion; that is, description and interpretation of field notes are interwoven.

THEORETICAL PERSPECTIVE

The perspective on emotions and emotional experience applied here draws from interpretive and interactionist theories associated with the works of Denzin (1977, 1984, 1985, 1990a), Goffman (1967), Gordon (1981, 1985, 1989), Harre (1986), Hochschild (1979, 1983), Lewis and Saarni (1985), Power (1985, 1986), Saarni and Harris (1989), Sartre (1939/62, 1943/56), Shott (1979), and others. *Emotions* are understood as persons' self-feelings, experienced bodily, consciously, and in persons' social worlds (Denzin, 1984). Emotions are "emerging acts under construction and definition by the individual" (Gordon, 1985, p. 141), "grounded in the practical activities that locate individuals in the world" (Denzin, 1984, p. 32). *Emotional culture* is "a group's set of daily beliefs, vocabulary, regulative norms, and other ideational resources pertaining to emotion" (Gordon, 1989, p. 322). I add "daily practices" to this definition, as they provide the settings for emotional interaction and are indicative of these beliefs and norms.

Children's emotional socialization is intricately tied to the emergence of their social selves (Gordon, 1985). Infants are immediately drawn into the emotional culture; their gestures, cries, vocalizations, and actions call out to their caregivers. As parents, siblings, and strangers respond, infants become partners in the give and take of human relationships (Saarni, 1989; Snow, 1989). These reciprocal relationships, formed and grounded in interactive episodes, are the nexus of socialization. As Pawl (1990a, 1990b) noted, it is in the context of relationships that the needs and wishes of very young children are met, or not. It is in the context of relationships that infants and toddlers continue to develop expectations about how the world is, how adults in that world behave, and their own place in the social world.

While children are active participants in their socialization, the meanings they assign to their experiences and feelings are largely dependent on the meanings given to them through their caregivers' responses and gestures. To a great extent, children come to see and feel about themselves as they perceive their primary caregivers to feel about them.[2] Caregivers, then, are significant emotional associates in children's lives, defining the emotional culture in which children develop understandings about themselves, others, and their worlds.

In this study, I examine minor epiphanic emotional experiences for children in the care of adults who manage their daily activities and routines. Epiphanic experience refers to those moments in the lives of children and their caregivers which may seem insignificant in themselves and their temporality, but which may be symbolically representative of major tensions, conflicts, or ruptures in their relationships (Denzin, 1989a). I contend that these epiphanic emotional experiences profoundly affect, momentarily and cumulatively, the meanings children give to themselves and their present and later experiences.

METHODOLOGICAL PERSPECTIVE

Emotions and emotional relationships are not static phenomena: "They cannot be taken out of context, classified, and quantified. They are processual . . . grounded in both time and place" (Power, 1986, p. 261). Developing an understanding of children's emotional experiences necessitates entering their social worlds—in this case, the child care center. The methodological perspective of this investigation is, therefore, also primarily interpretive and interactionist (see, among others, Blumer, 1969; Caputo, 1987; Denzin, 1989a, 1989b; Mills, 1959; Packer, 1985; Sartre, 1960/63; Van Manen, 1990). Through description and interpretation, the situated lived experiences of the children and their caregivers are made meaningful and understandable by bringing them before the reader (Denzin, 1989a).

In general, interpretive and interactionist theories posit the fundamentally relational, social aspect of our existence and the inescapable fact that human beings are part of the world they study. Children and their caregivers are meaning-makers engaged in joint acts and are constructed and constrained by the specific and at-large social situations in which they find themselves. Interpretations and understandings of situated, ongoing, everyday life experiences of particular individuals are developed within the immediate contexts in which they occur. Far from being detached and neutral, interpretation begins from concerned engagement (Packer & Addison, 1989a, 1989b). The understandings that emerge are viewed as social constructions, value-laden, historically specific, grounded in experience, and always incomplete.

My immersion into the worlds of the infants and toddlers I discuss here involved more than seven years of participant-observation in twelve infant and toddler classrooms in six licensed day care centers.[3] I observed in these programs every week as I supervised practicum students. In addition to my own observations, a considerable number of field notes was recorded by practicum and independent study students enrolled in the university's child care training program. Observations occurred throughout the day, from children's arrival until their departure. Participatory involvement in these classrooms included having conversations with caregivers, talking and playing with the children, holding and comforting crying babies, intervening when safety was threatened, and helping out in whatever ways I could when situations became hectic.

The field notes herein represent repeatedly observed situations, within and across all these centers over the years, and provide the foundation for my interpretations and understandings. By their presentation, I invite the reader to see, hear, and experience what my students and I have witnessed. I have, at times, drawn composite pictures, combining two or three similar incidents. I readily admit to the poeticizing activity and evocative intent of interpretive ethnographic research (Clifford, 1986; Van Manen, 1990). I have attempted to be faithful to the words and gestures of those observed, yet recognize that there are considerable experience, thought, and emotion that exist beyond this narrative which cannot be represented directly (Clifford, 1986; Denzin, 1990b; Tyler, 1986). The aim is to describe what there is that seems to matter (Coles, 1967).

EMOTIONAL CULTURE: DAILY PRACTICES

The day care center is, for the children described herein, their lived and felt space for up to ten hours each day. All the aspects of these children's lives—sleeping, playing, and eating—are conducted in one place and according to the shared authority of two or three caregivers. The children's experiences are dictated primarily by schedules of custodial routines, although play may be allowed between these events (Leavitt, 1991, 1994). These daily routines are teeming with possibilities for emotional interactions. Consider the following situations recorded before and after lunchtime:

The caregiver had gathered the toddlers together on the carpet for a story before lunch. About halfway through the story, she stopped reading and told Caleb to go wash his hands and face. He shook his head and said "No!" The caregiver told Caleb he had to go. He protested again. The caregiver put down her book, picked up Caleb and carried him to the bathroom, as the other children watched. Caleb cried and struggled throughout this process, during which I suggested to the caregiver that Caleb might want to hear the rest of the story before washing up. She responded, "His face is dirty. He has to wash up." The other children waited for the caregiver to return. When they returned to the group, the caregiver resumed reading the story, interrupting herself periodically to call on other children to wash. Caleb sat with a frown on his face and did not show interest in the story.

When the toddlers were done eating their lunch, they were reminded to stay seated until called to wash their hands and brush their teeth. They were called in the order they finished eating. Several children finished eating about the same time, so some of them waited a long time to be called, doing nothing but sitting. When a toddler got up out of his chair, he was told to go back and sit down until he was called. Carrie, on her own initiative, got out of her seat and waited by the sink. The caregiver refused to let Carrie wash her hands and brush her teeth because she hadn't waited to be called. Carrie began to cry; it was clear that she was quite upset. The caregiver told Carrie she needed to sit down until she was called. Carrie continued to cry; the caregiver did not try to comfort Carrie or help her back to her seat. After about five more minutes of continued crying, the caregiver told Carrie to lie down on her cot, without washing or brushing.

In repeated situations such as these, the management of children takes precedence over their emotional selves. Caregivers appear emotionally disengaged; they seem to go through the motions of managing children's routines, as if only children's bodies and physical needs required attention. Consider the field notes below:

The toddlers were required to be quiet, and sit with their hands on their laps before they were served lunch. They were not allowed or encouraged to serve themselves. Some children were refused food until they stopped making "noise." Some had been crying, others were talking. The adults talked to each other while they served the food and during lunchtime. No reasons were given to the children about why they shouldn't talk. When the children's plates were empty, they were given more food, without being asked first. Afterwards, their plates were taken away, also without consulting them.

Lena (5 months) was sitting on the floor playing with some toys. The caregiver decided to change her diaper and approached Lena from behind, abruptly and wordlessly picked her up, and laid her on the changing table. Lena squirmed while being changed. The caregiver did not talk to Lena or give her a toy to hold onto and distract her. A few times Lena gurgled and cooed. The caregiver did not respond. She changed Lena's diaper without looking at her face; the caregiver's movements seemed almost robotic, without expression. When finished with the task, she put Lena back down on the floor, also without a word.

In these episodes, social relations between the children and their caregivers are atomized and fragmented. They share a common field of activity, but are emotionally isolated. Caregivers interact *at* rather than *with* children, although, as in the excerpt below, caregivers interact with each other.

It was nap time. The adults sat in the room and talked with each other. They did not lower their voices. Toddlers who were unable to sleep lay on their cots unattended by the caregivers. As more children started to wake up, the adults continued to sit and talk with each other. When the toddlers sought attention from the adults, looking toward and calling to them, they were ignored or dismissed. The children were required to stay on their cots, silent and waiting.

The negative reciprocity of this situation is apparent in the caregivers' external preoccupation. The children's attempts to communicate with their caregivers were ignored, discounted, or denied. To the extent caregivers are unconnected with the children present and regard them as "nonpersons" (Goffman, 1967), children are objectified (see Leavitt and Power, 1989). To be objectified "is to be totalized, defined, judged, limited—incorporated into a system of ends that one has not chosen—and at the mercy of an alien consciousness" (Schroeder, 1984, p. 176). The field notes below illustrate:

The toddlers were playing in the large motor area. Three caregivers sat on the floor watching the children play. Two-year-old Vicki arrived with her mother, who told the caregivers Vicki had been awake since 3:30 that morning. Vicki sat and absently watched the others; she did not respond to the adults' initiations. Her eyes started to close. One caregiver said to another that if Vicki fell asleep before lunch, she wouldn't sleep during nap time. Suddenly, this caregiver grabbed Vicki from behind and shook her, saying, "Wake up, Vicki, wake up!" Vicki began to cry. The caregiver told her, "But Vicki, if you sleep now, you won't take your nap." Vicki continued to scream and cry. The caregiver said, "Vicki, stop it now, no reason to cry."

In the above situation, Vicki was at the "mercy" of her caregiver who failed to recognize and respond to Vicki's physical and emotional state. Vicki was to be managed according to the "system of ends"—the daily schedule—which had little relation to her own individual needs and choices. In this way, she was objectified, alienated, and left powerless. The excerpt below describes a similar situation:

I was sitting on the floor reading books to some of the children when Marissa (22 months) arrived this morning. Apparently her mother left her in the hallway outside the room door and Marissa started screaming. The caregiver brought Marissa into the room and shut the door. Marissa threw herself on the floor, screaming and kicking. The caregiver matter-of-factly told her to stop crying, but Marissa continued. The caregiver tried to get Marissa's snowsuit off but had a difficult time as Marissa continued to cry and did not cooperate. As the caregiver pulled the last leg off, Marissa arched her back so that she fell backwards onto the floor and hit her head. Her screaming escalated in volume and intensity. The caregiver, who had been wordless throughout the undressing, put Marissa's suit away and said, "Stop it already, Marissa." Marissa continued to cry. The second caregiver, who had been sitting nearby at a table cutting paper, rose from her chair and wordlessly grabbed Marissa by her forearm, lifted her off the floor, carried her to the hallway, returned to the room without Marissa, slammed the door, and said, "That is so we don't kill her." We could hear Marissa continue to scream through the door. A few minutes later the first caregiver went out to bring Marissa back into the room. Marissa was left by the door, inside now, screaming. The adults ignored her. Unable to refrain from intervening, I went over to Marissa and asked her, "Would you like me to hold you?" She nodded her head "yes" in response.

I picked her up and she immediately stopped crying. I continued to comfort her, and eventually engaged her in some play.

   This child's separation from her parent was a stressful one this day, as it often is for toddlers. The mother might have come into the room with her child, but since she did not, a challenge was presented for the caregivers. The caregivers failed to acknowledge Marissa's feelings with a simple statement such as, "You're upset your mom left you in the hall. Come on in and let's see what I can do to help you to feel better." Instead, the caregivers continued to manipulate Marissa bodily, rejected her emotionally, and failed to explain their actions.

   The caregivers in the situations described failed to project themselves empathetically into the children's worlds. The empathic capacity involves connecting one's own experience to that of others, and through that connection, gaining understanding of their feelings.[4] Caregivers merely have to imagine the realness of the children's experiences for themselves, to consider how things might look and feel to the child (Denzin, 1984).[5] The following field notes provide a (rarely observed) contrast to the situations thus far described:

Avon (8 weeks) needed his diaper changed. Once on the changing table he began to cry. The caregiver explained to Avon that he needed his diaper changed, but Avon persisted in his crying. The caregiver tried again to calm him by telling him he was dirty and that she was going to change him and make him feel comfortable again. Avon continued to cry hard. The caregiver then stopped the diaper changing process and rubbed Avon's tummy in an attempt to soothe him. In a soothing tone she told Avon there was no need to be upset or afraid, she only wanted to make him more comfortable. As Avon calmed, the caregiver told him she needed to take off his clothes because they were wet. She proceeded to do this, then cleaned him up and put a fresh diaper and clothes on. All the while she continued to talk soothingly to Avon, with comments such as "I think you're all clean now," and "Gee, I hope these p.j.'s fit you." By the time she had finished, Avon was a clean, happy baby again.

   This caregiver attempted to view the experience from the child's perspective, to consider how the world seemed to appear and feel to Avon. She respected, rather than discounted or denied, Avon's feelings and responded with soothing reassurances. Such situations contrast dramatically with those in which emotional disengagement inhibits caregivers' abilities to comprehend and respond to the perspectives of children. This inability, in turn, further disengages them from the children. As Hochschild (1983) wrote, "it is from feeling that we learn the self-relevance of what we see, remember, or imagine" (p. 196). "When we lose access to feeling, we lose a central means of interpreting the world around us" (p. 188).

EMOTIONAL CULTURE: REGULATIVE NORMS

"Regulative norms" pertaining to emotion in these day care centers emerge in the daily practices of caregivers and are made clear over time and with repeated experience. In recurring emotional episodes, children learn from their caregivers what is acceptable and unacceptable behavior; they learn what Hochschild (1979, 1983) calls the "feelings rules" and how to do "emotion work," that is, to manage their feelings and emotional expressions to correspond with the adults' expectations. These norms include prohibitions against crying, against initiating interactions, and against soliciting attention, affection, and comfort. Children are taught to deny their feelings and suppress their emotional expressions.

A dominant regulative norm, or feeling rule, in these infant-toddler centers is that children are not to cry. Yet crying is a primary way nonverbal infants and toddlers express their feelings; they need to know they are accepted by adults even when they cry. But caregivers seemed to have little tolerance for children's crying, as suggested in the field notes presented thus far, and those below.

Letitia (8 months) had been lying on the carpet playing. After a while, she started to cry. The caregiver, who was not involved with other infants, yelled from her chair, "Letitia! Be quiet!" Startled, Letitia stopped crying momentarily, but began again. No one made another effort to calm her. I finally decided to pick her up myself, which quieted her.

Rory (17 months) cried as his mother left the room. His crying escalated as he pressed his face to the window in the door. Occasionally he turned around to look at the two caregivers, who ignored him. Rory's face and eyes were red. After ten minutes a caregiver went and stood over him, commanding, "Calm down!" Rory stopped crying, looked at her, she looked at him, and he resumed his crying. She told him again to calm down. He continued to cry. She walked away, saying "someone take me out of here!" After another fifteen minutes the center director, having noticed the scene through the windows, entered the room and picked up and held Rory. He quieted immediately. She stayed with him, and after a few minutes was able to interest him in some toys. Still teary-eyed and whimpering, he gradually responded.

In this instance, one caregiver (the director) was willing to attend to and comfort Rory, illustrating the power of a responsive caregiver to calm, soothe, and redirect an unhappy toddler. This occurred, however, only after an extended period of inattention and rejection, and expressions of impatience by his primary caregiver. In another incident:

The toddlers were playing, except for Kyle (15 months) who was crying. As the toddler approached her, the caregiver knelt down, put her hands on Kyle's shoulders and said, "You must learn to smile. You're always crying. I'm not picking you up." She walked away from Kyle. He followed her and reached out to hold onto her leg. The caregiver, exasperated, said, "Will you just go away? Turn it off. I don't want to hear it." The child continued to stand there and cry.

The emotion work this caregiver expected from Kyle—learn to smile on demand; suppress your negative emotions—not only demonstrated her emotional insensitivity, but failed to help Kyle understand his emotions as he learns to manage them. It appears that caregivers are primarily interested in children's surface behaviors, not their feelings (Power, 1985). That toddlers *can* learn to control their emotions, or emotional expressions, to some extent is not at dispute here. The issue is whether adults *ought* to expect them to, and in what ways, and with what consequences. In these situations, children's emotional beings, their emotional expressions and responses, appear irrelevant. As a result, children's emotions were ignored, suppressed, denied, and left unclarified as they learned to reconstruct their behavior and emotional expressions in accord with the caregivers' demands. These young children learn very early the regulative norms pertaining to their emotional expressions and needs.

EMOTIONAL CULTURE: CAREGIVER BELIEFS

The regulative norms of the day care center are tied to caregivers' beliefs about children's behaviors and emotions, and their own roles as caregivers.[6] The idea that caregivers should be emotionally involved with children is contradicted by the expectation that they be "professional"—understood as an emotionally neutral role (Murphy, 1992; Power, 1987).[7] And so, as the field notes below demonstrate, caregivers distance themselves from children's emotional lives (White, 1983).

As I entered the room, Clarke (12 months) toddled over to me crying, tears streaming down his face. The caregiver was a few feet away, standing over the other five children playing on the carpet. I knelt to talk to Clarke. He reached out his arms to me, still crying. I said, "I think you need a hug," and held him. He quieted and clung to me. This was our first meeting—we were strangers. As I held Clarke, the caregiver matter-of-factly told me he had been crying all morning. She explained that he recently had been at his grandmother's, who, she believed, "held him all the time." She suggested that this was why he wanted to be held. But, she told me, she was not going to hold Clarke. When I left for the day I put Clarke down, and he began to cry vehemently again, despite my efforts to comfort him.

Janine (11 months) was standing outside her crib reaching into it through the bars. She was whimpering quietly. The longer she stood there the more frustrated she became. I walked over and saw that she was reaching for her pacifier. When I gave it to her, the caregiver took it away, saying she couldn't have it. Janine began to cry. When I asked the caregiver why Janine wasn't allowed to have her pacifier, she explained it was because Janine would share it with the other babies. To prevent this she was only allowed to have her pacifier in her crib. Although Janine continued to cry, she was not placed in her crib with the pacifier, or given a substitute object. Neither did the caregiver attempt to distract her by inviting her to play.

Kara (4 months) was crying. She lifted her arms up to me, her eyes brimming with tears. As I reached down to her, the caregiver said to me, "Don't pick her up. She does that to everyone at first. We don't need to spoil her." Kara continued to cry. I hugged her briefly and then tried to interest her in a toy. She continued to cry. The caregivers ignored her.

Kara may "do that to everyone at first," that is, reach out to every adult newcomer in the classroom, because she, like Janine and Clarke, have learned that her primary caregivers are emotionally unavailable to her. Kara continues to reach out to other adults in the search for one to whom she can turn for emotional sustenance and comfort.

"People act toward emotions according to the meanings they impute to them" (Gordon, 1985, p. 141; see also Blumer, 1969; Denzin, 1984). In the situations above, the caregivers were aware of the infants' emotional states, but they discounted, diminished, and disregarded the intensity and realness of children's feelings (see Reynolds, 1990). Caregivers were not too busy with other children or tasks, but, as a matter of principle—of belief in the myth of "spoiling"—they refused to respond. For these caregivers, the children's emotions had no legitimacy, meaning, or significance; children were rejected, abandoned, and emotionally isolated.

Caregivers' reactions to children also indicate a belief in children's abilities to control their behaviors and emotional expressions to either conform to, or willfully resist, adults' expectations:

Jolie (20 months) asked the practicum student to take her to the bathroom. Once there, the student discovered Jolie's pants were soaking wet. The student removed the toddler's clothes and helped her onto the toilet. While Jolie sat, the student related what happened to the caregiver, asking her to bring over some clean, dry clothing. The caregiver brought the clothes and tossed them on the floor by the child. Jolie looked up at the caregiver, who looked at her with disapproval and anger, saying, "Yuk, Jolie! I don't like what you are doing! Don't go to the bathroom in your pants. That is yukky!" She left without waiting for a response. The student finished dressing Jolie, who looked upset and bewildered.

Alex (18 months) responded to a conflict by biting another toddler, who promptly returned the bite. The caregiver told Alex that he "deserved" to be bitten. Alex was then punished by being placed in "time out." Afterwards, Alex approached the caregiver, indicating he wanted to be held. The caregiver refused, saying she "didn't want to" hold him.

The two caregivers above did not seem to consider developmental explanations for the children's behavior, or the consequences of their own responses. For example, biting is, although inappropriate, an age-typical behavior in toddlers with limited verbal ability to express their feelings of anger and frustration. Toileting is a skill that emerges over time and has as much to do with a child's physical development as it does with motivation. The adults' responses did not help the children to understand or change their behavior. Moreover, the adults refused to explain their actions or acknowledge and respond to the children's feelings. When caregivers are not responsive, children's emotions, and thus their *selves*, are denied legitimation.

Liljestrom's (1983) observation suggests another belief which may influence caregivers' responses to the children. She noted that, as a society, we degrade emotional life; emotions are considered irrational, private, and "childish" in the negative sense. It appears that even children may not be allowed this childishness. Punishment, by way of rejection, withholding of affection, refusal to forgive and comfort, as well as by other means (e.g., "time out"), was a common response of caregivers to children's emotional expressions.

Paul (2 years) was brought crying and screaming to the infant room. Apparently he had been spitting. The caregiver told him that if he was going to "act like a baby then [he] will be with the babies." She left him in a corner of the room by the changing table, where he continued to cry and shake. Another caregiver continued to call him a baby.

In this situation, the caregivers failed not only to offer support and understanding, but shamed and punished Paul for expressing his emotions. Like Jolie and Alex, who sought understanding, foregiveness, and comfort, the children in these situations have, in essence, been emotionally abandoned. In this way, children's emotional socialization takes place within the interplay of caregivers' beliefs (conscious or unconscious) and the regulative norms emerging in the daily practices of the day care center.

EMOTIONAL CULTURE: EMOTIONAL LABOR

The emotional culture of infant-toddler day care is influenced not only by the caregivers' beliefs and practices, but by their own experience of their work—their attempts to negotiate the terrain of caregiving. Loseke (1989) writes about family day care providers: "Regardless of the ideal that [caregivers] should be mothers who love the children they care for, economic transactions transform [them] into employees and necessarily distinguish them from mothers" (p. 323). As day care employees, caregivers are responsible for many babies close in age and confined to one place; they share their work with other non-related adult caregivers, and they are accountable to supervisors, parents, and state licensing agencies. Generally isolated from adult society, caregivers' days are filled with the constant crying of infants and their constant, unpredictable and demanding needs. Daily, caregivers face the drudgery of repeating routine tasks such as diaper changing and feeding. The competing and simultaneous demands placed on caregivers, as well as the lack of personal and institutional resources to meet them, compound the problematics of negotiating care. Caregivers' emotional distancing may evolve partly as attempts to resist the practical constraints imposed on them.

As caregivers' *work*, infants in day care become the objects of the caregivers' labor. As caregivers' work, emotional responsiveness becomes *emotional labor*: the publicly observable management of feelings sold for a wage (Hochschild, 1983). Emotional labor requires caregivers to induce or suppress feeling in order to sustain the appropriate surface appearances of expected emotions. Within this emotional labor lies the potential for negative reciprocity, estrangement, emotional disengagement, and alienation from oneself and others. In Noddings' words, "Caring disappears and only its illusion remains" (1984, p. 26).

To some extent, the emotional labor of caregivers is inherent to their task. In contrast to the mutual caring possible in adult relationships, "children cannot reciprocate care equally, they require a degree of selflessness and attention that is specific to them" (Grimshaw, 1986, p. 253). To be other-directed for such long hours can put considerable strain on the most well-intentioned caregivers' emotional capacities to care for children. The stress is compounded as caregivers are expected to develop a sense of investment in each child that enables them to sustain caring throughout each day and over time, but also release children each day to their parents, then every several months relinquish them to another set of caregivers. In short, caregivers are expected to emotionally engage intensely, to disengage gracefully, and to do both upon demand (Zigler & Lang, 1991).

The challenge presented for caregivers, then, centers on their ability to maintain their own sense of well-being while caring for the children (Gilligan, 1982; Hochschild, 1983). Too often, the pleasure may seem to belong all to the children; the caregiver may feel "conned" by the mythical lure of emotionally satisfying child caregiving. As the field notes below illustrate, the child care center can become a site of hostile and painful feelings in which the caregiver confronts the child as a hostile object (Rose, 1986):

Two caregivers sat on the floor with four infants. Alan (7 months) crawled over to them, excited. One caregiver said to him, "No, I don't want you—you weigh a ton. No Alan, you tub, get out of the way!" Then she said, "Go to Martha" [the other caregiver]. When Alan looked toward Martha, she said to him, "No-o-o, not me Alan, just stay there." Alan looked confused. Then the first caregiver lifted him into the playpen and said, "You play in here, Alan," and turned away. Alan tried to climb out of the playpen, but was yelled at.

The caregiver was giving Brad (6 months) his afternoon bottle. Brad was in an infant seat on a small table and the caregiver was seated in a chair beside it holding onto the bottle. Brad was drinking his milk slowly, gazing at the ceiling where mobiles hung. The caregiver repeatedly jabbed the bottle in and out of Brad's mouth and moved it back and forth, saying, "Come on, Brad, you're not the only baby in the world or in this room. Stop messing around and get to drinking."

As caregivers attempt to cope with the emotional labor of their work, they may withhold themselves and their own emotionality as an act of self-protection. Unable to draw upon their own capacity for feeling, caregivers are then unable to respond to the children empathetically. Caregivers react to children's demands passively; they stop caring and become remote and detached (Hochschild, 1983). As Noddings (1984) pointed out, if the caregiver "is not supported and cared-for, she may be entirely lost as one-caring" (p. 100). Clearly, the children suffer this loss.

EMOTIONAL CULTURE: CONSTRUCTION OF THE "ANTI-SELF"

The crying child who is comforted begins to realize that she is not alone with her private experiences. She begins to realize that they are expressed to others and can be shared with them. Here is the cornerstone of the social structuring of experience that we call the "self." (Cahill, 1990, p. 2)

The child's self is constructed in the interpersonal relationships that bind her to others; she is known in the experience of connection and is defined by the responsiveness of human engagement (Gilligan, 1988; Mead, 1934/62; Packer, 1987). To the extent children's emotions, and their selves, are not given meaning through recognition and response, caregivers facilitate each child's loss of self. Despite the amount of time they are grouped together, the caregivers and children are emotionally isolated; the emotional culture is impoverished. These descriptions of the emotional culture of these day care programs suggest the *absence of care*.

The emotional isolation and depersonalization described here are not acceptable for *child care*. Regardless of the possibilities for unconditional love these infants and toddlers may receive from their parents during non-day care hours, the consequences for children spending as much as ten hours each day with emotionally uninvolved or hostile caregivers may have far-reaching implications. At the same time children create, differentiate, and individuate themselves, they come to understand themselves in the mirror of what others have constructed as a world (Wartofsky, 1983). Steele's (1990) autobiographical account of teacher-inflicted punishment presents a moving statement of the consequences for children's selves:

As children we are all wounded in some way and to some degree by the wild world we encounter. From these wounds a disbelieving *anti-self* is born, an internal antagonist saboteur that embraces the world's negative view of us, that believes our wounds are justified by our own unworthiness, and that entrenches itself as a lifelong voice of doubt. (p. 36)

As *singular* events, any one of these emotional interactions may not be decisive and deterministic of children's future emotional development and understandings; there is some evidence that later experiences ameliorate earlier ones (see Kagan, 1984). Nevertheless, "every experience lives on in further experiences" (Dewey, 1938, p. 28). *Repeated* emotional experiences are integrated into children's understandings about themselves, others, and the world they share (Denzin, 1984). In this way, "the experiences and feelings of childhood endure" (Bowman, 1989, p. 450); they become part of children's biographies. The experiences I have described contribute significantly to the sedimentation of emotional meanings for these children, providing the emotional foundation for future interactions and relationships.

CONCLUSION

The field notes herein illuminate problematic emotional socialization within infant-toddler day care centers. The meanings and significance of the interactions described in this text are tied to the children's interpretations of these events as they experience and make sense of them. The "effects" of caregivers' actions and inaction toward children may lie less in the set of actions per se than in the child's construction of those actions (see Kagan, Kearsley, & Zelazo, 1980). In this study, I have endeavored to see the world through these children's eyes in order to understand the meanings of their experiences for them. I have attempted to give voice to the experiences of society's often silenced, ignored, or invisible members—our youngest children.

p77806

This interpretation of problematic emotional experiences within infant-toddler day care centers is, of course, unfinished, to be taken up again (see Denzin, 1984, p. 9). As we continue to place our youngest children in group care settings, it is important to consider under what conditions caring relations and emotional responsiveness can be sustained. Emotionally responsive caregiving requires attention to feeling, involvement, connection, compassion, respect, comfort, and nurturance—realms of experience neglected across our culture. Consequently, the endeavor to humanize the child care setting may depend upon fundamental changes in our beliefs and commitments. At the least, attention to the meanings in the phrase *child care* is a call for what Noddings (1984) described as an existential "awareness of and commitment to what we are doing" (p. 35). Children's daily lived experiences and their own capacities to care are at stake here.

NOTES

1. This chapter is a substantial revision of excerpts from a larger ethnographic study (Leavitt, 1994).

2. See Berger and Luckmann (1967) on the "reflected self," Cooley (1922) on the "looking-glass self," Sartre (1943/56) on "the Other's look," and Mead (1934/62) on taking the attitude of the other.

3. These centers represent a range of program types: church-based non-profit, for-profit chains, corporate-sponsored, and proprietary. Four of these centers accept infants at six weeks of age, the two others, between 15 and 24 months. All are open for a ten-to-twelve-hour day. Centers 1 and 2 were privately owned, enrolling about 55–75 children each. In center 1, the clientele tended toward the "professional," two-working-parents family. Center 2 served a broader range, including low-income and single parents; this center has recently gone out of business. Centers 3 and 4 are non-profit and housed in churches; they serve a variety of families and are partially subsidized by federal funds. Center 3 is one of the largest local centers, enrolling as many as 176 children, a considerable proportion from low-income, culturally diverse, and single-parent families. Center 4 has a capacity for 71 children and serves a considerable number of academic and professional families, although it is the only one of the six with a sliding fee scale. Center 5 is the newest, a corporate-sponsored program with a capacity for 142 children. Center 6 is a for-profit program affiliated with a national chain, with a capacity for 123 children.

4. See Schutz (1967) on intersubjective understanding, putting oneself in the place of the other and identifying our lived experience with the other's. See Denzin (1984) regarding emotional intersubjectivity and emotional embracement. Shott (1979) defines empathy as imagining how another feels or what another's situation is like.

5. See Bowman's (1989) article calling for a blend of scientific and personal knowledge in the practice of child care, and the critical necessity of empathy in understanding young children.

SOUTH PUGET SOUND LIBRARY

6. My interpretations of caregivers' beliefs are inferred from my observations of and interactions with them. I have yet to engage caregivers in a more in-depth dialogue about their beliefs and practices (see Leavitt, 1993a, 1993b, 1994.)

7. See Lief and Fox (1963) regarding the idea of "detached concern" in the caring professions, and Katz (1980) regarding the "optimum detachment" called for in early childhood programs. Vandenberg (1987) also observed that words like "love, care and compassion" do not occur in our professional texts: "We use more professional and technical sounding terms like attachment, prosocial behavior and social skills management" (p. 8).

REFERENCES

Berger, P., & Luckmann, T. (1967). *The social construction of reality*. New York: Anchor.

Blumer, H. (1969). *Symbolic interactionism: Perspective and method*. Berkeley: University of California Press.

Bowman, B. (1989). Self-reflection as an element of professionalism. *Teachers College Record, 90* (3), 444–451.

Cahill, S. (1990, April). *Emotionality, morality, selves, and societies*. Comments prepared for the "Sociology of Emotions in Post-Modern America" session of the 1990 annual meetings of the Midwest Sociological Society, Chicago, Ill.

Caputo, J. (1987). *Radical hermeneutics: Repetition, deconstruction, and the hermeneutic project*. Bloomington: University of Indiana Press.

Clifford, J. (1986). Introduction: partial truths. In J. Clifford & G. Marcus (Eds.), *Writing culture: The poetics and politics of ethnography* (pp. 1–26). Berkeley: University of California Press.

Coles, R. (1967). *Children of crisis, vol. 2: Migrants, sharecroppers, mountaineers*. Boston: Little, Brown.

Cooley, C. H. (1922). *Human nature and the social order*. New York: Scribner.

Denzin, N. K. (1977). *Childhood socialization*. San Francisco: Jossey-Bass.

Denzin, N. K. (1984). *On understanding emotion*. San Francisco: Jossey-Bass.

Denzin, N. K. (1985). Emotion as lived experience. *Symbolic Interaction 8*, (2), 223–240.

Denzin, N. K. (1989a). *Interpretive interactionism*. Newbury Park, Calif.: Sage.

Denzin, N. K. (1989b). *The research act: A theoretical introduction to sociological methods*. Englewood Cliffs, N.J.: Prentice Hall.

Denzin, N. K. (1990a). On understanding emotion: The interpretive-cultural agenda. In T. D. Kemper (Ed.), *Research agendas in the sociology of emotions* (pp. 85–116). Albany: State University of New York Press.

Denzin, N. K. (1990b). Harold and Agnes: A feminist narrative undoing. *Sociological Theory 8*, 198–216.

Dewey, J. (1938). *Experience and education*. New York: Macmillan.

Friedman, S. (1990). NICHD infant child-care network: The national study of young children's lives. *Zero to Three, 10* (3), 21–23.

Gilligan, C. (1982). *In a different voice: Psychological theory and women's development*. Cambridge, Mass.: Harvard University Press.

SOUTH PUGET SOUND LIBRARY

Gilligan, C. (1988). Remapping the moral domain: New images of self in relation-
    ship. In C. Gilligan, J. Ward, J. Taylor, & B. Bardige (Eds.), *Mapping the
    moral domain* (pp. 3–19). Cambridge, Mass.: Harvard University Press.
Goffman, E. (1967). *Interaction ritual: Essays on face-to-face behavior*. New
    York: Pantheon Books/Random House.
Gordon, S. L. (1981). The sociology of sentiments and emotions. In M. Rosenberg
    & R. H. Turner (Eds.), *Social psychology: Sociological perspectives*
    (pp. 562–592). New York: Basic Books.
Gordon, S. L. (1985). Micro-sociological theories of emotion. In H. J. Helle & S. N.
    Eisenstadt (Eds.), *Micro-sociological theory: Perspectives on sociological
    theory, vol. 2* (pp. 133–147). Beverly Hills, Calif.: Sage.
Gordon, S. (1989). The socialization of children's emotions: Emotional culture,
    competence, and exposure. In C. Saarni & P. L. Harris (Eds.), *Children's
    understanding of emotions* (pp. 319–349). Cambridge, Mass.: Cambridge
    University Press.
Grimshaw, J. (1986). *Philosophy and feminist thinking*. Minneapolis: University
    of Minnesota Press.
Guttentag, R. (1987). From another perspective. *Zero to Three, 8* (2), 21.
Harre, R. (Ed.). (1986). *The social construction of emotions*. Oxford: Basil Black-
    well.
Hochschild, A. R. (1979). Emotion work, feeling rules, and social structure. *Amer-
    ican Journal of Sociology, 85*, 551–575.
Hochschild, A. R. (1983). *The managed heart: The commercialization of human
    feeling*. Berkeley: University of California Press.
Kagan, J. (1984). *The nature of the child*. New York: Basic.
Kagan, J., Kearsley, R., & Zelazo, P. (1980). *Infancy: Its place in human devel-
    opment*. Cambridge, Mass.: Harvard University Press.
Katz, L. (1980). Mothering and teaching—some significant distinctions. In L. Katz
    (Ed.), *Current topics in early childhood education, vol. 3* (pp. 47–63).
    Norwood, N.J.: Ablex.
Leavitt, R. L. (1991). Power and resistance in infant-toddler day care centers. In
    S. Cahill (Ed.), *Sociological studies of child development, vol. 4* (pp. 91–
    112). Greenwich, Conn.: JAI.
Leavitt, R. L. (1993a, April). Studying children in day care: Personal reflections
    and ethical dilemmas. Paper presented at the annual meeting of the Amer-
    ican Educational Research Association, Atlanta.
Leavitt, R. L. (1993b). Conversations with caregivers: An inquiry into the work of
    caregiving. Unpublished research proposal.
Leavitt, R. L. (1994). *Power and emotion in infant-toddler day care*. Albany: State
    University of New York Press.
Leavitt, R. L., & Power, M. B. (1989). Emotional socialization in the postmodern
    era: Children in day care. *Social Psychology Quarterly, 52* (1), 35–43.
Lewis, M., & Saarni, C. (Eds.). (1985). *The socialization of emotions*. New York:
    Plenum Press.
Lief, H. I., & Fox, R. C. (1963). Training for "detached concern" in medical stu-
    dents. In H. I. Lief, V. F. Lief, & N. R. Lief (Eds.), *The psychological basis
    of medical practice* (pp. 12–35). New York: Harper & Row.
Liljestrom, R. (1983). The public child, the commercial child, and our child. In

F. S. Kessel & A. W. Siegel (Eds.), *The child and other cultural inventions* (pp. 124–152). New York: Praeger.

Loseke, D. (1989). If only my mother lived down the street. In J. M. Henslin (Ed.), *Marriage and family in a changing society* (pp. 317–328). New York: Free Press.

Mead, G. H. (1934/62). *Mind, self, and society*. Chicago: University of Chicago Press.

Mills, C. W. (1959). *The sociological imagination*. New York: Oxford University Press.

Murphy, L. B. (1992). Sympathetic behavior in very young children. *Zero to Three, 12* (4), 1–5.

Neugebauer, R. (1994). Impressive growth projected for centers into the 21st century. *Child Care Information Exchange, 95*, 80–87.

Noddings, N. (1984). *Caring: A feminine approach to ethics and moral education*. Berkeley: University of California Press.

Packer, M. (1985). Hermeneutic inquiry in the study of human conduct. *American Psychologist, 40* (10), 1081–1093.

Packer, M. (April 1987). *Interpretive research and social development in developmental psychology*. Paper presented at the Biennial Meeting of the Society for Research in Child Development, Baltimore, Md.

Packer, M., & Addison, R. (1989a). Introduction. In M. Packer & R. Addison (Eds.), *Entering the circle: Hermeneutic investigation in psychology* (pp. 13–36). Albany: State University of New York Press.

Packer, M., & Addison, R. (1989b). Evaluating an interpretive account. In M. Packer & R. Addison (Eds.), *Entering the circle: Hermeneutic investigation in psychology*. Albany: State University of New York Press.

Pawl, J. (1990a). Infants in day care: reflections on experiences, expectations and relationships. *Zero to Three, 10* (3), 1–6.

Pawl, J. (1990b). Attending to the emotional well being of children, families and caregivers: Contributions of infant mental health specialists to child care. *Zero to Three, 10* (3), 7.

Power, M. B. (1985). The ritualization of emotional conduct in early childhood. In N. K. Denzin (Ed.), *Studies in symbolic interaction, vol. 6* (pp. 213–227). Greenwich, Conn.: JAI.

Power, M. B. (1986). Socializing emotionality in early childhood: The influence of emotional associates. In P. Adler & P. Adler (Eds.), *Sociological studies of child development, vol. 1* (pp. 259–282). Greenwich, Conn.: JAI.

Power, M. B. (1987). *Interpretive interactionism and early childhood socialization*. Paper presented at the Stone Society for the Study of Symbolic Interaction Symposium, Urbana, Ill.

Reynolds, E. (1990). *Guiding young children: A child-centered approach*. Mountain View, Calif.: Mayfield.

Rose, H. (1986). Women's work: Women's knowledge. In J. Mitchell & A. Oakley (Eds.), *What is feminism?* (pp. 151–183). Oxford: Basil Blackwell.

Saarni, C. (1989). Children's understanding and strategic control of emotional expression in social transactions. In C. Saarni & P. L. Harris (Eds.), *Children's understanding of emotion* (pp. 181–208). New York: Cambridge University Press.

Saarni, C., & Harris, P. (Eds.). (1989). *Children's understanding of emotion.* New York: Cambridge University Press.

Sartre, J. P. (1960/63). *Search for a method.* (H. E. Barnes, Trans.). New York: Knopf. (Original work published 1960).

Sartre, J. P. (1943/56). *Being and nothingness.* (H. E. Barnes, Trans.). New York: Simon & Schuster. (Original work published 1943).

Sartre, J. P. (1939/62). *Sketch for a theory of the emotions.* (P. Mariet, Trans.). London: Methuen. (Original work published 1939).

Scheler, M. (1913/70). *The nature of sympathy.* (P. Heath, Trans.) Hamden, Conn.: Archon Books, Shoe String Press. (Original work published 1913).

Schroeder, W. R. (1984). *Sartre and his predecessors.* London: Routledge & Kegan Paul.

Schutz, A. (1967). *The phenomenology of the social world.* Evanston, Ill.: Northwestern University Press.

Shott, S. (1979). Emotion and social life: A symbolic interactionist analysis. *American Journal of Sociology, 84,* 1317–1334.

Snow, C. (1989). *Infant development.* Englewood Cliffs, N.J.: Prentice Hall.

Steele, S. (1990). The "unseen agent" of low self-esteem. *Education Week, 10* (5), 36.

Tyler, S. A. (1986). Postmodern ethnography: From document of the occult to occult document. In J. Clifford & G. Marcus (Eds.), *Writing culture: The poetics and politics of ethnography* (pp. 122–140). Berkeley, Calif.: University of California Press.

Vanderberg, B. (1987, April). *Developmental psychology and the death of god.* Paper presented at the Biennial Meeting of the Society for Research in Child Development, Baltimore, Md.

Van Manen, M. (1990). *Researching lived experience: Human science for an action sensitive pedagogy.* London, Ontario, Canada: University of Western Ontario Press.

Wartofsky, M. (1983). The child's construction of the world and the world's construction of the child: From historical epistemology to historical psychology. In F. Kessel & A. Siegel (Eds.), *The child and other cultural inventions* (pp. 188–215). New York: Praeger.

White, S. (1983). Psychology as a moral science. In F. Kessel & A. Siegel (Eds.), *The child and other cultural inventions* (pp. 1–25). New York: Praeger.

Zigler, E., & Lang, M. (1991). *Child care choices: Balancing the needs of children, families, and society.* New York: Free Press.

Chapter 2

Family Day Care as Mothering: A Study of Providers' Perspectives

MARGARET K. NELSON

INTRODUCTION

In debates about the federal and state role in provisions for child care services, the issue of quality emerges repeatedly as a key unresolved question. There are two separate areas of discussion. The first is whether quality control should rest with federal or state agencies. Two times in the recent past a state role in setting standards for child care was favored over federal authority: in 1980 the Federal Interagency Day Care Requirements were withdrawn, and in 1990 the Child Care and Development Block Grant again left regulation with the states. The second issue concerns the content rather than the location of regulatory activity. Common themes exist in proposed regulations as well as in actual state licensing provisions. In fact, controversy more often revolves around specific numbers and means of enforcement than about the overall characteristics of quality care for young children. These characteristics include: low staff: child ratios; small group size (especially for very young children); health and safety precautions; staff training in areas such as child development and early childhood education; and a program of care that includes developmentally appropriate activities to promote social, intellectual, emotional, and physical development (Morgan, 1986; Young & Zigler, 1986).

The ideals identified in the child care literature generally come from "experts" in the field, including individuals and organizations concerned about the care of young children as well as individuals and organizations that conduct research about the effects of non-parental child care. The question of whether those persons who actually offer care to young children work with the same definition of quality is only rarely considered. In part, the ideals of individual child care providers can be ignored because it is assumed that the training incorporated into the definition of quality care will engender appropriate ideologies while the regulatory mechanisms will ensure compliance with minimal standards.

This paper seeks to reverse the usual direction of understanding with respect to ideologies of child care and to uncover a "bottom up" analysis of the definition of quality. The particular focus is family day care. Family day care, defined as "non-residential care provided in a private home other than the child's own" (Fosburg, 1981, p. 1), is a popular form of out-of-the-home care, especially for very young children (Hofferth, et al. 1990).[1] As this paper will show, family day care providers work with their own unique definition of quality care, a definition that in some ways is very similar to, but in other ways differs greatly from, that proposed by the experts.

In what follows, I first describe the methods for this study. I then show how family day care providers construct an ideal of good care that draws on mothering as an analogy, downplaying training and programmatic concerns while accentuating love and affection. I then suggest that this style emerges both from the structural constraints of family day care and from experiential learning, and I demonstrate how this style of care leaves providers ill-prepared to cope with failure. In the conclusion, I discuss how these findings have implications for the design of support services for family day care providers. I also suggest that a similar method could be used to practical effect in other contexts.

METHODS AND SAMPLE CHARACTERISTICS

Data Collection

This study was conducted in Vermont where the organization of family day care offers three legal alternatives. Licensing is required of providers with more than six full-time non-resident children. Because almost all licensed day care occurs in formal centers rather than private homes, no licensed providers are included in this analysis. Registration is required of those who offer care to children from more than two different families and may legally include six full-time children of preschool age and four part-time school-age children. Women caring for (any number of) children from no more than two different families may remain unregistered. Those who care for more than this number and fail to register constitute the "illegal" population of family day care providers (Vermont Department of Social and Rehabilitation Services, 1985). A 1985 study of child care in Vermont estimated that approximately 75 percent of all children under the age of six with parents in the labor force were in (legal or illegal) unregulated care (Davenport, 1985).

This study uses two complementary approaches to explore the experiences of registered and unregistered family day care providers. In the summer of 1986, I mailed a questionnaire to each of the 463 registered day care providers in Vermont; responses were received from 225 providers (a response rate of 49 percent). The following summer I distributed questionnaires to 105 unregistered family day care providers.[2] The questionnaires covered a range of issues including the number of years the women had been providing child care, reasons for opening a day care home, attitudes toward child care, problems, and background information. These questionnaires offer a description of the demographic characteristics of family day care providers; they also provide a starting point for an analysis of self-definitions and priorities.

The richer, more nuanced, understanding of the meaning of child care to family day care providers emerged from a second research method. Over a two-year period, I conducted lengthy semi-structured interviews with thirty registered day care providers (twenty-one of whom had also completed questionnaires) and forty unregistered day care providers (ten of whom had also completed questionnaires).

For both the distribution of the questionnaire and the interviews, registered providers were identified through lists made available by the state. Locating unregistered family day care providers posed greater problems. First, they do not appear on any published lists. Second, many unregistered providers attempt to maintain low visibility: if they are not reporting their incomes or if they are caring for more than the legal number of children, they actively seek to avoid recognition by state officials. The initial research strategy was to use advertisements that providers had placed in two local newspapers during the six months before the research started. Unfortunately, a number of those who had advertised were no longer offering child care and some were now registered providers. I also drove through various areas in three counties and stopped in such places as general stores, parks, and post offices to ask about recommendations for names of family day care providers. In addition, I asked people with children in family day care for the names of their day care providers and for the names of other parents with children in this kind of care. These three techniques provided an initial list of candidates for questionnaire distribution and interviews. Providers who agreed to participate in the study were asked to recommend others. The use of snowball sampling, then, constituted a fourth strategy.

Interviewing Strategies

Interviews were initiated with a telephone call in which I identified myself and explained that I was "writing a book about the daily experiences of family day care providers." I usually included the name of the person who had recommended that provider. Using a specific name seemed to make a difference: although my response rate as a whole was very high (only four women refused to be interviewed), I had total success in those cases where I could draw on a personal contact. In initial telephone calls, I would not only establish a specific time for the interview, but I would seek to answer any questions the provider had about the nature of the study, and I would promise confidentiality.

Questions in the interviews themselves dealt with a wide range of issues, including relations with children and parents, the impact of the work on members of the provider's family, and sources of stress and satisfaction. Most interviews began with my briefly restating what I had said on the telephone, that I was interested in the experiences of family day care providers and that I was writing a book on the subject. I would formally begin the questioning by asking the woman how she came to be offering family day care in her home. This proved to be a useful starting point because the responses would generally include information about the provider's stage of life (whether she had children, was married, etc.), her interests in entering the occupation (whether she chose the occupation in order to stay home with her children or for some other reason), and her current attitude toward the work (whether she was satisfied and planning to remain in it or dissatisfied and seeking a change). This information enabled me to ask subsequent questions in a more knowledgeable way and to tailor questions to the specific situation of the individual. The initial question also allowed the providers to offer their own definitions of their motives and interests.

Because I was particularly interested in allowing the description of family day care to emerge from the point of view of the providers themselves, all of the questions in the interview were open-ended. In many cases, the questions were designed specifically to pursue and enrich the definitions of issues that had emerged from my analysis of the questionnaire data. For example, providers were asked in the questionnaire to indicate their agreement with the statement, "I think my role as a family day care provider is to be like a mother to the children I care for." Response options ranged from "strongly agree" to "strongly disagree." Armed with the finding (reported below) that many providers agreed with this statement, I sought to uncover the more precise meaning of being "like a mother" in the context of a family day care home. Hence I would ask questions that pursued this topic: "Could you tell me how you feel about the children in your care?" "What do you want to be offering to the children in your care?" "Can you talk about the ways in which you feel differently about the children you care for and your own children?" Areas of concern raised by women in the beginning of the study were pursued in subsequent interviews, and probing questions were designed to engender a fuller discussion of issues touched on superficially. This method precludes the possibility of using these data in a quantitative manner because not all interviews covered precisely the same material. However, with this method, I feel confident that I am analyzing the experiences of family day care providers in a manner that reflects their reality rather than imposing an outsider's perspective.

Each interview lasted at least one hour, many ran for several hours. All of the interviews were conducted in the provider's home. Although I made an effort to carry out interviews during a time when the children would be napping (so that there would be fewer interruptions), I found myself becoming a participant-observer in the operation of family day care homes. I watched providers settle disputes with children, attend to their ongoing needs, and find distractions for them so the interview could continue. I was also called into service myself: I changed diapers, comforted children frightened by the momentary absence of the day care provider to answer the doorbell or telephone, and (at the end of many interviews) taught children how to record their voices and listen to themselves on a tape.

All interviews were transcribed. The analysis that follows relies on both the *content* of the respondent's answers and the *form* of those answers. I noted hesitations, halting explanations, and resistance to answering specific questions.

Sample Characteristics

The family day care providers in this study were almost uniformly married women (86 percent) with children of their own (96 percent). Over half (56 percent) of the women had at least one child of preschool age and therefore cared simultaneously for both their own and non-resident children. The women in the study ranged in age from 21 to 71 with a mean of 34.5. The number of years of involvement in the occupation extended from recent initiates who had been working for less than a year to one woman who had been offering care for twenty-three years; the median number of years as a family day care provider was three. Most (94 percent) of the women had completed a high school education, and half of the women had some education beyond high school. The median household income for all providers fell in the response category of $20,000 to $25,000 at a time when the median family income in the state (for a married couple with a wife in the labor force and a child under the age of six) was $21,137 (U.S. Bureau of the Census, 1980); the median household income among the comparable group of family day care providers (i.e., married with a child under the age of six) fell between $25,000 and $30,000. With one exception, all of the women who were interviewed were white.

DEFINITIONS OF QUALITY

Family Day Care as Mothering

The family day care providers in this study work with a definite definition of quality care—one that in part resembles the definition of the "experts" but one that deviates from it as well. To a great extent, this definition is based on a cultural ideal of mothering.

First, the women viewed the development of personal and intimate relationships as an essential component of family day care: seventy-five of the questionnaire respondents agreed strongly with the statement "a family day care provider should be like a mother to the children in her care." When interviewed about their feelings toward the children, the women use familial analogies: "They are my part-time kids"; I'm trying to give the children a sense of family"; "I'm like a second mom"; "I think of them as extended members of my family"; "These guys are like my own kids"; "I'm offering closeness and security—my motherhood."

Moreover, most family day care providers wanted to create the same environment they assume prevails in a home with a mother present. Eighty-one percent of the questionnaire respondents felt it was "very important" to provide "a homelike atmosphere." Again, interviews confirmed and elucidated this approach: "I try to make the child comfortable here"; "I try to give them the experiences I gave to my own children"; "I want this to be a nurturing place"; "They should be at home here"; "I like this being just like a home." When I asked, "What do you do with the children?" the analogy to a mother's care emerged again:

I don't schedule the day. They do their thing and I do mine around whatever they are doing. . . . If the ironing's got to be done, the ironing gets done. If the laundry's got to be done—I don't do all of these things after they leave at night. I don't do a thing any different than I did when I was home with my own two. What's got to be done gets done.

Although most women cannot find time to attend to much housework, some can, and they see their actions as beneficial to the children: "They see you doing these things and it's just like mom."

The manner in which providers use these terms suggests that they believe their meanings are obvious, that everyone knows what kind of care a mother offers and what a home is. As providers talk, they reveal the specific content of the ideal with which they work and the ways in which it approximates their own definition of good mothering.

As in expert definitions, safety is paramount: the providers believe it is important to keep the children safe and to attend to their everyday needs during the hours of care. Most of the family day care providers, when asked to describe their style of child care or what they are trying to accomplish with the children, also mention discipline:

I expect the child to respect me as a person and I, in return, respect them as an individual, their privacy. If they want to be left alone, fine. I try to encourage manners, politeness, sharing with other children, as well as playing together in a group. Just generally learning to respect other people's property.

But neither safety nor discipline necessitates constant interaction. The majority of family day care providers is convinced that a home is a place where children should play, learn through playing, and can be left alone for periods of time to amuse themselves. They may read to the children or bring out toys and equipment. But, in contrast to a definition of quality that includes developmental activities focused on intellectual stimulation, most do not believe that instruction should be the core of a child's day: only 24 percent of the questionnaire respondents said that it was "very important" to offer children a structured or planned day; only 39 percent indicated that they thought it was "very important" to include "educational activities" in the daily round of events (see Enarson, 1990; Marzollo, 1987). In fact, a substantial number of the providers think that too much emphasis on "ABC's" is inappropriate and unnecessary for young children: "I'm not one who feels [preschool education] is important." Providers do, however, stress other kinds of learning, particularly the development of social skills: 53 percent of questionnaire respondents said they thought this was "very important." As one provider said, "You teach them everything they have to know about life." And another provider contrasted this kind of teaching with the emphasis on education and drew a boundary between her responsibility and that of parents: "I don't spend a lot time trying to teach the kids. I tell [the parents] that is their job. I teach them what life is about."

When women were asked to speak about the concrete differences they perceived between the care they give and that offered to children in a day care center, they were quite articulate and insistent: they responded that day care centers neither encourage the "warmth, love, and intimacy" nor offer the "one-on-one" care of a family setting. Some providers suggested that because day care centers, like schools, follow a schedule of activities, they do not allow for a free-flowing responsiveness to the individual child's needs and interests. Almost all of the women interviewed believed that a home is the preferable location for the daily care of young children. Indeed, many of the providers were motivated to start offering care to other children because they wanted to ensure that their own children could remain at home.

Homelike care thus refers to the kind of activities that prevail; it also refers to the pacing of these activities and the attentiveness and affection that make this pacing responsive to children's needs. And, not surprisingly, most providers believe that the enactment of this ideal requires small groups of children. In fact, only a very small percentage of the day care homes included in this study operated beyond the legal limits (six children), whether or not the provider had placed herself within the regulatory system. But a small group size did not emerge from an abstract or "expert" definition of quality care: it followed as a logical consequence of enacting a specific ideal in which the provider believed that she should be "like a mother" to the children in her care. This is an ideal that assumes a commonality among all homes and among all mothers. Family day care providers know well that the children in their care come to them from very different backgrounds, from families with widely varying material resources and caregiving styles. In asserting a shared notion of homelike care, they deny that these differences are significant. They embrace instead some common core that they believe defines mothering whether for their own or someone else's child.

Sources of the Provider's Style of Care

This construction of family day care as mothering has roots in the structural constraints within which providers offer their services and in the kind of prior experiences available to the women who do this work. By definition, family day care providers remain at home and merge paid and unpaid care in a single setting. This makes it difficult for the provider to distinguish between what she is doing for her *own* children and what she is doing for the children who come to her on a daily basis. There is also a material underpinning to the emphasis on homelike care. A preschool pedagogy is expensive (Bernstein, 1977). Although the providers spend weekends scouring garage sales for toys and equipment, they cannot afford to spend too much on these items. As one woman said, "I'm a *home* day care. I can only do so much with what I can afford. I can't buy luxurious things."

There is also a pragmatic underpinning to this kind of care. Most day care centers and preschools divide children into single-age groups (in order to lessen the variations in the kinds of demands to which they are called to respond) and tie parents to specified schedules (in order to reduce the frequency with which they are interrupted). Thus they are equipped to plan activities appropriate for a narrow range of children and to follow a schedule. Family day care providers don't have these luxuries: "It's hard with the little ones [around] to sit down and work on our alphabet. . . . I leave that up to the mother to do at home."

The isolation in which they work makes it difficult to go on field trips ("We go to the playground—but that is hard unless you have someone with you") or to maintain an energetic level of activity ("In a center workers have a break, and therefore children have a person with more gusto. I can't keep up that level"). The work surrounding meal preparation and cleaning takes time that might otherwise be devoted to interaction with the children. Because their work space is also their living space, they have obligations to make the day care "invisible" at the end of the day. They cannot totally rearrange the house to meet children's needs or leave unfinished activities in place (Nelson, 1990a).

As noted above, much of the prescriptive literature focuses on the importance of specific training for child care providers. The providers in this study, however, emphasize experience rather than training: it is through the former that they believe they have acquired the skills necessary to perform competently the role they have defined.

Many providers, when asked how they learned to care for children, begin with a discussion of their own mothers' care for them. Providers also draw on their own early experiences of caring for young children. While conforming to society's expectations for young girls, they had innumerable opportunities to develop caregiving skills. In answer to the question, "What kind of training have you had?" one woman said:

Training? I was the oldest of eleven children—does that count? I have brothers and sisters at home right now that are like my own. I potty trained them, I broke them of their bottle, I nurtured them, I gave them all the things that they needed. . . . I felt I was ready [to start caring for children]. I come from a big family— there was lots of us around.

Another woman, when asked whether she had ever cared for children before, answered, "Just my whole life. My mother was sick when my younger sister was born and I babysat . . . from the time I was eight."

Most significantly, family day care providers talk about learning from the experience of caring for their *own* children. As one woman said, "I've been told—and I feel—that [my own children] are great kids. . . . The way I raised them is what I do with the kids I babysit for . . . and [my children] are doing fine so far." Because they see the work as an extension of mothering, they believe they are prepared to handle the job without receiving formal training.[3] One woman laughed at a question about her qualifications:

A woman came the other day and she was asking, "What special training do you have in dealing with children?" And I said, "I'm the mother of six children, that's all the special training that I feel like I need." As far as taking a book that tells me how to deal with children . . . I don't want that. I don't believe in book-raising children.

As these comments suggest, for many providers there is no clear distinction between their current activities and their personal histories of more casual caregiving. They learned early that they were supposed to be nurturant, to be altruistic, to share their love (and their homes) with others. Some women could not answer the question of why they opened a family day care home without reference to these earlier experiences; others could not even identify the moment at which they began to offer family day care as such because they started so informally. When urged to identify the source of their ability to care for children, they point to concrete experiences. Yet, because most of this experiential learning is so much a part of their everyday lives, they believe they are simply doing something that comes naturally to all women. Thus both their commitment to caregiving and their ability to do so effectively are presented as apparently innate parts of being a woman/mother (see DeVault, 1991). If they acknowledge that child care does not come easily to all women ("I don't think that everyone is cut out to do this"), they deny that it requires a cultivated set of abilities. "I don't have any skills," said one woman; "Anyone who has been a mother can do this," added another.

Yet, no matter how casually they begin, or how adamantly they claim that they rely on "common sense" alone, as women persevere in the occupation, they also (and contradictorily) acknowledge that they have acquired a distinct body of knowledge and set of skills.[4] They mention learning to deal with crises and injuries, learning about developmental stages, and learning how to manage the complexities of relating to a wide range of ages. Some mention specific skills that ease the burden of their work: "I have gotten better at putting them to bed—I know that sounds funny but it could be difficult. I am also better at learning how long their attention span is." Some women say that they have become more flexible over time in response to their newfound ability to assess accurately children's moods: "I used to go with a routine and stick to that. Now I am looser than I used to be because I have learned how to be and to get the same thing accomplished while being looser." Many women speak about having become more patient. The definition of patience that one respondent (a provider for twenty-three years) gave me suggests that this aspect of the caregiver's experience is particularly complex:

Patience is understanding the individuality of all of these children. . . . I could have another 181 [children] and each one of them would be different again. There's no two that need the same amount of loving or need the same amount of reprimanding. Each one needs a little extra something of some sort which is fun finding with that individual. I think [that is part of the challenge].

The Limits of Mothering

Family day care providers seem to accept the role of substitute mother for their paid caregiving, and they experience that activity much as mothers do. As they give the children the security of a home, five days a week, for eight or nine hours each day, sometimes over a period of several years, family day care providers "learn to love" the children. Seventy-seven percent of the questionnaire respondents agreed with the statement, "I get emotionally involved with the children in my care." And they speak about both the rewards and satisfactions and the problems and discontents of their work in terms similar to those of mothers (Boulton, 1983; Glenn, Chang, & Forcey, 1994; O'Barr, Pope, & Wyer, 1990).

The conflation of the mother role with the provider role was so complete that when I asked, "Do you feel differently about your own children and the other children in your care?" the answer I almost uniformly received was, "I treat them all the same." Tellingly, in emphasizing external behavior (the way the children are treated), the providers avoided answering the question about the way they *felt* about the children. It is a form of denial that their feelings for their own children differed from their feelings for their clients.[5] Having dismissed professional caregiving, the provider embraces mothering. Having done so, she cannot easily speak about the manner in which she deviates from this ideal.

But a contradiction is present. Mothering is the most desirable style for a family day care provider, but it is a style she must adopt incompletely. Among the social group from which these providers are drawn— white, working- and middle-class women—motherhood confers the exclusive privileges of claiming, molding, and keeping; neither these women nor their clients believe that other people's children can be claimed, molded, and kept.[6] To think that one can do so with other people's children creates a situation where disappointment is inevitable. And this style of motherhood is neither motivated by financial gain nor limited in time. Yet a day care provider who refuses reimbursement, or fails to identify the normal hours in which she will give care, invites exploitation. The family day care provider cannot answer a question about feelings directly because there is no direct way to describe how one maintains an ideal by deviating from it. We can hear this confusion when providers are prodded to differentiate between the care they give other people's children for pay and the care they offer their own. The women invariably use a "but" to describe their feelings: "I love these children, *but* they're not my own"; "I enjoy caring for children, *but* it is a job for me."

Providers do not explicitly acknowledge that the care they offer is different from mothering. Yet the emotional component of that care, what I call the feeling rule of "detached attachment," is characterized by some limits drawn around the caregivers' emotional engagement with the children (Hochschild, 1975, 1983).

Providers frequently referred to the detachment they have created and the emotional labor in maintaining it: "I reserve something, knowing that they're not mine"; "I hold back a little"; "I don't want to get too attached." Almost every provider could talk about one child to whom she had become overly attached. Almost every provider spoke about not letting this happen again:

I won't take one on from six months and watch it grow up like that again if I've got any feeling that they're going to be taken away from me. . . . I felt that I was doing a good job and I enjoyed [the child] just as much as [the parents] did, watching it grow up and being a part of its life. Maybe I did get too attached.

But if providers settle on a form of detachment out of necessity—so that they can accept interference in their caregiving, so that they don't get hurt by loss, so that they don't make decisions that are not in their own best interests—it is clear that this resolution is partial at best. Detached attachment has to be recreated daily; it is difficult to sustain emotionally; and it may even, on occasion, conflict with their ability to offer good care. One provider who had left the occupation for center-based care explained at length how caregiving in this new setting freed her from this struggle and enabled her to offer better care:

I think that's part of what was making me burned out. I really felt that was where some of it was, from letting myself become too attached to the children. You have to keep a little bit of distance. Because, I think the fact that I had them here all the time they became . . . so much a part of my family that made it kind of crazy. . . . I haven't distanced myself from any of the children [at the center], but I don't have the hours with them. I think that makes a difference. . . . In a three-hour span you can't get as close. And you always know that there's somebody else that can take over there, whereas [at home] there wasn't. I was their sole person for support, authority, love, or whatever.

Another, in talking about the emotional labor involved in maintaining a detached attachment, made it clear that the process is difficult and continuous:

Question: Can you talk about your feelings toward the children?
Answer: I get very attached and yet I try to keep myself somewhat removed. The

first year was hard because I got frustrated . . . because I cared for them so much. I wished I could go home and tuck them in. You know, you see a little guy come at 7 in the morning and you know he's not going to bed until 10 o'clock, it breaks your heart. Or to wake him up at the end of nap time when he's the first one to go to sleep. That's the caring I feel for them. I like to hold them if they cry. They need that.

Question: You said you hold yourself back a little from loving the children, can you talk more about that?

Answer: I'm afraid to get too emotionally involved with them because it hurts if I see things happening in their private lives. I try not to look at them as my own kids because if I do, it's hard to explain. I want to love them and treat them with lots of care, but I want to hold back a bit and not mother them too much because if I do the mothers resent that to some degree.

Question: So how do you hold back?

Answer: It is hard to describe. Maybe I don't hold them as much as when I had my own kids because there are six of them. I guess I don't hold back as much as I think I hold back. To me what happens here is just like when my three were at home. . . . It's as much as a family setting as I can give, but it's still not a family setting. . . . I'm doing with the kids what I did with mine. So maybe I'm not holding back as much as I think.

The provider has to find a balance between attachment and distance. The balance must be recreated daily because the provider doubts her ability to be detached, to remain detached, even while it is a perspective she seeks to adopt.

EXPERIENCES OF FAILURE

Providers can speak easily about mothering the children who come to them for care; they speak less easily about the ways in which they feel differently about children in their care and their own children. Providers are even more reluctant to speak about occasions on which the care they give has failed to achieve the level of quality—which for providers means at least some degree of attachment—they hold as their ideal. At one level, this reluctance should not be surprising. No one enjoys discussing failures and inadequacies. However, some approaches to caregiving or education explicitly leave room for failure. A teacher might, for example, speak about using certain techniques that work with some kinds of individuals but are less successful with others. Or one might acknowledge the limits of one's training: if an individual has not received the skills for dealing with disturbed children or slow learners, she might claim insufficient preparation for the challenges of a specific individual. Moreover, caregiving in an institutional setting offers alternative sources of attention and interaction: if a given caregiver is less successful on the whole or is having momentary difficulty with a client, another can offer relief (Lundgren & Browner, 1990). But mothering as a stance—even when modified by detachment—assumes and builds on a commitment and capacity to nurture and love *all* the children in one's care and to have that love reciprocated. Having located her skills in the capacity to learn from experience and challenge, the family day care provider believes she should be able to adapt to any child encountered. In the isolation of a family day care home, there is no relief from a difficult interaction with a child; the entire responsibility rests with the single provider. This isolation precludes ongoing support; no one can say you did a good job or offer constructive criticism. Thus family day care providers are both ideologically and structurally unprepared for failure.

As suggested above, conversations with providers about "failure" are uncomfortable. An assertion that there "was never a child they could not care for" often turns into a reluctant admission that "there was one child once" followed by a halting, difficult discussion of how they made the choice to tell a parent that they could no longer offer care.

To a certain extent, providers seek to protect themselves from failure by screening clients. One provider said that she "sort of filters out people on the phone—assessing the way they are, the questions they ask, and the things that are important to them." Parents who are simply seeking the cheapest possible care might be eliminated in this manner. Many providers also ask that parents interested in using their services come for an interview, and if they don't like what they see (either in terms of the mother or the child), they sometimes use the subterfuge of high rates. One provider said:

I did have this one girl come with her daughter, and I knew when she came in the door that I did not want to watch this girl's daughter. . . . The daughter was off the wall. The mother kept saying, "Don't do that" [and] the kid would not listen. And I'm thinking to myself, how am I going to get out of this. . . . So right as she is getting ready to leave . . . I told her I charged $4 an hour—which was a lie. . . . I did not want her to even consider me. . . . I didn't know how [else] to get out of it.

But these precautions cannot always work, and most providers have found themselves in the situation where they have to refuse to continue to care for a child with whom they have already established a relationship.

Three different justificatory strategies can be identified in the providers' explanations for their own decision to sever a relationship with a child. They include: a refusal to become the primary caregiver in situations where they define the real parent as being inadequate; a concern for ensuring adequate care to all children; and an acknowledgment that, quite simply, sometimes love fails to emerge. These strategies are not mutually exclusive; providers draw on more than a single explanation.

In some cases, providers shift the burden of responsibility away from themselves onto the "other" mother. In so doing, the provider explicitly acknowledges that her mothering must be complementary. Becoming primary would threaten the detachment that she strives to achieve. Providers speak with pain about the times in which they seek to free themselves from dealing with abused and neglected children whom they believe would be too costly in emotional terms, either because they could become too important to the child or because the child could become too important to them:

I had a child I took care of for a couple of years . . . and once she came and she had a mark on her bottom . . . and she went down for her nap and she woke up and she still had the mark and that really just blew my mind. Instant tears and the whole thing because I had become very attached to the little girl at that point. I had to remove myself from the situation because I couldn't deal with it any more. . . . I was scared of being *too* attached to the child.

One time I did have a state child . . . and it just pulled at my heart. . . . When the little girl came she just reeked and I bathed her. You know, I had fixed her up so cute. But I can't do that every day. I just don't have the time. And the next day she said to me, "Would you bathe me again?" I just cried over her but . . . I thought, I really can't do this. It's too hard alone.

Although providers speak about these kinds of situations with guilt ("I could have done him some good"), ultimately they have to acknowledge that their fragile stance depends on some modicum of distance and on having the other mother available to do her share.

Inadequate primary mothering can be too absent; it can also be too present. "Too present" mothering confronts the provider with a child who has too many demands, too many expectations. In these cases, a provider has to acknowledge that, although she offers the one-on-one care of a home, she cannot reproduce the conditions of a home in which there is but a single child and a single mother. Hence a child that has come to expect constant attention cannot be included:

I had only one child who was too difficult to care for. The parents had been very overprotective, and the child could not leave her mother. She would cry unless she was being held.

I had one child who was hard to care for. He had stayed with his great grand-mother, and he had been held all the time and he expected that.

A displacement onto the other mother is often conjoined in providers' discussions with a second justificatory strategy: the demands of a single child (whether deriving from overprotection or a lack of adequate care) can jeopardize the care given to other children. In using this strategy, providers look to the total picture and the threat that a single difficult child can pose to overall quality. Bad modeling is a common theme:

The child would mock me, and the other kids would pick up on it.
He was very disruptive, and it upset the other children.
He was swearing, and others kids picked it up.

Even if the child's behavior is not being imitated, the disruption of a single difficult child may detract from the attention available to the other children and the time required for the provider's ongoing tasks:

Tomorrow will be the first time refusing a child. I went through a lot of guilt about it. But I had to realize that I was at my limits. . . . I haven't told the mother yet. . . . I love the little boy and I will miss him. But he needs constant supervision, or else he is in trouble.

Finally, and perhaps most problematically, providers acknowledge that sometimes love fails to emerge. Because love constitutes a centerpiece of what they have to offer, they cannot keep with them children to whom they fail to get attached. Neither the child nor the provider, they suggest, can profit in such a situation:

I did sit for a child I didn't like. I had a boy who had a strange personality. We would have clashed if I kept him, but the mother stopped working. He wasn't lovable, and I couldn't hold him and hug him. The mother's older kids had problems—probably she was making the same mistake again. I might have told the mother it wasn't working out. I don't think there's anything wrong with people having personality clashes. The thing is with a kid you don't want to hurt their feelings. I wouldn't want my kid in a home where he wasn't at least liked, let alone loved. And I wouldn't want someone to give their kids a piece of candy and not mine.

None of these strategies is satisfactory. As suggested above, failure torments providers. Their self definition as mothers makes (what they believe is) a dereliction of responsibility especially problematic; their isolation and lack of training leaves them with few resources for redefining, and sometimes even understanding, unsatisfactory relationships with children. If providers find some comfort in the justifications they compose when *they* initiate the severing of ties, they are much less well equipped to deal with occasions when *parents* take the initiative. Although all children eventually move beyond the need for daily care and are therefore, in a sense, "lost" to the providers, normal or maturational losses can be taken in stride. The provider can believe she has done her job well when children are ready to move on. But those losses that are precipitated because the parent senses that the provider's care is no longer adequate threaten the provider's self-confidence. As the following two quotes demonstrate, because they combine loss with questions about the adequacy of care, providers speak about these occasions with a special anguish:

> The mother decided she would get someone closer. That really hurt my feelings. I felt that I was not a good sitter. I even asked my husband, "Why is she taking him away from me?"

> One day she called me up and said she wasn't going to bring him back because she didn't think he was happy here. And that really bothered me, and I asked, "Why don't you think he's happy here? What do you want me to do?" And she said, "It's nothing to do with you. I just don't think he is happy here. He doesn't want to go." . . . I was upset because I thought I did something wrong. I thought I had let his crying bother me too much. . . . I started to wonder whether I should be taking care of other people's kids.

In attempting to deal with such situations, a provider might even rewrite history. One mother, in recommending the name of a person to interview, told me that because her daughter had been unhappy with a particular provider, she had decided to take both of her children elsewhere. The provider told a somewhat different version of the events, a version in which *she* had initiated the separation herself:

> I lost two [children] about six months ago. The little girl was having trouble at home, and we just couldn't pinpoint what it was at home. . . . And all of a sudden here one day she threw up . . . and she didn't make it to the bathroom. . . . "I'm coming," I said, and I thought, "I'm not going to make it to her." I had her since she was an infant . . . and I've gone over it time and time again. But after that day she was really afraid to come. I kept her for six weeks [more] and finally said to the mother, "She is so frightened and I hate to be the one to tell you this, why don't you try another baby sitter." I was crushed. I miss them something wicked. . . . It was like I had let her down, because we were very close and she always enjoyed coming. Not being able to figure it out is what troubles me.

Although there is no way to discover who actually made the final move to change caregivers, the provider's discussion reveals not only the belief that *she* solved the problem but also an anguished realization that no matter who made the decision, her own skills were inadequate in this particular case.

In sum, although a family day care provider can find a basis on which to justify her own decision to sever ties with children who pose problems of attachment, she is totally unprotected when the adequacy of her mothering is at stake. When a child fails to thrive in her care, or when a parent believes that to be the case, the family day care provider is left only with self-doubt.

CONCLUSION

Most family day care providers develop a definition of quality care that takes into account both the structural conditions in which they work—a situation of isolation in the individual's home—and the experiential knowledge they have accumulated over years of giving care to children. The developed ideal of family day care as "homelike" with a role for the provider as being "like a mother" includes both affection and distance, attachment and detachment. When providers talk about this ideal, they reveal that it is difficult to sustain. They have to struggle to maintain the "proper" feelings. This ideal also leaves little room for coping with situations that "fail." Although they might be able to justify their own decision to refuse to offer care, they have few resources to draw on to help bolster their confidence when they perceive themselves, or are perceived by others, as having failed to maintain the quality care for which they strive.

Those providers who have agreed to work within a regulatory network speak of that system primarily in terms of constraint rather than assistance; those who maintain their own autonomy often speak of the fear of unnecessary or burdensome rules (Enarson, 1990; Nelson, 1990b). Regardless of their accuracy, these attitudes suggest that the concerns that predominate from the "top" (although informed by expert opinion about the needs of children) are not perceived as accurately reflecting the concerns and interests of family day care providers. Yet family day care providers clearly have problematic areas in their relations with, and their feelings about, the children in their care. The data that testify to these problems might be used as the basis for designing resources that might make regulation more attractive, and of more direct use, to family day care providers. Such resources might include training programs that focus on methods for handling difficult children and guidelines to use when refusing to offer care. They might also incorporate group discussions about how providers experience failure and advice about how to cope with their feelings of inadequacy in those situations. Such resources would clearly serve the concrete ongoing needs of family day care providers.[7]

Qualitative data thus have practical use. Although such data can never reveal everything one might want to know about a given population, the methods of this study can be applied to other settings as a way of discovering the constructed definitions and meanings with which different kinds of caregivers work. The findings of such analyses can reveal, as they did in this case, problematic areas and issues of central concern. They might also bring about a mediated definition of quality care, a definition that incorporates the perspective of caregivers as well as those of experts and the clients they seek to represent. Those engaged in hands-on care might benefit from this process both by receiving acknowledgment of their point of view and by the development of assistance with problematic issues in their daily routines. So too might the children who are the recipients of this care benefit from a process that supports their caregivers and thus seeks to ensure that the job of caregiving is done well.

NOTES

1. The Hofferth et al. (1990) study separates "family day care" and care by relatives in a home other than the child's. It is difficult, therefore, to know which relative care involves women such as the ones I am describing in this study. In 1990, 18.6 percent of children under age five with employed mothers were in family day care; an additional 11.3 percent of these children were being cared for by relatives in a home other than their own. In contrast, 26.5 percent of these children were cared for in a child care center.

2. In the course of distributing questionnaires to unregistered providers, I picked up an additional 10 registered providers, bringing the total for that group to 235.

3. Even those who had undergone extensive training to become nurses or teachers, when asked what skills they drew on, mentioned motherhood before their occupation.

4. This body of knowledge and set of skills are very similar to those that Sara Ruddick (1984) defines as "Maternal thinking."

5. Alternatively, this answer might be taken as an indication of the difficulty of separating treatment and feeling. Caregiving involves instrumental tasks and emotions. We care for someone because we care about them; when we care about someone we take care of their needs. Yet, if it were just this difficulty, we might find that mothers could not separate the tasks and the emotions. However, most mothers can separate the two easily (e.g., I love my child but I hate changing diapers, getting up in the middle of the night, and losing contact with the adult world).

6. In communities where mothering has a more collective aspect, these ideals might be very different (Collins, 1990).

7. This is not meant to imply that these are the only resources family day care providers need. Clearly they need others as well. For example, they need financial assistance, respite support, and health care insurance. The resources under discussion here are those that would respond to the particular set of issues discussed in this paper. See Nelson (1990a) for a more complete set of recommendations.

REFERENCES

Bernstein, B. (1977). Class pedagogies: Visible and invisible. In J. Karabel & A. H. Halsey (Eds.), *Power and ideology in education* (pp. 511–534). New York: Oxford University Press.

Boulton, M. G. (1983). *On being a mother: A study of women with pre-school children*. London: Tavistock.

Collins, P. H. (1990). *Black feminist thought: Knowledge, consciousness and the politics of empowerment*. Boston: Unwin Hyman.

Davenport, A. (1985). *The economics of child care*. Montpelier, Vt.: The Governor's Commission on the Status of Women's Childcare Task Force.

DeVault, M. (1991). *Feeding the family: The social organization of caring as gendered work*. Chicago: University of Chicago Press.

Enarson, E. (1990). Experts and caregivers: Perspectives on underground childcare. In E. K. Abel & M. K. Nelson (Eds.), *Circles of care: Work and identity in women's lives* (pp. 233–245). Albany: State University of New York Press.

Fosburg, S. (1981). *Family day care in the United States: Summary of findings, vol. 1*. Washington, D.C.: U.S. Government Printing Office, U.S. Department of Health and Human Services.

Glenn, E. N., Chang, G., & Forcey, L. R. (1994). *Mothering: Ideology, experience and agency*. New York: Routledge.

Hochschild, A. R. (1975). The sociology of feelings and emotion: Selected possibilities. In M. Millman & R. M. Kanter (Eds.), *Another voice: Feminist perspectives on social life and social science* (pp. 280–307). Garden City, N.J.: Anchor/Doubleday.

Hochschild, A. R. (1983). *The managed heart: The commercialization of human feeling*. Berkeley: University of California Press.

Hofferth, S. L., et al. (1990). *National child care survey, 1990*. Washington, D.C.: The Urban Institute.

Lundgren, R. I., & Browner, C. H. (1990). Caring for the institutionalized mentally retarded: Work culture and work-based social support. In E. K. Abel & M. K. Nelson (Eds.), *Circles of care: Work and identity in women's lives* (pp. 150–172). Albany: State University of New York Press.

Marzollo, J. (1987, April). Child-care workers speak up. *Parents' Magazine, 62*, 114–118.

Morgan, G. (1986). Supplemental care for young children. In T. W. Youngman & T. B. Brazelton (Eds.), *In support of families* (pp. 156–174). Cambridge, Mass.: Harvard University Press.

Nelson, M. K. (1990a). *Negotiated care: The experience of family day care providers*. Philadelphia: Temple University Press.

Nelson, M. K. (1990b). The regulation controversy in family day care: The perspective of providers. In J. S. Hyde & M. J. Essex (Eds.), *Parental leave and child care: Setting a research and policy agenda* (pp. 354–372). Philadelphia: Temple University Press.

O'Barr, J. F., Pope, D., & Wyer, M. (1990). *Ties that bind: Essays on mothering and patriarchy*. Chicago: University of Chicago Press.

Ruddick, S. (1984). Maternal thinking. In J. Trebilcot (Ed.), *Mothering: Essays in feminist theory* (pp. 213–230). Totowa, N.J.: Rowman and Allanheld.

U.S. Bureau of the Census (1980). *1980 Census: Vermont*. Washington, D.C.: U.S. Government Printing Office.

Vermont Department of Social and Rehabilitation Services (1985). *Journal for family day care homes*. Montpelier, Vt.

Young, K. T., & Zigler, E. (1986). Infant and toddler day care: Regulations and policy implications. *American Journal of Orthopsychiatry, 56* (1), 43–55.

Chapter 3

Heart, Mind, and Soul: Head Start as a Reminder of the Powerful Function of Schools for Their Communities

Maike Philipsen and Jo Agnew

INTRODUCTION

This is the story of a Head Start program in a poor, rural, predominantly African-American community we call Centerville. Except for a GED program, it is the only educational institution in town. That was not always so. During the 1960s and 1970s, Centerville lost its elementary schools through consolidation and desegregation efforts.

The question that undergirds the research described here was: How do the educational experiences of Head Start students compare with those of older students who attend schools located outside of the Centerville community? In what ways, in other words, do mothers and teachers of young children in Head Start perceive "their" school, "their" teachers, the curriculum, and the general purpose and effectiveness of Head Start in comparison with the world of schooling experienced by older students and their mothers.

Not all of the older students we interviewed attended Head Start when they were young children. This study, then, is not a longitudinal study of Head Start graduates but an effort to compare the educational experiences of two groups of students from the same town.

The vast body of literature on Head Start is controversial in terms of the long-term effects of early childhood intervention. While some studies suggest that cognitive gains are in danger of waning over time (Westinghouse Learning Corporation, 1969; Bronfenbrenner, 1974), other research demonstrates the positive long-term effects of Head Start programs related to children's health, nutrition, grade retention, socioemotional traits, school adjustment, and family life (McKey, Condelli, Ganson, Barrett, McConkey, & Plantz, 1985; Hale, Seitz, & Zigler, 1990). It is clear in the research, however, that Head Start programs alone are no guarantee that children will be able to break out of the cycle of poverty. If students leaving Head Start are forced to attend schools that they do not consider their own, and if they grow up in a social context without employment opportunities and without role models of people for whom education has paid off, the cycle of poverty is likely to continue. A comprehensive study of Head Start needs to take into account what happens to students once they leave the program and become part of a school system that was not designed to meet their needs.

By contrasting the educational experiences of young children enrolled in Head Start, on the one hand, with those of older students, high school graduates and dropouts, on the other, it is our goal to highlight necessary elements not only for successful early childhood education but for successful education of minority students in general. By portraying the educational experiences of the older students, we may be able to reveal crucial barriers to successful education of students who are not (in some cases no longer) enrolled in a Head Start program. The issue is not whether Head Start programs should be dismantled because they presumably fail to produce long-lasting positive effects, but how students can be assisted once they leave Head Start. We agree with Zigler and Styfco's note of caution:

The expansion of Head Start is certainly justified by the large body of evidence on the benefits of quality early intervention. Yet many people have read too much into this literature, to the point that they view preschool education in general, and Head Start in particular, as the definitive solution to major national problems in education, business, and the social structure. (1993, p. 17)

By studying the Head Start program in the general context of schooling in Centerville, it became obvious how important it is for community members to send *their* children to *their* schools, located in *their* community and knowing that common values are shared by parents, teachers, and community members alike. The Head Start program in Centerville illustrates that schooling for African-American children has the potential to be a nurturing, strengthening, educational experience in a racist society in which minority children not only need to start ahead but need support along the way.

By employing a comparative perspective, looking at both the Head Start program in town and the educational experiences of older black students who are bused out of their community every day, we also discovered what the community lost when it lost its schools. The closings of the town's own elementary schools are widely perceived by Centerville's inhabitants as a devastating turning point, as if "the heart was torn out" of their community. The Head Start program in Centerville serves as a powerful reminder of the important function of schools for a community. Other researchers have described the connections between schools and communities. Peshkin notes that "An anthropological view of schooling inclines us toward the concept of education as cultural transmission, functioning to maintain communities, social structures, and values" (1982a, p. 50). Jarrett concurs: "It is evident that the school is, and always has been, a primary agency for socialization. The child is inducted into the mores and folkways of their society through the schooling process" (1991, p. 55).

Our study was conducted in a rural town in north-central North Carolina. Centerville's population of 1,500 is 78 percent African-American. The town lacks an economically productive infrastructure and thus provides limited employment opportunities for its inhabitants. People commute in order to work. Roughly 50 percent of the population live below the official poverty line.

In 1969 the white school in town was closed as part of a countywide (and statewide) consolidation effort. The attendance lines split the town along its central street, sending Centerville's white students to two different schools and ending the historical alignment of school and community for the white residents. In 1972 school desegregation resulted in the closing of the black school in Centerville. The Head Start program in Centerville was established in 1967 and has served the Centerville community since then. Today only preschool children go to school in their own town. Older students are being bused to a number of predominantly white schools in three neighboring communities: Larox, Stepford, and Crestmore. To this date, black students are regularly reassigned to allow these schools to meet their desired racial mixes.

This paper is based on an ethnographic study of the educational history of Centerville. The authors were members of a research team that was invited by the mayor of Centerville to document long-term effects of the local school closings. Besides the local Head Start program, team members visited churches, homes, and production sites in town, as well as schools in the neighboring communities. We participated in festivals and went to GED classes and community programs. We conducted approximately fifty in-depth interviews, collected archival data in order to construct an educational history of the town, and have recently produced a video using oral history techniques to reconstruct the history of and capture current educational values in Centerville.

It was the team's goal both to respond to the initial request of the mayor and to pursue any research interests that would emerge during the course of the study. We started our project with broad sensitizing questions, yet without a clearly defined research agenda. It was only in the course of the research process that different interests and foci emerged. One team member specialized in oral histories with teachers of the formerly segregated school; one dealt with the relations between the town's history of land ownership, educational resources, and patterns of schooling; a third member investigated the town's discourse about race; while a fourth member focused on the phenomenon of denial concerning race and gender relations as well as historical events (for an overview of the larger study, see Baynes-Jeffries, Blount, Desimone, McCullough-Garrett, Nix, & Philipsen, 1993).

The authors of this paper initially had two foci: Maike Philipsen researched the educational experiences of female high school students, recent graduates, and dropouts in Centerville; Jo Agnew studied the local Head Start program. In sharing findings, it became obvious that while the Head Start children seem to thrive in their school, and while both mothers and teachers involved in Head Start perceive their institution to be a valuable educational experience for their children, older students who are bused out of their community in order to attend schools in predominantly white neighborhoods do not do well at all.

Teachers and principals speak with great concern about the older students from Centerville. The educational performance of a great many of them is considered to be poor, and a high percentage never graduate. The question that poses itself is: how do we account for the differences between the educational experiences of young children and those of older students? In order to shed light on this question, we will first look at the reality and meaning of the local Head Start program from the perspectives of both teachers and mothers of young children. In a second step we will focus on the educational experiences of high school students, graduates, and dropouts.

METHODOLOGY: AN ETHNOGRAPHIC CASE STUDY

Qualitative researchers aspire to enrich the human discourse (Geertz, 1973) by providing interpretations—or partial accounts—of certain matters. They generally do not strive to discover an objective "Truth" that, given the appropriate sample, control, and method, is generalizable to a larger population. Qualitative research is based on the assumption that social phenomena are dynamic; they change over time because human behavior is both unpredictable and at least partially shaped by the free will of social agents (Cziko, 1989; Eisner, 1988). In other words, since people make choices, albeit within certain social constraints, they adapt their behavior to newly evolving circumstances.

This study provides the authors' partial accounts of the educational values and experiences of two groups of students in Centerville. These partial accounts, however, do not stand alone. They are embedded in and were enriched by the accounts constructed by other members of our research team. During the planning and fieldwork period of the larger study, the team met regularly to exchange conceptual and methodological ideas, experiences, and findings from the field. By means of re-searcher triangulation we thus intended to "check and balance" our individual, partial accounts and construct a holistic story of education in Centerville. As a group, we employed several different kinds of data col-lection: in-depth interviews, observations, participation in communal events (Labor Day festival, gospel festival, church services, youth "rap sessions"), and document analysis (newspapers, town council minutes, dropout data). We visited homes and community programs, and invited community members to view and debate the content of a video on ed-ucation in Centerville which we had produced.

Consequently, we triangulated our study in terms of data sources and methods of data collection. It was our policy that "all researchers own all data," which permitted each member of the team to make use of reports, transcripts, and primary documents collected by others. While each individual team member pursued his/her own focus, in short, we all conceptualized our studies to strive for the "ideal and moral imper-ative to learn all, to take all into account, and to tell all" (Noblit & Engel, 1991, p. 123).

While it is beyond the scope of this chapter to describe all the meth-odological details of our studies, we will lay out with some specificity the processes we used for interviewing. We conducted in-depth, open-ended interviews with a wide variety of Centerville inhabitants: mothers and teachers of Head Start participants, young women between the ages of fourteen and twenty-six who either still attended school or had grad-uated or had dropped out of school, and women between forty and sev-enty years of age who had school-aged children or grandchildren and had lived in Centerville all their lives. Most interviews were individual conversations; some were group interviews. Most were conducted in pri-vate settings (the interviewees' homes) or in Centerville's Head Start facility, and lasted between one and two hours. All interviews required written consent, and the majority was tape-recorded and transcribed ver-batim. Interview guides served as outlines of the issues we wanted to ex-plore. These issues were not always tackled in a particular order, and the actual wording of questions varied a great deal across different inter-views. We dropped and added questions spontaneously depending on the flow of the conversation. In a way, the interview guides served as a basic "checklist" to ensure that all relevant topics were being covered. All interviews were prearranged, either by phone or during face-to-face encounters, such as at festivals or in church. Our sampling methods are best described as "snow-ball" sampling: we asked interviewees for relatives and acquaintances who might possibly be willing to talk to us. In the interviews, we generally avoided dichotomous questions (questions that invite "yes" or "no" answers) and "why questions" (questions presuming cause-effect relationships). Rather, we asked what Michael Quinn Patton calls "truly open-ended questions" which

permit respondents to respond in their own terms. [They do] not presuppose which dimension of feeling or thought will be salient to the interviewee. The truly open-ended question allows the person being interviewed to select from among the person's full repertoire of possible responses. (1990, pp. 295–296)

Our questions were meant to serve as "catalysts" for the interviewees to express their opinions and experiences in whatever way they chose. By asking a broad "open" question as, for example, "what do you think about education?", we "allowed" the participants to choose the direction of their answers. Their answers could be generalizations, or they could take the form of concrete examples in regard to their educational experiences. Participants could talk about ideals or limitations, about hopes, disappointments, wishes, or plans. Consequently, the interviews routinely "fanned out" in different directions on the basis of a given question. The interviewees determined how to answer the questions, and we followed up on their answers and probed deeper. It was as important to understand why our interviewees answered in a certain manner as to know what they actually said.

HEAD START IN CENTERVILLE: THE EDUCATIONAL EXPERIENCES OF YOUNGER STUDENTS

Head Start is based on the belief that "education is the solution" to breaking the cycle of poverty (Zigler and Styfco, 1993, p. 9). Head Start programs were originally developed in communities much like Centerville with a high concentration of low-income families. Head Start was initiated twenty-seven years ago in Centerville and has, over that time, drawn large numbers of children from the Centerville community. Clearly, however, the cycle of poverty has not been broken in this community. What, then, does the Head Start program mean to the teachers and mothers of young children in Centerville? The following vignette constructed from field notes and interview data introduces our discussion of this question.

As the class of 1993 Head Start graduates marches along with their teachers into the school gym, several mothers and grandmothers with their cameras and camcorders are busily recording this very special event in Centerville. Soon the piano starts playing Michael Jackson's "We are the world; we are the children; there will be a better day . . . " (Jackson, 1992). The four-year-olds stand up and sing their hearts out, while the audience nods and smiles, clapping along with the children.

The president of the Chamber of Commerce congratulates the graduates. She tells their families that their children are getting an important head start in life. "With a good education," she says, "they can do anything. They can become the leaders in their community."

The coordinator of the Centerville Head Start Center hands out awards of excellence to two teachers. She talks about how much these teachers have done to help the students and proceeds to read a letter from a parent about a teacher: "Mrs. B is a religious person, and she is real strict. It is important to her that the children learn. And she takes the time to make them really learn. She knows they have the ability to learn and shows concern for each child from the very start."

The coordinator announces the recipients of the outstanding volunteer service awards, given to several mothers of Head Start children. One of these mothers walks up to the microphone on stage and thanks the teachers, telling the audience that her children are learning so much from the Head Start staff. She feels it was very important that her kids learned to write the ABC's, learned about black history, and had the opportunity to go on many great field trips.

Soon it is time for each graduate to march across the stage to receive a diploma and then proceed down a special runway which has been decorated with banners, streamers, and balloons. The audience enthusiastically cheers for each child. As soon as everyone has received his/her diploma, a veteran teacher who had been with the Centerville Head Start Center for over twenty-five years asks her class to lead the audience in singing all the verses to "He's got the whole world in his hands." There is an ambience of much warmth, cooperation, and caring in this graduation, reflecting a sense of belonging and togetherness. Obviously, this graduation means a lot to those present. All are dressed in their Sunday best from tiny babies to elderly grandmothers.

After the ceremony, mothers of graduates are saying their goodbyes to teachers and staff at the center. One of the mothers cries as she hugs her child's teacher. She says: "Mrs. B., will you come and visit us? We will miss you so; we love our school."

Such poignant moments indicate the meaning of Head Start to the teachers and mothers of young children in this community. Analysis revealed that these moments are grounded in one major theme: attachment. The data of the study revealed that mothers and teachers of young children in Centerville are deeply connected to and involved with their school, a school located in their community and run by teachers who share the children's racial background. Forty of the fifty Head Start students who live in Centerville are African American; five of the six teachers assigned to the Centerville Head Start program are also African

American. The black students, in short, are exposed daily to black role models.

Head Start in Centerville is generally perceived as a positive experience by all those involved. Besides the deep sense of belonging to the school shared by children, parents, and teachers alike, the Head Start curriculum is recognized as relevant to the students' lives. Teachers teach what the parents believe their children need to know before they enter public elementary schools. The mothers present at the graduation ceremony displayed a sense of pride in their children's learning and accomplishments.

Parents are certain that Head start teachers deeply care about their children. One mother of a Head Start student felt this caring was demonstrated in the teachers' strictness: "They were real strict. It was important to them that the kids were learning, and I liked teachers like that. Not just someone that's going to pass my kids on by. Teachers who will make my kids really learn because they know they've got the ability." Teachers are trusted to fulfill their mission of preparing Centerville's young children for the future. Not only do Centerville's mothers routinely get involved in the center's activities, but they also allow teachers into their homes as part of the home-based program of Head Start. One grandmother of a Head Start student described the teacher-parent cooperation as close: "Ya know, Head Start works with the whole family, not just the children but also the mothers and fathers and sometimes even the grandparents like me. I take care of the kids when their mother works and get to visit with the Head Start teacher who comes to our house."

Yet another striking feature characterizes the meaning of Head Start for those involved: the culture of Head Start is constructed as a collective orientation, an orientation within which the needs of the group are stressed and communal values rather than individuality are emphasized (for similar findings see Lubeck, 1985). Observations of teacher-student interactions and analysis of children's songs provide the evidence that the theme of "if we only stick together we will be o.k." is a consistent feature of daily life in Centerville's Head Start Center.

Along with the sense of belonging and togetherness prevalent at the Head Start in Centerville, there is also a sense of cultural congruence. The Head Start curriculum—what was being taught and how it was being taught—coincided with and reinforced values taught at home. One of the teachers mentioned specifically that the Head Start curriculum was culturally congruent for the children from Centerville. Said she: "We encourage the children to be outgoing and express their emotions. We talk a lot about black history, too. We teach them to work together."

She stressed that many former students find that they get punished for being expressive, labeled as troublemakers, or simply ignored once they leave Head Start and begin attending public schools outside their community. In a way, then, culturally congruent education—if confined to early childhood education—has its limitations. As Lubeck noted: "though highly functional within a black kinship network, these social interactions may not prepare children to adapt to the specific requirements of American schooling" (1985, p. 113).

Our overall impression of the Head Start program in Centerville is that it provides a kind of temporary haven where the teachers and mothers work very hard to help their children feel a positive attachment to schooling. And, although their hard work does not seem to pay off in a school society dominated by white culture, it must not be ignored. This Head Start program serves as an example of what schooling in general could provide for all children and families: a positive experience where an initial sense of cultural identity and strength is tied to positive attitudes toward school.

BEING BUSED OUT OF CENTERVILLE: THE EDUCATIONAL EXPERIENCES OF THE OLDER STUDENTS

In contrast to the young children in Centerville's Head Start program, schooling is not portrayed as a positive experience for the older students who are being bused to schools in predominantly white communities. The students from Centerville feel deeply alienated from the schools they attend. They do not have a sense of belonging to the predominantly white communities in which the schools are located. This attitude is reflected in the way members of the older generations in Centerville feel about the schools to which their children are being bused. As mothers of high school students pointed out:

A lot of the parents don't have a lot of contact with teachers. They don't go to PTA meetings. . . . A lot of our parents here—of course, you know that Centerville is 75 percent black—a lot of our parents don't go to school. They have their own idea of what's going on in school. They feel like their children are not treated fairly. And it's not going to do us any good to go to that school anyway.

You send your kids over to Crestmore, and they're like: "Oh, you're not from here. We don't like you from down there." I think that's a big part of the problem.

An assistant principal of one of the high schools serving Centerville students in Larox, seven miles west of Centerville, stated, "The students from Centerville don't feel as if this is their school. And the parents say, 'No one has ever invited me to come to this school.' "

Centerville parents and students lack a sense of belonging to the schools. The schools themselves have, in the students' eyes, little if anything to do with "living." While the mothers of the Head Start children were convinced that the Head Start curriculum was designed to offer their children useful skills, the older students cannot see much usefulness in the curriculum offered in their schools. What defines school for them—academic subjects, after-school activities—does not seem relevant to their problem-ridden situations outside of school. As the students from Centerville see it, schools do not provide the space to talk about "things that really matter." Schools do not support adolescents during the difficult period of growing up. Rather, schools silence—or even push out—those students who have the most severe personal problems.

The students from Centerville feel distant from their predominantly white teachers. Teachers are perceived to be non-supportive, particularly for those students who need special help. They are seen as lacking creativity in presenting the subject matter, and as generally not being very interested in their students. The mothers and grandmothers of these older students repeatedly stressed that parents can no longer send their children to schools that they trust—schools in which teachers conduct classes according to values that parents support. The following criticisms forcefully reveal these frustrations:

We did better not being in integrated schools because black kids have picked up the culture of the white kids. That's like picking up the culture of people you're not used to. That causes stress.

Desegregation turned out to be a one-way street. Only the blacks have taken over the white values, and no whites took over black values.

Both the contemporary Head Start program in Centerville and the former all-black schools prior to desegregation are described as places where black teachers and administrators serve(d) as both authority figures and role models for students. Adults in the integrated schools in Larox, Crestmore, and Stepford, however, do not.

Another significant ingredient of schooling that—while still existent for the young children attending Head Start—was lost once the all-black school was closed is a sense among Centerville's parents that teachers care for the young. The culturally sanctioned ways of disciplining children in school and conducting the daily business of teaching were fundamentally different from what our interviewees perceive as the non-caring and liberal pedagogy of today's teachers in faraway schools. As one mother whose daughter attends a school in Larox said, "I think those teachers used to be more into what they were doing than a lot of teachers now. They saw to it that things got done. And now it's sort of like this: 'you do it or you just get left behind.' "

Teachers of the past are described as having had a mission, or as having assumed "moral responsibility for the education of children" (Noblit, 1993, p. 27). Today's teachers are suspected to be performing without commitment. The following quotes from conversations with members of the older generations in Centerville reveal these understandings:

The teachers were more interested in you learning than they seem to be now. To tell you the truth, some of teachers now—they're just, it's just like any other job. Like any other job—looking for a paycheck. Just a paycheck.

Teachers nowadays—well, you teach yourself. When I was going to school teachers taught us, but now you teach yourself when you go to school. It's more like you work on your own.

There is much to indicate that the distrust of black parents and grandparents toward today's teachers is far-reaching and intense. In fact, the mothers and grandmothers in our study question the very essence of today's teaching profession. They do not feel that their children are taught by "professionals." Said one parent, "When I was going to school the teachers didn't joke around with the kids and all. They were very professional. Now sometimes in school you can't tell who the teacher is and who the students are."

"Being professional" means running teacher-centered classrooms, and "professionalism" is tightly connected to issues of discipline and control, both of which today's teachers, in the eyes of the people in Centerville, have lost. As a mother explained, "It seems like today everybody's having a party, you know? It doesn't look like there is any structure. . . . Seems like everybody is just 'I go my way, you go yours.' "

How do members of the older generations in Centerville construct the concept of caring with power—or, as George Noblit calls it, "moral authority" (1993, p. 37) that undergirds much of their criticism of today's schools? Centerville's parents believe today's older students do not really get affirmation that anybody cares for them. Schools outside the Centerville community, for instance, fail to provide children with the sense that "somebody cares about you." The failure of today's schools to provide firm discipline and control is unequivocally considered to be a clear indication of the lack of caring:

I think in order to have control you have to enforce rules, and do the things that's necessary in order to let the kids know that you care about them. If kids feel that they can get away with everything, like sneaking away from school, then they feel "I don't need to be there."

And for the older students in Centerville, "feeling as if nobody cares about me" translates into "not caring about yourself":

I feel that they had a better handle on the kids when I grew up than they have now. . . . And the kids, a lot of them could care less. And they always tell me "Well, nobody don't care anything about me."

While there are also many white parents and grandparents who mourn the loss of discipline and control in our schools, this loss has its own particular meaning for black parents. With the loss of their own (i.e., black) teachers, they lost their own forms of discipline and control. But beyond that, black parents also strongly believe that by giving up strict enforcement of discipline, order, and control, teachers lost (or gave up) their mission of truly caring for black students. They lost their moral authority. They are not seen as truly caring because they are not in control, not in charge, not "on top of things"—they do not regulate, oversee, and discipline to the extent necessary to make sure that students learn, behave, and ultimately succeed. In essence, parents and other older community members in Centerville are convinced that they have lost the essential tool that would allow their children "to make it out there" in a basically hostile and racist environment.

Another factor that keeps black students from Centerville at "the bottom" in terms of academic performance is black peer culture. While peers are considered valuable by Centerville's students since they help make school bearable and at least vaguely interesting, peers are also seen as influences that routinely discourage individual students from striving to "do good" in school. Academic achievement is largely associated with what John Ogbu (1988) has described as the stigmatization of "acting white." Two former students describe this phenomenon as follows:

The majority of students I hung out with were white. I had seen earlier that I wasn't doing my work if I hung out with my buddies from around the neighborhood. . . . And I did better when I was around white people. . . . And I caught a nickname. They called me Zebra. It was for a black guy trying to be white. I was called that for trying to be with my white friends.

But when you're in school, there are kids who are not striving for what you want, and they try to do little things to hold you back or stop you from trying to achieve. . . . It's kind of hard because sometimes you just have to block out your friends and block everyone else in order to get what you strive for.

Rarely do those students who would like to excel "against all odds" actually resist pressure from peers. Most of them are afraid to step out of their peer culture. Students who are seen as turning against their peers frequently face a number of unpleasant sanctions. Since students from Centerville form a minority in the schools they attend, they depend on their own peers in terms of forming an in-group identity in school. Alienating one's peer group by trying to be a good student is widely perceived as running the risk of losing a vital plot of social ground to stand on.

While the young children in Centerville's Head Start program seem to feel positively recognized in school, the older students experience school as a place of stigmatization and stratification. They have to endure various forms of racism directed against all black students, and they have to cope with a number of racial barriers that are gender-specific. Black boys take the brunt of stereotyping and discrimination against black students: boys are a priori labeled as "bad," while black girls are expected to be "nice." On the other hand, black girls see that black boys are at least challenged to excel in one area: athletics. Black girls, however, are neither challenged with any special expectations to achieve, nor do they get much support from their teachers when they need extra help.

The young women from Centerville, however, not only experience forms of stratification in school that are based on race and gender, they also experience stratification based on class. It is more than obvious to the vast majority of black students that they are poor—particularly when they compare themselves to their white peers who almost always come from more affluent families.

The experience of "classification systems" in school along the lines of race, class, and gender has decisive effects on how the young women from Centerville craft their own identities, and on how they make decisions concerning their futures. They decide, for instance, not to rely on males as future breadwinners. Or they foster the dream that they will one day be able to "outdo" those who are currently better off in material terms. Only a few female students are determined to achieve in school and in this way possibly overcome racial stereotypes and low expectations toward black students. Schooling, in summary, is not seen as a "jumping board" into a world where everybody—regardless of race, class, or gender—has equal chances to succeed. On the contrary, school is experienced as yet another place where hierarchical and unequal relationships are lived and perpetuated. And while the young children in Centerville's Head Start program are being told during their graduation ceremony that they will be able to do anything if only they get a good education, the older students have already realized that the world is not that wide open for them.

Another factor that significantly shaped the educational experience of the older students in Centerville is the daily routine of being bused out of their community to predominantly white schools. Busing has many consequences for the students from Centerville. It is not merely inconvenient. Depending on buses also prevents students and parents who do not have access to private transportation from attending events that take place outside of the regular school schedule (after-school activities, PTA meetings, tutoring sessions, etc.). In addition, busing is perceived as simply unfair: it is always the black students who have to leave their community. White students are not being bused to Centerville.

Students from Centerville, moreover, are not only bused out of their community, they are also frequently reassigned to different schools in order to allow these schools to meet their desired racial mixes. Students lose academically when they have to "start over" at a new school. Students and parents also lose any ties they might have established with a particular school if they are forced to leave and start over at another school.

The problems of both busing and school transfers could be solved if a school was reestablished in Centerville. And yet, while the older generation in Centerville readily embraces that idea, most of our younger interviewees are indifferent toward it, or even oppose it outright. They have been effectively "socialized away" from their community—a community which, in their eyes, has nothing to offer anyway. They prefer to "escape" to neighboring towns rather than "get stuck" in Centerville. The combination of community deterioration and busing—both of which "cut the roots" out from under Centerville's students—has effectively undermined any stable sense of belonging among the young. While the school in pre-desegregated Centerville apparently did its share in keeping the black community together, the politics of busing has helped in socializing the young away from their community. What busing has not accomplished, however, is to provide them with a sense that they can "make it" somewhere else.

CONCLUSION: HEAD START AS A POWERFUL REMINDER OF THE IMPORTANCE OF SCHOOLS FOR A COMMUNITY

This study, in summary, demonstrates that schooling and communities are organically related. The Head Start program in Centerville serves as a powerful example that the school is not isolated from the community it serves (Lubeck, 1985, p. 9). To be sure, structural economic conditions led to a cycle of poverty in Centerville that could not be broken merely by one educational program such as Head Start. Yet, what Head Start does provide are powerful lessons that schooling can be perceived as a positive experience by both parents and teachers.

Head Start in Centerville provides young children with an environment accepted by their parents as genuinely caring and educationally enhancing. Mothers get actively involved in a program they trust and consider invaluable for their children. Cooperation between community and school is close and intense. Parents feel that their children are being taught a foundation of knowledge and skills necessary "to make it out there."

Most of these positive realities for young children in Centerville are lost for the older students. The Centerville community provides a good example of the general phenomenon that "schools have grown increasingly out of touch with the social and cultural reality in which they are embedded and in which the participants live. This mismatch between institutions and context is profound" (LeCompte & Dworkin, 1991, p. 2).

For a wide range of reasons, older students feel alienated from the schools they attend: they have to switch schools frequently due to racially motivated reassignments; they perceive themselves to be outsiders at predominantly white schools in predominantly white communities; they are largely indifferent toward a curriculum which, in their eyes, is irrelevant to the reality of their lives; they feel that their (white) teachers do not care for them, while their own peers discourage them from achieving. Instead of cooperating closely with teachers, Centerville's parents stay away from schools which they, by and large, do not perceive to be their own.

The Head Start program for the young children in Centerville reemphasizes the bond between community and schooling and provides a "foundation of hope" for both children and parents in terms of the children's educational future. However, the busing experience of the older students effectively socializes them away from their community without providing them with the reassurance that they have good chances to be successful somewhere else.

Head Start could be described as a temporary haven for both mothers and children; while it does not prepare children adequately for schooling in a predominantly white setting, it does provide the children with an initial sense of identity and strength. Looking at it another way, Head Start provides an example of what schooling in general could provide for children, parents, and the community. And yet, the positive effects of Head Start are in danger once the powerful triad of community, school, and students is broken. Further, the young children's enthusiasm for their school and for education in general is bound to wane given the dismal socioeconomic conditions in their community, lack of employment opportunities, and absence of role models for whom education has indeed "paid off." The fragility of Head Start's success serves as an illustration of Apple's statement: "In this economy, the people of color, women, and the young are most at risk" (1989, p. 3).

The Head Start program in Centerville serves as the last reminder of what the community of Centerville lost when its schools were closed during desegregation. As Peshkin notes, such a loss is significant:

Though far from new to American education in general, consolidation and centralization are innovations for any particular school district. They clearly involve changes of a non-trivial nature, in that they affect a community by closing its school and affect a group of children by necessitating their accommodation to new children, new teachers, new physical settings, and, possibly, new routines, procedures, and expectations. (Peshkin, 1982b, p. 166)

One could argue with Lightfoot that "though the Brown decision focused on schooling, it disregarded the development of children and perspectives of families and communities" (1980, p. 4). In the specific case of Centerville, by losing its schools, the black community is perceived as having lost education as a vehicle for social mobility. They have lost an essential tool in their struggle to keep up in an ever-changing and highly competitive world. They lost their most powerful tool in the struggle for equality. As Joseph pointed out, even during the days of all-black schools, "The American dream . . . never worked for Blacks" (1988, p. 174). And yet education symbolizes hope. It is seen to have played a crucial role in all the social, political, and economic gains blacks have achieved since the days of slavery. In a way, education could properly be called the structural underpinning of everything that has been cause for pride within the black community, from emancipation in the post-Civil War period to civil rights struggles in the fifties and sixties (Kluger, 1977).

But education no longer has the same meaning it used to have. Except for the Head Start program, the black community in Centerville no longer has control over the one institution that carried the main burden of preparing the young for their future in a hostile white environment. They lost their school which provided children with sanctioned values, role models, meaning, and, most important, a sense of caring. They lost the institution that provided parents with a sense of involvement and control over their children, and their children's future.

Discipline, control, and caring inherently carry with them vital political aspects. While these issues are primarily discussed in terms of schooling, they have much wider ranging implications: a measure of control over their own lives is lost, and, with it, a certain degree of hope concerning the future.

REFERENCES

Apple, M. (1989). *Teachers and texts*. New York and London: Routledge.
Baynes-Jeffries, R., Blount, J., Desimone, L., McCullough-Garrett, A., Nix, M., & Philipsen, M. (1993). Deep understandings: A conversation about race,

community, and schooling in a rural African-American town. *The Journal of Negro Education, 62* (4), 403–440.

Bronfenbrenner, U. (1974). *A report of longitudinal evaluations of preschool programs, vol. 2: Is early intervention effective?* Washington, D.C.: Department of Health, Education, and Welfare (HDEW Pub. No. OHD 74-25).

Cziko, G. A. (1989). Unpredictability and indeterminism in human behavior: Arguments and implications for educational research. *Educational Researcher, 18* (3), 17–25.

Eisner, E. W. (1988). The primacy of experience and the politics of method. *Educational Researcher, 17,* 15–20.

Geertz, C. (1973). *The interpretation of cultures.* New York: Basic Books.

Hale, B. A., Seitz, V., and Zigler, E. (1990). Health service and Head Start: A forgotten formula. *Journal of Applied Developmental Psychology, 11,* 47–58.

Jackson, M. (1992). Will You Be There? *Dangerous Album.* New York: Sony Music Distribution.

Jarrett, J. L. (1991). *The teaching of values: Caring and appreciation.* New York: Routledge.

Joseph, G. I. (1988). Black feminist pedagogy and schooling in capitalist white America. In M. Cole (Ed.), *Bowles and Gintis revisited* (pp. 174–186). London: Falmer.

Kluger, R. (1977). *Simple justice: The history of Brown v. Board of Education and black America's struggle for equality.* New York: Vintage Books.

LeCompte, M., and Dworkin, A. (1991). *Giving up on school.* Newbury Park, Calif.: Corwin Press.

Lightfoot, S. L. (1980). Families as educators: The forgotten people of Brown. In D. Bell (Ed.), *Shades of Brown* (pp. 3–19). New York and London: Teachers College Press.

Lubeck, S. (1985). *Sandbox society.* London and Philadelphia: Falmer.

McKey, R. H., Condelli, L., Ganson, H., Barrett, B., McConkey, C., & Plantz, M. (1985). *The impact of Head Start on children, families, and communities: Final report of the Head Start evaluation, synthesis, and utilization project.* Washington, D.C.: U.S. Government Printing Office (DHHS Pub. No. OHDS 85-31193).

Noblit, G. W. (1993). Power and caring. *American Educational Research Journal, 30* (1), 23–38.

Noblit, G. W., and Engel, J. D. (1991). The Holistic injunction: An ideal and a moral imperative for qualitative research. *Qualitative Health Review, 1* (1), 123–130.

Ogbu, J. U., (1988). Class stratification, racial stratification, and schooling. In L. Weis (Ed.), *Class, race, and gender in American education* (pp. 163–182). Albany: State University of New York Press.

Patton, M. Q. (1990). *Qualitative evaluation and research methods.* Newbury Park, Calif.: Sage Publications.

Peshkin, A. (1982a). The researcher and subjectivity: Reflections of an ethnography of school and community. In G. Spindler (Ed.), *Doing the ethnography of schooling* (pp. 48–67). New York: Holt, Rinehart, & Winston.

Peshkin, A. (1982b). *The imperfect union.* Chicago: University of Chicago Press.

Westinghouse Learning Corporation (1969). *The impact of Head Start: An eval-*

uation of the effects of Head Start on children's cognitive and affective development. Executive summary. Washington, D.C.: Clearinghouse for Federal Scientific and Technical Information (EDO36321).

Zigler, E., and Styfco, S. J. (1993). *Head Start and beyond.* New Haven and London: Yale University Press.

Chapter 4

Life History of a First Grade Teacher: A Narrative of Culturally Sensitive Teaching Practice

Mary E. Hauser

This chapter tells a story about Janet Dillon, a first grade teacher in a multiethnic school. Janet is a teacher from whom we can learn some lessons about teaching young children. She seems to embody a sensitivity to the cultural differences of her first graders that is usually only described in textbooks. She models the kind of cultural sensitivity that provides a variety of ways for young children to experience and then to practice the attitudes, knowledge, and skills necessary for effective living in a complex, diverse world. In Janet's classroom all who enter are greeted by a "welcome" sign printed in six languages (Russian, Lao, Hmong, Khmer, Spanish, and English). She encourages students to use their home language in conversations with one another, and she arranges her classroom physically and "psychologically" so that students have spaces to work with others in whatever language seems to fit the activity. This kind of structure fosters the development of initiative and industry, important psychosocial tasks for children of this age. Fluent in Spanish, she also expresses interest in learning common words in the other home languages of the students. These glimpses of her practice intrigued me, and I found myself spending more and more time in her classroom in the course of a larger research project I was conducting at her school. This chapter is also about how qualitative research, in this instance life history research, can inform our knowledge of best practices with young children. Such knowledge needs to come from those who enact appropriate curricula on a daily basis. For too long the experiences and the voices of teachers, especially teachers of young children, have been marginalized in educational research. It seems that the younger the child taught, the less important is the voice of the teacher. However, this volume and others (e.g., Ayers, 1989; Genishi, 1992; Schubert & Ayers, 1992) are now helping to demonstrate the importance of the experiences of teachers of young children. Their experiences and voices are not decontextualized from the mainstream of educational practice as are those of many researchers. What they tell us can resonate with our experiences and knowledge in a meaningful way. We are learning the value of building theory from the practices of accomplished teachers.

Janet is a European-American woman who strongly identifies herself as a member of mainstream American culture. Indeed, 87 percent of the teachers in the United States are European American and 72 percent are female (Ordovensky, 1992). Janet's culturally sensitive teaching practice led me to wonder about the course of its development and to consider using a life history approach to understand the personal and professional experiences that led her to work with minority students in a way that we often think only minority teachers are able to do. Much literature validates the importance of a match between the cultures of students and teacher. As an example, McGroarty observes that "although sharing minority identity does not automatically ensure similarity of experience, it can provide important insights into the educational situation of students from non-mainstream backgrounds" (1986, p. 314). Cultural congruence between students and teachers is considered by many to be an advantage in the classroom. The fact that minority children fail in school is attributed (correctly in many instances) to a mismatch between the cultures of the students and the teacher. Language, dialects, gestural systems, and participation structures through which children make sense with each other are not the same as the codes used by the teachers who generally come from a more powerful social group (Trueba, 1989).

Because Janet does not share a minority ethnicity with her students, understanding how she developed the views that guide her practice may inform the preparation of future teachers. By far the largest number of education students are from European-American backgrounds. They are being trained to teach in classrooms where, by the year 2000, the majority of their students will not share that background. Learning from teachers like Janet can influence teacher educators to change their practice to prepare preservice teachers more effectively for a culturally diverse world.

Connelly and Clandinin (1990) wrote that "by listening to participant stories of their experience of teaching and learning, we hope to write narratives of what it means to educate and be educated." This is an important goal of this project.

SETTING THE CONTEXT

These are reflections by Janet, reflections on her experience as a learner that directly affect how she teaches first grade.

I know myself, where I work best, and where I read my best and where I do my best, and it's not sitting in an assigned seat.

I do remember in junior high and high school getting together in groups, which was the only way I could learn. It wasn't encouraged by the teachers, but we decided we had to do it.

I can't stand to do that drill, I know they must go crazy. It reminds me of Spanish language class where you have to do irregular verb drills: *yo soy, tu eres, el es, nosotros somos, Vosotros sois, ellos son.*

I went to a very exclusive public high school in southern California. Very very white. I was the only one with brown eyes. I felt a lot of prejudice in high school and college. But you don't know anything until you get out of the country. That's probably when I got the biggest awareness of what it's like for other people, immigrants or anybody else.

Learning happens more when you have a partner. If you choose to work independently, that's fine, but if you need help. . . . That's kind of what comes from the bilingual way of learning.

Throughout my conversations with Janet, her use of her own experiences to shape her teaching practice was evident. She seemed to be naturally reflective about what she did in the classroom. While inviting someone to recreate the story of their personal and professional experiences is also an invitation to reflect and examine that experience, it seems that those who choose to write and tell their stories are practically by definition those who tend to be self-reflective (Ayers, 1989, p. 129).

METHODOLOGY

My choice of methodology for this research was based on determining what I felt was the best way to answer my need to understand what personal and professional life experiences were salient in shaping Janet's teaching practice. I saw in Janet an example of what I considered effective teaching of young immigrant and refugee children. Since Janet did not consciously connect educational theory to what she did in the classroom, I wanted to understand just what it was that did guide her practice.

When the intent is to capture one person's interpretation of his or her life, the study is called a *life history* (Bogdan & Biklan, 1992, p. 3). There are in the literature, however, an often confusing array of ways to describe and identify research that could be used to understand teachers' lives. For example, Goodson (1992) sees a basic distinction between *life story* and *life history*. Life story is the story told about a life, and life history includes a wider range of evidence thereby locating the story within its historical context (Goodson, 1992, p. 6). Middleton (1993) employs a similar concept of life history in her research in that she includes analysis of the relationships between individuals' educational life histories and their historical and material contexts that both "shape and constrain our possibilities and release our educational imaginations" (p. 9).

Narrative is another frequently used term in the literature. Polkinghorne (1988, p. 13) describes narrative as an organizational scheme expressed in story form that connects individual human actions and events in a meaningful composite. "Narrative" is also used by Connelly and Clandinin (1988, 1990). They see the telling of stories as creating meaning from one's past experiences as well as creating meaning for the future. Witherell and Noddings (1991) also observe that narrative plays an important role in the formation of the self. Part of their description of narrative includes the idea that narrative demonstrates the embeddedness of our work in our cultural experience. Ayers (1989) prefers the term *life-narrative*. His methodology combines interviews and observations as well as interpretive activities that allow teachers to express themselves through other materials (such as paper or clay). Merriam (1991) uses the term *case study* and describes the methodology as being particularistic, descriptive, and heuristic in nature.

Despite the variation in terminology and different points of emphasis, common themes are apparent in these methods. One is the value of life history to let the reader enter and then understand the lives and work of others. Another is this perspective's power to connect with possibilities in other situations. Indeed, Plummer's (1983) view is that the "possibility" can occur for the interviewee as well as for the reader. Because the interview represents an intervention in the life of the interviewee, it can bring about a change in the way a person thinks about life and can stimulate change.

As research tools, life histories provide descriptions of real people, in real situations, struggling with real problems. Stories remove the anonymity of statistical samples and carefully controlled treatments. They connect us with the humanity that is what the business of teaching and learning is all about (Witherell & Noddings, 1991, p. 280).

To gather data for Janet's story, I interviewed her on several occasions over the period of a year. One set of interviews utilized questions from the in-depth interview procedure suggested by Seidman (1991). Questions are designed to lead to intersubjective understanding, enabling the interviewer to understand what an action or event means to the person interviewed. The initial question, "How did you come to teach these students?", provides a life history context for the experience under study.

A variation is to ask the person to tell as much as possible about her life leading up to the present time. This allows the person to trace the progress of experience, training, or education that prepared her for what she is doing now. The focus then moves to describing the details of her experience with the question, "What is it like for you to teach?" Requests for elaboration or clarification from the interviewer are then used to enlarge the discussion of the work beyond a chronology of what is done each day. Other questions situate the person's work in her personal context of meaning: "What is the meaning of what you do for you? How do you understand it in your life?"

The interviews were like conversations because, as Janet talked, I responded with stories from my own experience. As I will discuss in the analysis section, the data became mutually shared knowledge, rooted in the intersubjectivity of our interactions. While this technique could raise eyebrows concerning validity with readers who are more familiar with positivistic research, qualitative researchers control possible problems by carefully describing the role of the interviewer in the process.

I also taped interviews with several of Janet's teaching colleagues and interviewed the brother to whom she is closest in age and with whom she shared most of her experiences while growing up. These interviews elaborated the context in which the life story (i.e., the chronology she related) would be placed. Janet read this account and provided feedback before it was presented in its final form.

The hours I spent in her classroom observing and participating were an important part of learning about Janet. I was a substitute teacher on some occasions and served as an extra pair of hands for a variety of activities. I heeded the warning of Connelly and Clandinin (1988, p. 21): "if the studies looking into the past of teachers do not investigate the future through inquiry into classrooms, then the implications of an auto- or biographical study for future courses of action are speculative at most." I tried to get a balanced picture of Janet in order to avoid the pitfalls that studies of teachers' thinking that are cut off in their methodology from the past and future cannot avoid (Connelly and Clandinin, 1988).

THE SCHOOL CULTURE

Janet teaches at Brand School in West Bank, a small city that is part of a large north-central California metropolitan area. This school (K–5, about 350 students the year of the study) has been the focus of a larger research project, studying how cultural transmission is accomplished in a culturally diverse learning environment. The students at this school speak seven home languages, and 46 percent have limited English proficiency as defined by annual testing. Of Janet's twenty-seven students, sixteen have Lao, Hmong, or Khmer as home languages, and three speak English, four Spanish, and four Russian.

The Laotian and Cambodian families have been in the United States from less than one year to ten years. They were not the educated and/or influential Southeast Asian refugees who arrived with the first groups. Most lived on farms and small villages in their home countries, and few had any schooling. As a result they have been less successful in finding their place in American culture. About 70 percent of the families at the school receive AFDC funds (Hauser, 1990).

While West Bank was characterized by ethnic diversity even before the influx of families from Laos and Cambodia, cultural groups have remained fairly separate. Some residents describe the town as one where there is a "live-and-let-live" attitude, but certain areas have better reputations than others depending on the socioeconomic status and ethnicity of the groups who live there.

Brand's teaching and support staff does not reflect the ethnic diversity of the community. There are thirteen classroom teachers and seven specialists. All are European American with the exception of one Hispanic teacher, one Native American teacher, and the Chapter One teacher who is Vietnamese. Janet's teaching practice deviated the most from the school focus on "Americanizing" the students. Those processes have been documented in the larger study (Hauser, 1990).

JANET'S STORY

Janet did not share any childhood stories that foreshadowed her teaching career. But her older brother remembers that she was always tolerant of her younger brother from early on. When her younger brother would mess up the doll house she was playing in with a friend, she would clean things up without much complaint. Janet's older brother thinks that dealing with situations like this helped her to develop an understanding and love for kids. Janet's father had a third grade education, and her mother finished high school. It was her brother's impression that their parents were not able to be as helpful as they could have been in supporting their children's education because they did not understand the importance of school. He remembered: "They didn't have the background to help us with school work. We didn't have the books at home."

Their parents encouraged saving money, planning for the future, and not taking risks. One message that was given was that you can't always be happy. The immigrant background of both parents could have been a factor in these attitudes, according to Janet. Her mother was Portuguese, and she knew no English when she arrived in the United States at the age of three. Her father was Czech. Learning English quickly and fitting in were emphasized when Janet's mother went to school. "My mother still remembers the struggle of adapting. That must have been tough if she still remembers it and talks about it today," recalled Janet. So strong was the desire to become assimilated into American culture that some of her mother's relatives still resist all questions about their homeland. "They just wanted to be identified as Americans," Janet related.

In high school, Janet recounted that she was the only dark-haired, dark-eyed student and people wondered why she didn't go to the neighboring high school where all the Mexicans went. Janet noted: "When I dated the son of a rancher one summer, his friends told him that I wouldn't be a good person to get involved with because I was related to the people (my grandparents) who picked the grapes on his father's ranch." She became proficient in Spanish during high school, although her family thought it was not a good language to learn. They thought if she was going to learn a language, it should be Portuguese. She explained:

Later on when my grandmother learned I was interviewing for a job to teach in a Spanish bilingual program she was upset. She thought it was an insult to the family. The worst thing that anyone could do was to refer to her or her family members as Mexicans, and it was devastating to her to have her granddaughter teaching Mexicans.

Janet took Spanish originally because there was a "cute guy" in the class, and she persisted because she found she had an ear for it and found it interesting. (She told me that the "cute guy" did not keep up his Spanish and really regrets it because he is now an immigration lawyer.)

It was in high school that Janet had the only teachers she remembers favorably. They were a group of men who taught history, economics, and geography classes:

They team taught. I liked their style. They were really dedicated. They did worry a lot about the kids but didn't let the kids know it. I often heard them talking because I worked in their department doing typing. I also tutored a couple of their children. They had a camaraderie, a kind of family feeling.

But not all high school memories were fond. A counselor did not help her to set career goals when he told her she probably wouldn't make it at the State University:

I remember his name, Mr. Hills. He said that I should just go to junior college because I would flunk out at State and shouldn't waste my money because I was just going to be a housewife and raise kids anyway. I was devastated by that. I went back recently to tell him, "See—look what I have done." But he wasn't there anymore.

She entered college with a Spanish major and the thought of becoming a U.N. interpreter or working in an embassy, "some international stuff," but she found that she really could not attain the necessary grasp of the language. So she changed to an English major, not really knowing what she wanted for a career. She did investigate being a flight attendant. Her father worked in the mechanical department of a major airline which provided a connection for her. However, since nothing in the international field came up, the easiest thing that presented itself was teaching:

There weren't enough jobs in teaching then, but there were jobs in bilingual ed—that just seemed to work. So I was placed in a bilingual classroom for a student participation class. But I still didn't want to do it. But when I got back from the Peace Corps, I decided that I was best suited for it. And then once I got into student teaching, I decided that I really liked it.

A job that she had all through college, however, ended up influencing her choice of teaching as a career. "It helped me to be more interested in kids," she reported. She worked as a playground aide, classroom aide, and clerical aide at a school in Los Angeles in which all the students were African American. "It was a tough neighborhood, but the kids were neat and there were good teachers," was how she recalled it. Later on, as she reflected on the direction that her career has taken her, she decided that she would still like to do something international, "but it would have to be something with kids. I couldn't do a desk job."

Janet signed up for the Peace Corps after graduating from college to take advantage (she thought) of an opportunity to get a master's degree while serving. She was to teach English in Colombia, but she got assigned to agriculture and health services in Paraguay:

I was really depressed; I couldn't do it. I kept thinking this isn't what I want to do. I have no experience with this agriculture. I was supposed to teach people how to survive and I wasn't surviving. When I got home, I really felt guilty, though. It was like I had deserted. I was one of the kids of the Kennedy generation, you know, go and help the world. It was one of the things that I really wanted to accomplish in my life and I feel real bad after all these years that I didn't complete the term . . . but they did misrepresent themselves about the Colombia program.

After recovering from the trauma of leaving the Peace Corps before her term was up, Janet returned to college to get her teaching credential (California has a fifth-year certification program). In her words:

Actually I just lucked into it (the bilingual program). Everything was fate. I got a job in an L.A. suburb as an ESL [English as a second language] specialist with Samoan and Tongan kids. Then I went into bilingual education and picked up the extra credential through USC as I went along. That program lasted about five years.

After moving to northern California, she taught in a Spanish bilingual program for several years. She has taught in migrant programs, in "regular" classes, and for the past three years in FIRST STEPS, a self-contained ESL classroom for first graders who have no or limited English proficiency. She is also a trainer for the state of California to prepare teachers for a certificate in second language development.

This chronology was difficult to piece together because Janet is a stream of consciousness speaker. She easily pursues tangents of conversations that are interesting or have emotional impact for her. A colleague described her as "spontaneous," stating that "she is very open with her thought process." Janet has something to say about every topic that is introduced. Her manner is enthusiastic, vibrant, and positive, even when she is complaining about things. She consciously tries to keep a positive demeanor. Her strategy to deal with situations that make her upset is to "keep a low profile." The spontaneity was evident in her personal assessment of herself as well:

I would never stay in the same grade for more than five years. I do need the change. When this program settles, and gets running smoothly, then I think that is the time to be able to walk out and do something else. I like to be in on things, the changes, being part of the changes, the fact that progress is being made. I like to at least associate myself with the progress that is being made. If I find I am becoming one of the traditionalists, then I know I am getting old and I had better get out.

The events are only part of the story, of course, and I often asked her about the meaning of the experiences she was relating. This was her response to a question about her current position:

After having taught in a regular classroom and so many differing grades . . . I have done almost everything in teaching . . . and this is the most rewarding; [I] see the biggest gains, kids are the most enthusiastic, responsive, and I think that it makes me feel the best I have ever felt as a teacher. It makes me feel the best I have ever felt as a teacher because of the instant gratification you see when a kid picks up something . . . the rewards of teaching in this ESL class are much more obvious than in another class.

She was equally enthusiastic about a summer job she had just completed, Active Collaborative Teaching Coach in a migrant program:

I have found my niche in life. People are so receptive. They try all the ideas, they pick my brain. The are grateful for the ideas and materials I bring. It gives you credibility. Something you have to offer is valued.

Other comments that she made, including acknowledging the validation that she was receiving from being the subject of my interview, defined a strong need to be important in the lives of other people. But being important could not be equated with being better. Statements she made about her students indicated that she was not using a deficit model in her teaching: "They have so much potential. They are going to be as capable as anybody else, if not more so."

Those around her also sensed that she viewed children in terms of their strengths. Her brother commented: "She doesn't look at anybody as a failure." And from a colleague:

She listens. I think she changes her lesson design to meet the needs of the kids. And she listens to what they have to say. She is interested in what they have to say. She has a good sense of humor. She adapts; every day is a new day for the child, that kind of thing.

From another colleague:

If you can take that six hours that we have them and make that right, make them feel important, make their self-concept blossom, and that is, too, bringing in their cultures and accepting their cultures. That's why I like to teach here. Janet feels the same way.

The following excerpt from my field notes demonstrates her style of interaction with her students:

The bug collecting lesson: Students walked out (with partners) to the grassy area beyond the playground. They did not seem to stay in partners because they each had their own equipment (a clear plastic cup and a kid-sized magnifying glass). Some kids had more sophisticated carriers, and no one seemed to feel put out about the differences. They went where they wanted to. . . . Janet didn't give any directions about where they could look except to give permission to go to the tree at the far end of the grassy area. Most kids just had to show her their finds. She responded to each child, it seemed. She was interested, enthusiastic, excited about their finds. Everyone was expected to participate. But if they didn't come up with a bug, there was no penalty or disparaging remark. She didn't seem to be monitoring the class as a whole while she focused on the discoveries of the individual children. She had a cup to collect ladybugs to take home for her rose bushes, and many children gave her the lady bugs they found. There didn't seem to be any kids who she expected to be off task. When kids showed her what they found, she asked questions about size, shape, body parts, etc. She was the focus of their finds for the most part. They really wanted to share what they found with her. When it was time to go in, she asked a child to call those farthest away and then didn't monitor the result. They all came in.

Field note comments: She is very much in charge and gives procedural directions to the group but allows for a lot of individual autonomy in carrying out the task. She interacts with each child in turn as they come to her. Sometimes it is only validation. Sometimes it is a question. She doesn't seem to play favorites. She asks many children to do the favors and errands she needs. She shares herself with the children (her need for ladybugs for her roses).

ANALYSIS

I see some connections between Janet's personal and professional experiences and her teaching practice. Critical events often dramatically affect one's life choices or world view; they can be confidently identified as life-shaping experiences. But Janet did not describe her life as a series of critical events. As I reviewed my notes, it also seemed that she did not always tell her story confidently. She was hesitant at times to recount stories, thinking that they couldn't possibly be significant. Although I cautioned her otherwise, it was as if I, as the interviewer, was in charge of determining the value of her experiences. I was reminded that Polkinghorne (1988, p. 179) described stories that are told as incomplete; it is in the telling that meaning is established. What is related is not *the* literal story, rather it is a story constructed in the light of the person's present awareness. Casey (1992, p. 89) also writes about life history as a process in which the subject creates her own story. Janet's response to the value of her story is an example of how the nature of "traditional" educational research has not allowed teachers to see themselves as creators of valuable stories about teaching.

At the beginning of this story, I recorded Janet's words about her need to work with others to learn. Her personal need to learn collaboratively was reinforced by the strategies she learned in her bilingual teacher education program. It is not surprising that she organizes her classroom so that collaboration can happen. The pedagogical strategies as well as the physical structure in her classroom encourage kids to work with one another. During sustained silent reading, for example, students could read with partners if they chose to do so. She was often observed telling children to help one another to answer questions about their work. Janet usually allowed the children to pick their own table partners or to decide to work alone or with others for many class activities. As a result, her classroom was not as quiet as most. Even though she is aware of the negative image the noise projects to some colleagues in her building, she encourages the children to collaborate. Although she wants to be a faculty member who "gets along," her students' comfort in their learning environment guides her decisions about classroom climate. She is totally committed to helping her students develop their abilities. Because she believed it was important for her students to learn to function independently, she placed stress on facilitating their choice about interaction and collaboration, relying on the children to solve problems in ways other than getting all the answers from the teacher.

In getting to know Janet, we discovered that both of us had the experience of living in another culture. She had been in the Peace Corps, and I had lived and worked in China for a year. We agreed that these international experiences had been important to us in developing empathy for students for whom American culture was the "other culture." They were also important in helping us accept a wide range of differences in cultural practices. So significant to us were the periods spent outside of our own culture that we fantasized about requiring preservice teachers to have direct experience in a different culture in order to develop sensitivity to being an "other." Even though we were aware that direct experience is only one way of knowing, we felt that being an outsider in a culture would influence teachers' classroom practice.

Janet's recounting of her Peace Corps experience included the feeling of stress that came from not being able to communicate well. As a result, she emphasized the ESL part of her program and proudly pointed out students who had made gains in learning English. At the same time, she encouraged their communicating in their home languages within the classroom, working hard to provide the best possible balance of home language and English language practice.

Janet also recognizes the power of cultural differences in the learning process. She knows that learning is not as efficient when young children are expected to follow procedures in class that are outside of their previous life experience. This has led her to learn about the cultural experiences of her students so that she can adjust to their needs, rather than requiring adherence to what we consider a more traditional structure of elementary schooling. Her classroom culture was not as "institutionalized" as many. There was a feeling of informality in which students did not have a lot of "feet on the floor, backs straight, hands folded" rules to follow. Additionally, she actively connected the children's prior knowledge to her teaching themes, demonstrating that she valued their contribution to the work of the classroom.

What I described earlier as a natural ability to reflect has enabled her to use her life and educational experiences as a form of personal theory that determines how she works with children. For all of us, life experiences shape our teaching practice. Most often, however, the influences are implicit. Janet's are explicit. Schubert and Ayers (1992, p. ix) have made a similar observation:

We remain convinced that the conscientious teachers reflect seriously on their work. They think and feel carefully about what they do and why they do it. They use their experiences as a basis for fashioning responses to similar situations that they encounter.

PERSONAL REFLECTIONS

I now turn to the issue of subjectivity that must be addressed in any naturalistic inquiry. As I read and reread my field notes and interview transcriptions, I became uncomfortably aware of the fact that those words had become the reality from which the interpretive account would be extracted. Janet's reality had been filtered through those words. This story is ostensibly about Janet Dillon, but as soon as I made decisions about what words to use in the story, it also became a story about me. The things that I think are important became the focus of what I saw as important in her life. Child-centered education for young children and teaching practices that celebrate a multicultural, rather than an assimilative, perspective are my professional passions. That is the way I taught young children, that is what I emphasize in my work with teachers. Janet shared these views. We confirmed one another's ideas in our conversations; we sought one another out to complain, to share, to question. We compared stories of our conservative, middle-class backgrounds and speculated together about how our lives had changed. So in writing the story of Janet Dillon, I am also relating a part of my view of the world. Connelly and Clandinin (1990, p. 12) discuss this phenomena:

We need to listen closely to teachers and other learners and to the stories of their lives in and out of classrooms. We also need to tell our own stories as we live our collaborative researcher/teacher lives. Our own work then becomes one of learning to tell and live a new mutually constructed account of inquiry in teaching and learning. What emerges from this mutual relationship are new stories of teachers and learners as curriculum makers, stories that hold new possibilities for both researchers and teachers and for those who read their stories.

As Janet told her story, as I learned about it from others, as I wrote about it from my experience, it became a story that can inform the practice of those who work in early childhood education. There is no summary of research that is not presented without an agenda. Mine is to have this new story hold the following possibilities for those who read it:

a. *As an example* of the importance of understanding and using life experience in the education of teachers of young children. Any search for reform or restructuring of teaching and teacher education must explore more fully the lives of teachers and the values and constraints that shape them. Janet's story, as an example of life history research, helps us to understand the complexity of human interactions that are found in class-rooms. We can also see how classrooms are unique learning communities because we see the stamp of Janet's personal and professional knowledge and experience on everything that happens in her room. In my work in teacher education, stories of teachers' lives and experiences, such as those related by Ayers (1989) and Paley (1989), serve as powerful curric-ulum materials because they give students a vivid image of the reality of teaching.

b. *As a statement* supporting the viability of a multicultural perspective that is infused throughout the curriculum. This has been characterized as "education as multicultural" as opposed to the additive "multicultural education" concept. Because of Janet's life experience, she views herself providing more than just a "tourist curriculum." Her students and their life experiences are what she uses to make her classroom multicultural. She celebrates their differences; she does not make them invisible.

c. *As a vehicle* to rehumanize education. Teachers are not response columns in surveys, but human beings consciously shaping their practices with young children. As one researcher puts it, teachers should not be treated as if they are "cardboard cut-outs" (Beynon, 1985, p. 177) oc-cupying a space at the head of a classroom. Teachers are people; they are not a collective statistic. Casey argues that using life history research to understand the personal meaning of teaching prevents an instrumental view of instruction in which teachers are reduced to objects which can be manipulated for specific outcomes (1992, p. 188).

d. *As a case* for the necessity of recognizing the intersubjectivity of the naturalistic research process. The story told in a life history interview is not the same one that is reported. But the self-conscious declaration of purposes stated by the researcher and an explanation of the re-searcher/participant relationship help to ensure the validity of the story for the reader.

I learned a great deal from Janet Dillon. I learned some of the reasons she is able to work so effectively with her students from Laos, Cambodia, Russia, Mexico, and the United States. I learned about the power of life history to inform our knowledge of teaching. And I also learned about myself. Reconstructing her life history was a springboard for my own reflections and questions about my experience and its role in shaping my teaching practice. Intersubjectivity between researcher and participant has already been discussed. But what has not been mentioned is the meaning that is constructed by you, the reader. Writers tend to assume that readers are gender and experientially neutral, but they are not. As Barthes (1977) points out, the meaning of a text lies less in its origins than in its destination. Readers of texts are free to read what they want to read. So you can agree, but you are also free to resist, or to contribute your own readings. You can resist my intentions and contest my meanings. You, the reader, will bring yet another set of experiences to this story, and the intersubjectivity will be reconstructed in a different way. It is this process of reconstruction that enables you to connect with the story so that you can find meaning for your own experience. Janet and I, and now you, can use this life history to, as Middleton suggests (1993, p. 9), "release our educational imaginations."

REFERENCES

Ayers, W. (1989). *The good preschool teacher*. New York: Teachers College Press.

Ball, S., & Goodson, I. (1985). *Teachers' lives and careers*. Philadelphia: Falmer Press.

Barthes, R. (1977). *Image, music, text*. New York: Hill and Wang.

Beynon, T. (1985). Institutional change and career histories in a comprehensive school. In S. Ball and I. Goodson (Eds.), *Teachers' lives and careers* (pp. 158–179). Philadelphia: Falmer Press.

Bogdan, R., & Biklan, S. (1992). *Qualitative research for education: An introduction to theory and methods*. Boston: Allyn and Bacon.

Casey, K. (1992). Why do progressive women activists leave teaching? Theory, methodology and politics in life history research. In I. Goodson (Ed.), *Studying teachers' lives* (pp. 187–208). New York: Teachers College Press.

Connelly, F. M., & Clandinin, D. J. (1988). *Teachers as curriculum planners: Narratives of experience*. New York: Teachers College Press.

Connelly, F. M., & Clandinin, D. J. (1990). Stories of experience and narrative inquiry. *Educational Researcher, 19* (5), 2–14.

Genishi, C. (Ed.). (1992). *Ways of assessing children and curriculum: Stories of early childhood practice*. New York: Teachers College Press.

Goodson, I. (Ed.) (1992). *Studying teachers' lives*. New York: Teachers College Press.

Hauser, M. E. (1990). *Cultural transmission in a multicultural elementary school*. Unpublished doctoral dissertation, University of California, Santa Barbara.

McGroarty, M. (1986). Educators' responses to sociocultural diversity: Implications for practice. In *Beyond language: social and cultural factors in schooling language minority students*. Sacramento: California Department of Education.

Merriam. S. (1991). *Case study research in education: A qualitative approach*. San Francisco: Jossey-Bass.

Middleton, S. (1993). *Educating feminists: Life histories and pedagogy*. New York: Teachers College Press.

Ordovensky, P. (1992). *U.S.A. Today*, July 7, p. 1a.

Paley, V. (1989). *White teacher*. Cambridge, Mass.: Harvard University Press.

Plummer, K. (1983). *Documents of life: An introduction to the problems and literature of a humanistic method*. London: Allen and Unwin.

Polkinghorne, D. (1988). *Narrative knowing and the human sciences*. Albany: SUNY Press.

Schubert, W., & Ayers, W. (Eds.). (1992). *Teacher lore: Learning from our own experience*. New York: Longman.

Seidman, I. (1991). *Interviewing as qualitative research: A guide for researchers in education and the social sciences*. New York: Teachers College Press.

Trueba, H. (1989). *Raising silent voices: Educating the linguistic minorities for the 21st century*. New York: Newbury House.

Witherell, C., & Noddings, N. (Eds.). (1991). *Stories lives tell: Narrative and dialogue in education*. New York: Teachers College Press.

Chapter 5

Policy Issues in the Development of Child Care and Early Education Systems: The Need for Cross-National Comparison

SALLY LUBECK

Although differing in history, language, culture, and political systems, all advanced industrial societies have faced common problems in the late twentieth century, problems that have arisen, at least in part, because of dramatic shifts in the structure of work and family. These changes have raised policy questions, and the study of alternative systems of child care and education promises to be an important arena for future inquiry. This chapter contrasts the child care systems of two nations—the United States and the former German Democratic Republic—which devised radically different approaches for meeting the child care and education needs of young children.

POLICY QUESTIONS

The question of child care is itself intimately intertwined with attitudes toward female employment and the role of the state. In the United States and throughout much of Europe, the rate of women's labor force participation has increased, most dramatically for mothers of preschool- and school-aged children (e.g., Lubeck & Garrett, 1991; Moss, 1988, 1993). Fully 67 percent of U.S. mothers with children under age eighteen are now employed (Children's Defense Fund, 1992, p. 17), while in Europe, rates of maternal employment have been increasing rapidly. In 1991, 58 percent of mothers in the European Union (EU) with children under the age of ten were employed: "Highest levels (75% and over) are in Denmark and Portugal. Lowest levels (under 50%) are in Ireland (38%), Luxembourg (42%) and Spain (44%), Greece and Netherlands (46%). In between come Italy and UK (50–59%) and Germany, France and Belgium (60–69%)" (Moss, 1993, p. 1).[1]

Largely as a corollary to these trends, the numbers of children enrolled in preschool programs have burgeoned. Sixty-eight percent of U.S. children (3–5) were in some form of non-parental child care or early education program in 1991 (National Center for Education Statistics, 1993), while in nearly every nation in the European Union, the numbers of children in preschool programs have risen. At the end of the 1980s, 95 percent of French, Belgian, and East German children (3–6), 85 percent of Danish children (3–7), and 68 percent of West German children (3–6) were in preschool (Tietze & Paterak, 1993).

Particularly in the United States, these increases have been paralleled by other social changes: high rates of divorce (Beller & Chung, 1991), greatly increased numbers of children born out of wedlock (Martin & Bumpass, 1989), and rising poverty rates among young families (Children's Defense Fund, 1988; Edelman, 1989). Recent data from the National Center for Education Statistics (1993) indicate that the smallest percentage of U.S. children in preschool is from low-income families; the largest percentage comes from families with incomes exceeding $75,000. A major policy question, therefore, has been the role that the government should play in addressing the changing needs of its citizenry.

Public policy defines goals and some means of reaching those goals. Given the changes discussed above, nations have devised alternative means of addressing a number of policy issues:

• Should it be a matter of government policy to encourage or discourage female employment?

• Should government foster gender equity in both work and childrearing?

• Should the care and education of young children be the *private* responsibility of parents or a *public* responsibility of society?

• At what age should the government assume responsibility for the education of children?

Although a complete discussion of each of these issues is beyond the scope of this chapter, nations do address such questions in very different ways.

Government Support of Female Employment

In Hitler's Germany, women did not have rights separate from their husbands, and maternal employment was discouraged. Such public constraints reinforced the expectation that women take care of home and hearth. After World War II, Germany was, of course, divided into two nations, the (now former) German Democratic Republic (GDR), which became one of the communist bloc nations of Eastern Europe, and the Federal Republic of Germany, which remained part of Western Europe.

With a greatly depleted work force in the postwar era, the Federal Republic (West Germany) imported immigrant labor, and to this day professes little public support for maternal employment or public provision for children younger than three (Kamerman & Kahn, 1981; Tietze & Roßbach, 1993). By contrast, the German Democratic Republic (East Germany) encouraged female employment and gradually established public institutions for the care and education of young children. In the late 1980s, prior to unification of the Germanys, 90 percent of GDR women were in the work force or studying (Winkler, 1990), and most children aged one to ten were in publicly supported child care institutions for at least some portion of the day (*Frau & Politik*, 1990).

Although it is unwise to attribute observable differences between peoples solely to their experiences of either socialism or capitalism, it is striking that the peoples of two nations sharing a common heritage and language have developed very different attitudes toward female employment and extrafamilial child care. One recent study of West German fathers revealed that 80 percent held that "if there's a child, the father goes to work and the mother stays at home" (Moss, 1988, p. 34). Conversely, a study comparing gender-role attitudes in East and West Germany found that East Germans were much more likely to believe that "a working mother can establish just as warm and secure a relationship with her children as a mother who does not work." East Germans also dismissed the notion that "a preschool child is likely to suffer if his or her mother works" (Braun, Scott, & Alwin, 1992, p. 11). In this study, all attitudinal differences regarding gender roles between East and West Germans proved to be highly significant.

Government Support of Gender Equity and Shared Responsibility

Wage disparity and gender segregation are prominent topics in the literature on women and work, but, with the exception of the child support issue (through which fathers are expected to be financially responsible for children), the U.S. government has been virtually silent regarding policies that would encourage shared parenting. This is not the case in Sweden, where gender equity in childrearing has become a public policy issue (see, for example, Haas, 1991; Pleck, 1988). In 1991 Sweden guaranteed fifteen months of paid leave that could be taken by either parent after the birth of a child, and other Scandinavian countries have established paternity leave (Kamerman, 1991). Within the European Union, the Childcare Network has stated that "caring for and bringing up children should be regarded as a joint responsibility of the father and mother" (Moss, 1988) and recommended that the EU countries adopt a baseline standard guaranteeing three months non-transferable leave to each parent (Kamerman, 1989).

Private vs. Public Responsibility

There is a substantial amount of variability across nations regarding the degree and kind of responsibility for families and children that will be assumed by government. Of all industrialized nations, the United States and South Africa accept the *least* public responsibility for young children (Rosewater, 1989). The United States has virtually no program which supports all the society's young families.

There is no universal health insurance which guarantees that all pregnant women will receive adequate pre- and post-natal care or that all children will be immunized (Children's Defense Fund, 1992). Parental leave recently (August, 1993) became federal law with the passage of the Family and Medical Leave Act. However, the act only applies to firms with fifty or more employees and therefore does not cover most American workers. In North Carolina, for example, only six percent of the work force is currently eligible for leave under FMLA provisions (Lubeck, 1993a). There are no child allowances (Kamerman & Kahn, 1989), although recent changes in dependent care tax credits may develop into something like them (Kamerman, 1993). And there is little infrastructure currently in place for an early care and education system in which standards are uniform throughout the nation, much less one that provides universal care (O'Connell & Bloom, 1987).

Although the government plays an increasingly prominent role in people's lives, the ideology of private responsibility remains firmly etched in the collective American conscience. Childbearing and rearing are perceived to be a parental/family responsibility, and it is primarily parents who finance child care and early education for their children (Clifford & Russell, 1989). An exception is made, however, under the tenet of American law referred to as *parens patriae*. This doctrine states that the state should intervene only when parents cannot or will not care for their children (Grubb & Lazerson, 1982/88). Thus the inability to provide well for children, to afford child care or decent housing or needed health care, has been interpreted as a sign of individual rather than structural failure. It is a popular perception in the United States that increasing numbers of parents are failing their children and that increasing numbers of children are "at risk." However, in other nations such assumptions are not made as a matter of course. In some, all families are guaranteed some baseline of support. Although recent efforts to increase public responsibility for children in the United States have shown some success, the ideology of individualism and private responsibility continues to hamper the development of a coherent family policy.

In contrast, the German Democratic Republic was founded on the belief that the nation's resources should be equitably shared. Health care was free, and all children were fully immunized. In 1986 a "baby year" was introduced, guaranteeing job security and 70 percent of salary to the mother, father, or grandmother who stayed home with an infant (Barth, 1990).[2] Approximately 80 percent of those aged one to three were in *Krippen* (Barth, 1990; Boeckmann, 1993), while universal provision had been achieved for all children in need of care in *Kindergarten* (Ministerium für Volksbildung, 1989) and in after-school programs (*Horte*) for school-aged children (Edwards, 1985, p. 84). *Krippen* and *Kindergarten* were officially open thirteen hours a day, from 6:00 a.m. to 7:00 p.m.[3]

Public policy supported the idea of collective responsibility for the nation's children. All adults were to have the opportunity to work, and all forms of discrimination against women were to be systematically eliminated. Women were to be given equal access to education, training, employment, and political involvement. The 1946 "Law on the Democratization of the German School" promised educational equity (Edwards, 1985, p. 52), while the constitution of 1949 guaranteed women legal equality, the right to work, and the right to equal pay (Dennis, 1988, p. 56). In 1950 the law protecting mother and child became the foundation on which a comprehensive child care system was constructed (Edwards, 1985, p. 13). Although the ideological commitment to ending gender discrimination proved to be difficult to effect in practice (Lubeck, 1993b), the child care system nonetheless was founded both to enable women to work (indeed, under socialism, all able-bodied citizens were expected to be gainfully employed) and to foster the development and socialization of all the society's children (Boeckmann, 1993).

Age of Entry into the "Public" System

All industrialized nations now have a publicly funded system of education. Children typically enter the educational system some time between the ages of five and seven. Children in the Netherlands, Luxembourg, and Great Britain enter at age five; in Greece at 5 1/2; in Germany, France, Italy, Belgium, Ireland, Portugal, and Spain at age six; and in Denmark at age seven (Tietze & Paterak, 1993). With the gradual expansion of kindergartens in the United States, the vast majority of American children enter public schooling at age five (Robinson, 1987).

Increasing percentages of children aged three to six experience some form of preschooling. However, such programs are financed differently in different countries. Programs are heavily subsidized by local and federal governments in Belgium and France, for example, and open to all children. Consequently, 98 percent of French children aged three to five were in preschools in 1989, compared to 31 percent of U.S. children (Richardson & Marx, 1989, p. 13).

In this section, a number of policy questions have been raised. Rist (1994) has argued, however, that there are two levels at which decisions are made in the policymaking process:

The first involves the establishment of the broad parameters of government action, such as providing national health insurance, establishing a national energy policy, restructuring the national immigration laws, or reexamining the criteria for determining the safety and soundness of the country's financial institutions. At this level and in these instances, policy research input is likely to be quite small, if not nil. (p. 547)

The second level, according to Rist, is where there is interest in translating policy intentions into action, in moving from policy formulation to policy implementation. Rist believes that it is here that policy research is needed. Yet, if his advice is taken literally, most of the issues discussed above would not be on the table. His more constrained view of policy is undoubtedly pragmatic, but it limits discussion to questions that merely modify or extend the existing system. This chapter argues that, given the magnitude of the forces that are buffeting American families and children, a much more in-depth questioning of current policies is warranted. The next section suggests some of the ways in which the policies and programs of other nations can be studied.

CROSS-NATIONAL COMPARISON

It has been argued that all good studies in anthropology and sociology are comparative in nature (e.g., Mead & Wolfenstein, 1955; Grimshaw, 1973). Nonetheless, comparative work is an umbrella term for a variety of emphases and research approaches. Some research, such as the "Six Cultures" study, has involved research teams in different countries, teams committed to asking similar questions (in this case, about childrearing practices) and using comparable methods across social settings (Whiting, 1963). Another approach is to compare "after the fact." The Human Relations Area Files, for example, were established so that studies of various societies could be available for comparative work. Researchers can scan the files to find commonalities across studies which, at their inception, were not designed for specific comparison.

Kohn (1989) suggests that the term "cross-national" research should be restricted to that which systematically compares data from two or more nations. With this caveat, he distinguishes among four types: "Those in which nation is the *object* of study, those in which nation is the *context* of study, those in which nation is *unit of analysis*, and those that are *transnational* in character" (p. 20). The first type compares nations or institutions within nations for their own sake. The second type is primarily concerned with generalizing about how institutions operate or how social systems influence individual thinking and behavior. As *units of analysis*, countries are no longer of interest in and of themselves, but the characteristics of nations, such as gross national products, become variables for comparison. Finally, *transnational* research considers nations as parts of larger international systems.

While the study of children's development in varying cultural and social contexts has been of interest to anthropologists for some time (e.g., Mead & Wolfenstein, 1955; Whiting & Whiting, 1975; Whiting & Edwards, 1988), societal changes in the late twentieth century have stimulated interest in the study of the social institutions that support children's development and provide care for children while their parents work. At least two books are illustrative of the "nation as *object* of study" variety. Olmstead and Weikart (1989) profile how fourteen nations address child care and early education, while Melhuish and Moss (1991) illustrate how five nations do so. In each of these edited books, detailed information is provided, but little effort is made to understand commonalities and differences among the nations represented. By contrast, the *unit of analysis* approach is exemplified by Kamerman (1991) and by Lubeck (1989), both of whom display variations in the maternity/paternity leave provisions of a number of nations in tabular form. Here the variables themselves can be seen to be of consequence. Tietze and Ufermann (1989) and Tietze and Paterak (1993) also use this approach by summarizing preschool provisions cross-nationally. To date, there have been fewer efforts to study "nation as *context*" or "nations as components of larger international systems" (Kohn, 1989, p. 23).

What follows is a preliminary cross-national study of the "nation as context" type. Following Kohn (1989), such comparative work is further subdivided into two types: that which enables the researcher to make more general statements about how institutions appear to operate in the lives of families and children; and that which examines, in some detail, how social institutions such as child care settings might influence personality at the group level. The study of *Preschool in Three Cultures* (Tobin, Davidson, & Wu, 1989) is a good example of the latter. In comparing preschools in three societies—China, Japan, and the United States—the authors first give an insider's view of preschools, based on the descriptions and explanations of parents, teachers, and administrators in each country. Later, in analyzing questionnaire data, they seek to understand from the "outside" how preschooling affects individuals and families. They note, for example, that the Americans and Chinese surveyed considered it very important for children to learn to express themselves verbally, while the Japanese stressed listening over speaking: "the top Japanese answer to the question, 'What are the most important things for children to learn in preschool?' was 'sympathy, empathy, concern for others' " (p. 190). In contrast to the book by Tobin and his colleagues, the study which follows is of the former type and thus attempts to describe—and to contrast—how institutions operate.

COMPARING ALTERNATIVE APPROACHES TO EARLY CARE AND EDUCATION

The description which follows is a comparison of the child care and early education policies and programs of two nations. Specifically, the organization, financing, administration, and regulation of programs in the United States and the former German Democratic Republic are examined.

Due to political restrictions, little was known in the West about the child care system in the GDR, although it was reputed to be extensive. The Cold War effectively came to an end in November, 1989. Within a few months, it was agreed that the two Germanys were to be united, and complete unification was effected in October, 1990. Only for a few months (between November, 1989 and October, 1990) was it possible to move freely within the country, to speak openly with people, and to observe the GDR child care system while relatively intact. Data were collected on the child care system during the summer of 1990.[4] Soon after unification, administrative office buildings were converted to regional administrative units, and today the system has been modified and curtailed.

Since what had been written about GDR institutions was frequently dismissed in the West as propaganda, it seemed imperative to provide a living account of the child care system based on the reports of multiple informants within it. To that end, interviews were conducted with administrators in the Ministry of Education, the Ministry of Health, and the Ministry for Women and Families, as well as with the directors of *Krippen* and *Kindergarten*, the child care institutions for children aged one to three and three to six respectively. During the interviews, administrators and directors were asked to explain features of the system generally: how it developed; how it was financed, organized, administered, and regulated; and how issues of availability, affordability, quality, and compensation were addressed. Directors also were asked to provide specific information on their institutions (e.g., the number of children enrolled, the number of hours a teacher works per week, the schedule, curriculum, etc), as well as to give opinions (e.g., Do you think the medical care the children receive in the *Krippen* is adequate?).[5] In the discussion that follows, some of the most telling differences between the U.S. and GDR approaches to child care will be explored.

THE ORGANIZATION OF EARLY CARE AND EDUCATION

American child care is mainly organized at the community level (Morgan, 1987) and regulated by individual states. In the GDR the system was centralized at the federal level.

The United States

Child care and early education in the United States spring from separate roots and have multiple sponsors and diverse funding sources. What overall organizational structure exists has been referred to as a "patchwork" that is difficult to characterize (Morgan, 1987; Philips, 1991). To define the parameters of a highly decentralized system such as that which exists within the United States, it is necessary to describe its origins, to detail the diversity of care arrangements, to describe the role that government does play, and to note how costs and quality vary across types.

Historically, child care and early education evolved as two distinct forms, one as part of the child welfare system for children from poor families, the other rooted in the nursery school and early kindergarten movement for children of the middle and upper classes (Lazerson, 1972; Steinfels, 1973; Wrigley, 1989). In recent years the distinction between child care programs (traditionally full-day programs for the working poor) and nursery schools (part-day programs for the middle classes) has blurred, although inequities have been maintained.

Children aged birth to five, whose parents work, are cared for by different people in different settings. Typically children under the age of three have been in homes, while a larger proportion of three- and four-year-olds are in group-based arrangements (Lubeck & Garrett, 1991). The demand for infant care in group settings has been escalating, however. Programs are sponsored by a wide assortment of individuals, groups, parents, for-profit (e.g., franchises) and not-for-profit (e.g., churches) organizations and schools. Because most programs are locally run and administered, a sense of ownership by staff and parents is a hallmark of many programs. Moreover, the proliferation of options offers a wide range of choice, at least for those who can afford it.

The United States has adopted the notion of "kindergarten," but it differs from the German kindergarten in two principal respects: first, it is almost always for children five years of age; and, second, it is typically housed in public schools and is considered the first year of schooling. Approximately 92 percent of American children attend kindergarten (Robinson, 1987), which, in public schools, is free. After-school programs, where they exist, are typically sponsored by schools, community organizations, or state agencies.

The German Democratic Republic

The organization of programs in the German Democratic Republic presents an interesting contrast to the haphazard development of programs in the United States. Where many programs in the United States have been generated in response to changing demographics and market forces, programs in the GDR were the result of a centrally planned effort to equalize children's access to health, education, and care. Where U.S. programs, since their inception, have been class-based, GDR programs were intended to have a leveling effect, that is, to provide equally for the nation's children.

The newly formed German Democratic Republic, in line with socialist ideals, dedicated itself to the development of a comprehensive child care system so that women could seek employment. The child care system developed slowly over several decades (Weigl & Weber, 1991), but eventually policies and programs were coherent, providing both continuity over time and relative coherence across service sectors.

An administrator in the Ministry of Education described three types of sponsorship. First, there were state-run programs, organized through municipalities, urban districts, and districts. Second, there were company-run centers operated by large companies, but also in rural areas supported by farmers' cooperatives or by individual cooperatives. The companies were responsible for the construction and maintenance of the centers, and the state subsidized the centers by paying the teachers' salaries and providing toys, other materials, and food. The companies cooked the meals and maintained the institutions but still received support from the state. Payment was made annually, providing the same allotment to each slot. Finally, there were church-run centers. Churches could apply to have a center built and maintained, but they operated without financial support from the state. The official educational program was made available to the church-run centers, but its use was not mandatory. The company-run centers, by contrast, followed the same program as the state-run institutions. Mimeographed materials obtained from the ministry indicated that 85.8 percent of the kindergartens were state-run, 11.2 percent were run by companies, and three percent were sponsored by churches (Ministerium für Volksbildung, 1989).

Due to strong centralized control, programs looked alike, and they were described by directors in remarkably similar terms. The general feeling was that the child care institutions were a valuable societal resource. Nonetheless, directors also tended to identify similar problems, most of which reflected disenchantment with a large, bureaucratic superstructure.

Repeated complaints included: unnecessary paperwork, unduly strict measures of accountability, lack of local decision making power, limited resources, fluctuations in group size and staff-child ratios, long hours, low pay, and, what was often perceived as the consequence, high rates of teacher turnover (Lubeck, 1993b). Ironically, however, this level of uniformity also appeared to support equality of opportunity, a largely unrealized goal of the American system.

FINANCING

In the United States, most child care and early education programs are primarily financed by parents. Exceptions are federal programs such as Head Start or state-level programs for "at-risk" children or for children who qualify for special programs under the provisions of Public Law 94-142. Grubb and Lazerson (1982/88) have argued that this private/public split—a tradition of "private wealth and public squalor"—has historically characterized programs for American children (p. 49). In the GDR, programs for most young children were publicly financed, with parents contributing a small amount for food.

The United States

Child care in the United States is mainly financed by parents (Clifford & Russell, 1989). Costs for child care vary widely. A parent in Michigan may pay $1,000 per month for an infant in a center-based program. One woman I interviewed in North Carolina, an employee of a textile mill, paid $60 per month for a woman to care for both her infant twins.

Federal, state, and local funds are targeted to provide assistance to low-income families. Head Start, a program for (predominantly four-year-old) low-income children, is administered at the federal level; block grant monies for child care are distributed to states, and state and federal monies are then distributed to counties to be administered at the local level. Payments are parceled out to needy individuals to help pay for child care in whole or in part. Typically, the government requires that care be purchased in regulated homes or licensed centers. Waiting lists for these funds have been long, and many have never received services. Moreover, before the 1991 reforms, only about 16 percent of eligible children were served by Head Start. Today approximately 35 percent of children eligible for the program are served. State-sponsored programs for "at-risk" preschoolers have also expanded. The problem with all of these programs, however, is that they do not serve all in need, and they also frequently segregate children based on class and race.

The German Democratic Republic

The funding for the child care institutions in the former German Democratic Republic came primarily from public coffers, with parents contributing only a nominal amount for food. Nonetheless, figures on the cost per slot (*Platz*) of child care/early education in the GDR were difficult to obtain. The most intriguing figure for a nursery slot compares the cost with the average yearly wage of an industrial worker. Weigl and Weber (1991) maintain that each nursery slot cost the government 16,000M (12,800M plus annual operational costs averaging 3,200M), while the average yearly wage for a full-time worker in industry in 1987 was 14,796M (p. 47).

Nurseries, with higher staff-child ratios, were thought to be more expensive than the kindergartens, but no comparable figures were available for the kindergarten. Consequently, data were gathered on the number of kindergarten teachers with different levels of training, on the salary range for each level, on the number of children served (and the number of slots), and the cost per slot for maintenance and equipment (5,000M per slot). Calculations based on these figures, however, yielded a cost per slot that was less than half that of the Weigl & Weber figures for the *Krippen*. Their figures may include the cost for building new centers and/ or the cost of the extensive teacher training system. Because it is unclear exactly what was being calculated, however, it was not possible to compare costs of the two programs.

In the GDR, public, rather than private, monies or some combination thereof, were disseminated for child care. An administrator in the Ministry of Education explained how this was accomplished:

Besides those centers built and maintained by the cities and municipalities, all of this has been financed by the state budget. There were no parent contributions except this very small amount for food. Everything was paid by the central state budget. It all trickled down from the central state budget to the districts and then to the municipalities and the kindergarten received its budget from the municipality. Due to that, the same rules were applied for each center. It was determined in a centralized way how much money could be spent on food, for toys, and so on.

A kindergarten director, in turn, explained how she managed these funds:

Every institution has a budget. We have a certain budget for different things. For example, for play materials and activities I had 1,300M per year. I could order the material or buy it myself. Thus I had some cash in my office, 150M. If that was gone, I could report to the department and get more. I had this fixed amount that I had to deal with.

Asked if this sum was sufficient, the director explained further:

It worked pretty well. Sometimes, in some areas, it was scarce. For example, recently the costs for the laundry increased so that our money was not sufficient anymore. But I could always try to talk to the department and ask whether I could get additional funds. The cleaning of the sleeping bags or the blankets, which is done once a year, had to be done, and so the department had to give me that money. And that always worked out. They found ways. They transferred money from one kindergarten or school to the other so that we could get the extra money. But I could not buy toys without saying, no, we can't afford that this year. A doll stroller, for example, costs 150M, and that is a lot of money. So, if I have 1,300M, I cannot say that all the groups get doll strollers.

This sense of limitation was echoed in an interview with an administrator in the Ministry of Education:

The original idea was that there should be child care available in an equal amount for everybody. That is a good humanistic thought, but it led to minimization right away, because, naturally, you had to think about everybody, and then the total decreases more and more what is available for the individual, especially with the conditions of our economy.

Great efforts were made to provide equally for children, but, when resources diminished, the effect was pervasive.

In 1990 parents of nursery children were paying 80 Pfennige per day for food. Children had breakfast, lunch, and snack (*Kaffeestunde*) in the *Krippen*. Several directors commented that this fee no longer covered the cost. Parents in the kindergartens were being asked to provide breakfast and an afternoon snack. In addition, most paid 35 Pfennige for food and 17 Pfennige for milk each day. The actual amount parents paid was computed monthly, with sick days being subtracted. In the large combined nursery and kindergarten institutions that cooked their own food, parents did not have to provide any food. Instead they paid 2.50M per day per child. These figures, it should be remembered, represent only one point in time.

ADMINISTRATION AND REGULATION

Issues of administration and regulation focus on the direction and management of a child care system and on the rules dictated by those in authority. In a decentralized system, such as that in the United States, responsibility for administrative and regulatory functions is diffused throughout the system. In a centralized system, such as the GDR, the opposite is the case.

The United States

Especially since the "new federalism" fostered by the Reagan administration, many social and educational programs formerly overseen by the federal government have reverted to state control. States set their own standards which vary from state to state. In most, programs for children younger than three are administered by state departments of social services or human resources; programs for children older than three are administered by state departments of education or public instruction.

Typically, child care centers are licensed, while family day care homes are regulated. Requirements differ for each, but centers tend to be monitored, while homes are not, and, since most homes are not registered, it has been impossible to say how many exist at any given time or what quality of care is being provided. Most states have attempted to regulate structural features, such as staff-child ratios or group size or to require a certain number of hours of training for caregivers. Within center-based programs, staff-child ratios of 1:5 for toddlers and 1:10 for preschoolers are recommended, but not required, and interstate variability is great. For example, certain states require that there be one caregiver per three infants, while others allow a ratio of 1:7. The state of Idaho enforces no standards at all, except for programs that receive federal funds, while other states exclude church-run or half-day programs (Philips, 1991). States also vary in the amount and kind of training that is required, but many workers in child care settings have no training in child development. No state mandates a specific curriculum.

The German Democratic Republic

In stark contrast to developments in the United States, the administrative and regulatory system that evolved in the former German Democratic Republic was highly centralized, with all planning and decision making being done at the top and then passed down through a bureaucratic structure to programs at the bottom. Because the system was centrally planned, it achieved a degree of homogeneity that would be unthinkable in the United States.

The *Krippen* for children aged one to three were administered by the Ministry of Health; the *Kindergarten* for children aged three to six were administered by the Ministry of Education. However, the child care system was seen as the first step in the East German educational system (Fishman & Martin, 1987, p. 130), and health services (sick and well health care, immunizations, medication, etc.) were provided free of charge to children in both settings.

Program guidelines were also centrally determined. Staff-child ratios and group size were set by the state. In the spring of 1990, the official staff-child ratio became 1:5 in the nurseries and 1:10 in kindergartens. These ratios were supported when comparing national-level figures of the number of teachers employed and children served. However, directors described a variety of circumstances that could affect ratios and group size in profound ways, including fluctuations based on the numbers of children in the area in need of care, child and staff illness, guaranteed release time, vacations, and so on (Lubeck, 1993b).

All programs, except the relatively few run by churches, used the same state-mandated curriculum. Finally, three-fourths of all nursery teachers had received three years of training in a "medical technical school" (*medizinische Fachschule*) (Weigl & Weber, 1991, p. 50), and two-thirds of the kindergarten teachers were fully trained in an "educational technical college" (*pädagogische Fachschule*) (Ministerium für Volksbildung, 1989).

Teacher training involved both theoretical understanding and practical experience. Nursery students, for example, studied "educational theory, psychology, anatomy, physiology, hygiene, preventive health, nutrition, pediatrics, and general knowledge" (Weigl & Weber, 1991, pp. 50–51). Students also were required to spend time in the nurseries. Certain nurseries and kindergartens were selected to be teacher training institutions (*Ausbildungskrippen*). As the director of one such institution explained:

Our students' education takes three years. They [alternate theory and practice], going to school for three weeks and then having their practical training in the nursery for three weeks. This continues for two years, and the third year they start working in the nursery where they will work later, when they are finished with their education. We also have a teacher from the technical school, and she comes in and trains the future teachers. After these three years, they have to go through a practical examination and a theoretical one.

In theory, the GDR solved many of the problems that most plague the U.S. approach. Standards were uniform, most teachers were well trained, and nearly all children had the same curriculum, with teachers throughout the country expected to achieve the same goals for their children at each developmental level. As described above, however, the system also proved to be inflexible, and, just as in the United States, the low wages of the teachers contributed to high rates of teacher turnover.

CONCLUSIONS

Cross-national comparison offers a fruitful avenue of inquiry for those interested in seeing beyond the constraints and biases inherent in the exclusive focus on one's own cultural and social system. It makes it possible to track how macroeconomic shifts are affecting nations and to observe how, drawing on different histories and cultures, nations have devised novel policies and programs.[6] Although only an initial exploration of these issues, the "nation as context" comparison above suggests several advantages that might derive from using cross-national comparison as a means of addressing policy questions. First, such comparisons enable us to step outside our socially constructed consensus reality and to realize that children develop and families exist in a *political* context. The GDR created public institutions for nearly all children aged one to ten, while the French have created a system for all children aged three to five. By contrast, the United States continues to maintain a bifurcated or "two-tier" system of "private wealth and public squalor" (Grubb & Lazerson, 1982, p. 49). Yet to do so is a matter of choice. Poverty, as Michael Katz (1989) writes, "no longer is natural; it is a social product . . . poverty becomes not the product of scarcity, but of political economy" (p. 7).

For all its political repression and ultimate social implosion, the GDR was a nation that valued and made a commitment to children—to *all* the society's children, to their health, to their education, and to their general well-being. The contrast with the U.S. approach casts in relief the profound inequities that structure it to its core. Comparison sharpens the frequently blurred connections among our class-based economic system, the impact on families, and the differing opportunities available to children.

Second, the distancing afforded by cross-national comparison ruptures the smugness of "free market" tenets. If the GDR is now considered an economic failure, we must at least consider that the United States is becoming a social failure, with the gap between rich and poor widening, ever-growing numbers of children being reared in poverty, and women and children swelling the ranks of the homeless, as the most obvious signs. Third, comparison raises the question of whether social "problems" originate in people ("at-risk" children, "ineffectual" parents, etc.) or in the conditions of their lives. Fourth, it problematizes current reform efforts within the United States, clarifying how bound we are to the institutions we have, ever tinkering at the edges, rather than rethinking the enterprise as a whole. Finally, comparisons such as the one outlined above allow us to engage an institution such as child care as a whole, organically connected to the society of which it is a part, rather than as a technical-rational assemblage of variables or components seemingly responsive to individual manipulation.

The study of child and family policy from the *outside* is in its infancy. This brief survey of the child care policies and programs of two nations is intended to be suggestive of the type of research that might be done as cross-national analyses of the "nation as context" type. It has been suggested that different nations can be seen as laboratories for the study of children in different developmental contexts (Rogoff & Morelli, 1989). This chapter has argued that the policies of nations *create* different contexts, and thus more attention needs to be paid to the processes by which they come to be socially constructed. Much remains to be done.

NOTES

1. Cross-national data are often not strictly comparable. The U.S. Bureau of the Census typically reports on the child care arrangements of working mothers with children under the age of six and under the age of eighteen. The point of reference is always where the child is while the *mother* is working. The data here were based on analyses of the Labour Force Survey of the Statistical Office of the European Communities and report on the employment of mothers and fathers with children under ten years of age.

2. Before this time, twenty-six weeks of maternity leave were fully paid (Weigl & Weber, 1991, p. 46).

3. "Universal provision" here means that all parents who wanted services were able to get them. Although centers were officially open for thirteen hours a day, the ones visited in 1990 opened at 6:00 and closed at 5:30 or 6:00, by which time parents had come for their children.

4. Funding from the Spencer Foundation's Small Grants Program and the research assistance of Maike Philipsen are acknowledged and appreciated. Thanks are also extended to Hans-Günther Roßbach and Wolfgang Tietze for long conversations, frequent email messages, and much encouragement.

5. For a discussion of some of these issues, see Lubeck, 1993b.

6. There is a veritable minefield of potential problems in doing cross-national research (e.g., Elder, 1976; Berting, Geyer, & Jurkovich, 1979). Are the events we study comparable or are they rendered too decontextualized to characterize adequately the phenomena in question? At what level can comparisons be made—and who decides on their legitimacy? Although I take these issues seriously, a thorough discussion is beyond the scope of this chapter.

REFERENCES

Barth, A. (1990). Manchen wir besser. *Der Spiegel, 44* (9), 84–93.

Beller, A., & Chung, S. (1991). Child support and the feminization of poverty. In E. Anderson & R. Hula (Eds.), *The reconceptualization of family policy* (pp. 179–190). New York: Greenwood Press.

Berting, J., Geyer, F., & Jurkovich, R. (Eds.). (1979). *Problems in international comparative research in the social sciences.* Oxford: Pergamon Press.

Boeckmann, B. (1993). Das Früherziehungssystem in der ehemaligen DDR. In W. Tietze & H.-G. Roßbach (Eds.), *Erfahrungsfelder in her frühen Kindheit: Bestandsaufnahme, Perspektiven.* Freibug im Breisgau: Lambertus.

Braun, M., Scott, J., & Alwin, D. (1992). Economic necessity or self-actualization? Attitudes towards women's labour force participation in the East and West. *Occasional Papers of the ESRC Research Centre on Micro-social Change.* Paper 9. Colchester: University of Essex.

Children's Defense Fund (1988). *Vanishing dreams: The growing plight of America's young families*. Washington, D.C.: Children's Defense Fund.

Children's Defense Fund (1992). *The state of America's children, 1992*. Washington, D.C.: Children's Defense Fund.

Clifford, R., & Russell, S. (1989). Financing programs for preschool-aged children. *Theory into Practice, 28* (1), 19–27.

Dennis, M. (1988). *German Democratic Republic: Politics, economics and society*. London: Pinter.

Edelman, M. W. (1989). Children at risk. In F. Macchiarola & A. Gartner (Eds.), *Caring for America's children* (pp. 20–30). New York: The Academy of Political Science.

Elder, J. (1976). Comparative cross-national methodology. *Annual Review of Sociology, 2*, 209–230.

Edwards, G. (1985). *GDR society and social institutions*. New York: St. Martin's Press.

Fishman, S., & Martin, L. (1987). *Estranged twins: Education and society in the two Germanys*. New York: Praeger.

Frau & Politik (1990, April). Wieviel Platz für Kinder? *4*, 15.

Grimshaw, A. (1973). Comparative sociology: In what ways different from other sociologies? In M. Armer & A. Grimshaw (Eds.)., *Comparative social research: Methodological problems and strategies* (pp. 4–48). New York: Wiley & Sons.

Grubb, N., and Lazerson, M. (1982/88). *Broken promises: How Americans fail their children*. New York: Basic Books.

Haas, L. (1991). Equal parenthood and social policy: Lessons from a study of parental leave in Sweden. In J. Hyde & M. Essex (Eds.), *Parental leave and child care: Setting a research and policy agenda* (pp. 375–405). Philadelphia: Temple University Press.

Kamerman, S. (1989). An international overview of preschool programs. *Phi Delta Kappan, 71* (2), 135–137.

Kamerman, S. (1991). Parental leave and infant care: U.S. and international trends and issues, 1978–1988. In J. Hyde & M. Essex (Eds.), *Parental leave and child care: Setting a research and policy agenda* (pp. 11–23). Philadelphia: Temple University Press.

Kamerman, S. (1993). *Child and family policies in East and West Europe: Trends and issues*. Paper presented at the Conference on Social Safety Nets and Child Care Policy in Eastern Europe during the Transition to a Market Economy, Madison, Wisc.

Kamerman, S., & Kahn, A. (1978). *Family policy: Government and families in fourteen countries*. New York: Columbia University Press.

Kamerman, S., & Kahn, A. (1981). *Child care family benefits, and working parents: A study in comparative policy*. New York: Columbia University Press.

Kamerman, S., & Kahn, A. (1989). Has the United States learned from Europe? *Policy Studies Review, 8* (3), 581–598.

Katz, M. (1989). *The undeserving poor*. New York: Pantheon.

Kohn, M. (Ed.) (1989). Introduction. *Cross-national research in sociology*. Newbury Park, Calif.: Sage.

Lazerson, M. (1972). The historical antecedents of early childhood education. *The*

Center for Educational Policy Reprint Series, no. 18. Harvard Graduate School of Education, Cambridge, Mass.

Lubeck, S. (1989). A world of difference: American child care policy in cross-national perspective. *Educational Policy, 3* (4), 331–354.

Lubeck, S. (1993a, December). *An examination of leave policies at the time of childbirth*. Final report to the Mary Reynolds Babcock Foundation. Ann Arbor: University of Michigan.

Lubeck, S. (1993b). Die Suche nach einer neuen Zukunft für die Betreuung und Erziehung von Kindern: Eine Untersuchung politscher Entscheidungsmöglichkeiten im transnationalen Vergleich. In W. Tietze & H.-G. Roßbach (Eds.), *Erfahrungsfelder in der frühen Kindheit: Bestandsaufnahme, Perspektiven*. Freiburg im Breisgau: Lambertus.

Lubeck, S., & Garrett, P. (1991). Child care in America: Retrospect and prospect. In R. Hula & E. Anderson (Eds.), *The reconstruction of family policy* (pp. 191–202). Westport, Conn.: Greenwood Press.

Martin, T., & Bumpass, L. (1989). Recent trends in marital disruption. *Demography, 26* (1), 37–51.

Mead, M., & Wolfenstein, M. (1955). *Childhood in contemporary cultures*. Chicago: University of Chicago Press.

Melhuish, E., & Moss, P. (Eds.). (1991). *Day care for young children: International perspectives*. London: Tavistock/Routledge.

Ministerium für Volksbildung (1989). Mimeographed materials. Berlin: Ministerrat der Deutschen Demokratischen Republik.

Morgan. G. (1987, November). *Two visions: The future of day care and early childhood programs*. Unpublished manuscript. Wheelock College, Boston.

Moss, P. (1988, April). *Childcare and equality of opportunity: Consolidated report to the European Commission*. London: Thomas Coram Research Unit.

Moss, P. (1993, March). *Mothers, fathers and employment, 1985–1991*. London: Thomas Coram Research Unit.

National Center for Education Statistics (1993). *Profiles of preschool children's care and early education program participation*. Washington, D.C.: U.S. Department of Education.

O'Connell, M., & Bloom, D. (1987). *Juggling jobs and babies: America's child care challenge*. No. 12. Population Reference Bureau, Inc.

Olmstead, P., & Weikart, D. (1989). *How nations serve young children: Profile of child care and education in 14 countries*. Ypsilanti, Mich.: The High/Scope Press.

Philips, D. (1991). Day care for young children in the United States. In E. Melhuish & P. Moss (Eds.), *Day care for young children: International perspectives* (pp. 161–184). London: Tavistock/Routledge.

Pleck, J. (1988). Fathers and infant care leave. In E. Zigler & M. Frank (Eds.), *The parental leave crisis: Toward a national policy* (pp. 177–191). New Haven: Yale University Press.

Richardson, G., & Marx, E. (1989). *A welcome for every child: How France achieves quality in child care: Practical ideas for the United States*. New York: The French-American Foundation.

Rist, R. (1994). Influencing the policy process with qualitative research. In N.

Denzin & Y. Lincoln (Eds.), *Handbook of qualitative research* (pp. 545–557). Thousand Oaks, Calif.: Sage.

Robinson, S. (1987). Kindergarten in America: Five major trends. *Phi Delta Kappan, 69* 529–530.

Rogoff, B., & Morelli, G. (1989). Perspective on children's development from cultural psychology. *American Psychologist, 44* (2), 343–348.

Rosewater, A. (1989). Child and family trends: Beyond the numbers. In F. Macchiarola & A. Gartner (Eds.), *Caring for America's children* (pp. 4–19). New York: The Academy of Political Science.

Steinfels, M. (1973). *Who's minding the children? The history and politics of day care in America.* New York: Simon & Schuster.

Tietze, W., & Paterak, H. (1993). Hilfen für die Betreuung und Erziehung von Kindern im Vorschulalter in den Ländern der Europäischen Gemeinschaft. In W. Tietze & H.-G. Roßbach (Eds.), *Erfahrungsfelder in der frühen Kindheit: Bestandsaufnahme, Perspektiven* (pp. 272–315). Freiburg im Breisgau: Lambertus.

Tietze, W., & Roßbach, H.-G. (1993). Das Früerziehungssystem in der Bundesrepublik Deutschland (alte Bundesländer). In W. Tietze & H.-G. Roßbach (Eds.), *Erfahrungsfelder in der frühen Kindheit: Bestandsaufnahme, Perspektiven* (pp. 126–167). Freiburg im Breisgau: Lambertus.

Tietze, W., & Ufermann, K. (1989). An international perspective on schooling for 4-year-olds. *Theory into Practice, 28* (1), 69–77.

Tobin, J., Davidson, D., & Wu, D. (1989). *Preschool in three cultures: Japan, China, and the United States.* New Haven: Yale University Press.

Weigl, I., & Weber, C. (1991). Day care for young children in the German Democratic Republic. In E. Melhuish & P. Moss (Eds.), *Day care for young children: International Perspectives—Policy research in five international perspectives—Policy and research in countries* (pp. 46–55), London: Routledge.

Whiting, B. (1963). *Six cultures: Studies of child rearing.* New York: John Wiley & Sons.

Whiting, B., & Edwards, C. (1988). *Children of different worlds.* Cambridge: Cambridge University Press.

Whiting, B., & Whiting, J. (1975). *Children of six cultures.* Cambridge, Mass.: Harvard University Press.

Winkler, G. (Ed.). (1990). *Frauenreport '90.* Berlin: Die Wirtschaft.

Wrigley, J. (1989). Different care for different kids: Social class and child care policy. *Educational Policy, 3,* 421–439.

Chapter 6

Qualitative Research in Early Childhood Settings: A Review

Pamela C. Browning and
J. Amos Hatch

We learned some things as we put together this review of qualitative studies in early childhood settings. One is that relatively little research of this type has been done. We completed a large number of computer database searches using all of the descriptors we could think of, then followed up with descriptors developed from the articles we found. We continued by collecting articles, book chapters, and books referenced in the articles from the computer searches (and from articles and books that we know), then searched the references of these, and so on. Still, going back ten years, the number of published qualitative studies in U.S. early childhood contexts was relatively small. The field is new and open.

Another lesson is that much of the work in this new area of inquiry has been done by researchers from disciplines other than education. Anthropologists, sociologists, sociolinguists, and some social psychologists trained in qualitative methods have studied enculturation, socialization, behavior within institutions, language development, and other phenomena associated with young children. Fewer studies have been done by researchers whose interest is primarily in early childhood education and care, and these researchers are applying methods adapted from other fields with longer histories of qualitative work. This is not surprising, but it does point out a limitation in the scope of the research base and signals an opportunity for enriching what is known about early childhood settings.

The third lesson is related to the two above. When we studied the references of qualitative studies we found, we saw that most of the work cited was quantitative in nature. What this means to us is that much of the qualitative work being done represents early or initial attempts to study contexts and social phenomena that have previously only been studied using more quantitative means. Again, we see this as a limitation in that the field does not have a well-developed methodological or substantive research history. It also represents an opportunity to generate research strategies uniquely suited to early education and care settings and to examine previously unexplored territory in early childhood studies.

A final lesson, one that has shaped the form of this review, is that it is difficult to write a review of qualitative research using a traditional model of research reviews. The complex and often idiosyncratic nature of the methods and the narrative style of findings from qualitative studies make using the traditional format for reporting quantitative work awkward at best. In quantitative studies, research designs, sampling strategies, and statistical analysis procedures have been standardized and codified in ways that make it possible to summarize these in very few words. Similarly, findings are reported using terms and numbers that are relatively brief and straightforward (at least to those inside the quantitative research community). Qualitative methods are frequently adapted to the settings under investigation, and questions often emerge or change as studies progress, making codified descriptions of data gathering and analysis procedures difficult. Further, since understanding the contexts of a study is essential to interpreting the findings of a qualitative report, collapsing these into a few words in a review can distort important meanings generated in the study. Finally, since qualitative findings are descriptive in nature, shorthand versions like those found in traditional reviews of research are likely to leave out a great deal of the descriptive power.

Our way of dealing with, though not solving, the problems of reviewing qualitative studies has been to modify the traditional approach to research reviewing. We have chosen to identify several studies that we believe provide good examples of research done at different age levels within early childhood. Dividing the review into Pre-Kindergarten, Kindergarten, and Primary levels, we list several exemplary studies and use an annotated bibliographic style to describe the methods, contexts, and the nature of the findings of each. The goal is to give the reader a starting point for entering the qualitative literature of interest. We hope to provide enough detail so that the novice researcher or someone new to qualitative research can get a sense of how such work is done and what it can accomplish. We conclude with a brief section reviewing publications that discuss methods and ethics specific to qualitative research in early childhood settings.

STUDIES AT THE PRE-KINDERGARTEN LEVEL

In a comprehensive "ethnography of communication," Heath (1983) studied two culturally different communities in the Piedmont Carolinas. Observing and interviewing in homes, schools, and other community settings over a period of nine years, Heath studied differences in how children in the two communities learn to use language. She examined what these differences mean for teachers not from such communities and how knowledge of culturally different "ways with words" (p. 343) can enable teachers to bring those ways into the classroom.

Lubeck (1985) used passive participant observation and formal and informal interviews to compare processes through which preschool teachers in two culturally different settings transmit values, life experiences, and cultures. In a Head Start program serving black children and a preschool program for white children, Lubeck described differences in the uses of time, uses of space, nature of the curriculum, activities and materials, and patterns of interaction. She concluded that the transmission of a "collective" orientation organized the explanations for experiences provided at the black Head Start, while an "individualistic" perspective permeated the white preschool program.

Tobin, Wu, and Davidson (1989) utilized "multivocal ethnography" as a method for studying preschools in the United States, Japan, and China. The researchers began by videotaping segments of classroom life in preschool settings in each of the three cultures. They showed edited versions of the tapes to administrators, teachers, students, and parents, recording their "insider explanations" for what was shown on the videotapes. In addition, they recorded reactions to the tapes by foreign audiences, seeking "outsider explanations." The findings are a description and comparison of preschools in three cultures, told through the multiple voices of the participants.

Budwig, Strage, and Bamberg (1986) conducted a longitudinal study in which they used participant observation to study the interactive development of two white, middle-class two-year-old girls. The girls' play sessions were videotaped in their homes once a month for one year. The purpose of the study was to explore how "children begin to construct joint activities with their peers" (p. 101). The authors found that the mothers offered guidance while at the same time encouraging their children to assume increasing responsibility for constructing joint activities. They conclude that although caregivers scaffold their children's social activities, "actual social interaction with an age-mate also provides an important forum that contributes to the creation of communicative strategies necessary for constructing shared activities with others" (p. 103).

Heath (1985) explored the narrative play of SooJong, a two-year-old Korean girl born in the United States, through analysis of tape recordings of play sessions and field notes taken by the child's mother. Korean was spoken almost exclusively in the home, but SooJong attended an English-speaking nursery school. Heath concluded that SooJong instinctively realized that she would have to learn English in order to participate in the dramatic play at her nursery school so she practiced it at home in her play sessions. Heath suggested a developmental sequence in the acquisition of types of discourse for second-language learners.

Woodhouse (1988) used participant observation and interviews with mothers, staff, children, and administrators to examine the culture of a day care servicing children of young professionals. The purpose of the study was to identify the "potential impacts of changing roles and changing dependencies on women, children, and families" (p. 379). Woodhouse studied the four-year-old class of a day care in a country setting near a large eastern city. The characteristics of this day care culture led Woodhouse to speculate that the length of childhood is being shortened. She summarized: "Perhaps this shortening of childhood is the cultural response to the pushes and pulls on women—a response that needs to be carefully structured to avoid hurting children" (p. 382).

Johnson and Hatch (1990) studied the social and creative behavior of four "highly original" children in a preschool for 3-, 4-, and 5-year-olds. Three activity centers of the classroom were videotaped and observed by a passive participant observer one day per week for one school year; and teachers, parents, and instructional assistants were interviewed. The four children demonstrated in their classroom products and activities that they were highly original thinkers, but each had a different level of social competence and used different patterns of social behavior to negotiate interactions with their peers.

Friendship and peer culture were the focus of an extensive participant observation study completed in a university nursery school (Corsaro, 1985). One of the first of its type, the study detailed how peers construct their own culture in preschool. In his description, Corsaro included peer culture dimensions such as: conceptions of status, conceptions of role, the importance of play, friendship and social integration, and the protection of interactive space. The study provides a detailed description and rationale for field-entry strategies and data collection methods appropriate for participant observation studies in early childhood settings.

Corsaro (1988) used microethnographies of preschools in the United States and Italy to compare peer culture in the two settings. Corsaro used unobtrusive participant observation as well as informal interviews to collect data. He found control and communal sharing to be common in both settings. However, the Italian children's attempts to protect their interactive space varied somewhat from the routines established by the American children. Corsaro judged the differences to be reflective of the respective adult worlds and cultures.

A team of researchers from Ohio State University has conducted a series of studies in a university preschool serving three- to five-year-old children. The researchers utilized extensive videotaping, daily field notes by participant observers, retrospective teacher notes, and interviews to study peer culture. Children's play styles and object use were examined using data collected during the first two weeks of school (Elgas, Klein, Kantor, & Fernie, 1988). The findings suggested that "play periods are indeed social arenas in which the dynamics of the peer culture are enacted" (p. 152). The authors surmised that the peer culture of the preschool consisted of a hierarchical structure of subgroups and individuals and that objects played a part in gaining entry into a particular core subgroup.

In a separate article, Kantor, Elgas, and Fernie (1993) scrutinize a "salient play group within the peer culture of the preschool" (p. 131), exploring the requirements for membership in this core group. Samples of videotapes of the daily free-play period were used to examine the actions and interactions of three children—Bob, Lisa, and William—in the context of the core group. Bob and Lisa both became established members of the group, while William did not. The authors found that possession of a valued object (in this case, red rhythm sticks and capes) was necessary for group membership but did not ensure membership. They concluded: "If one is to be successful, he or she must fully understand the specific nature of what is valued: in this case, specific roles, themes, and objects, produced through particular attitudes, language, and social action" (p. 143).

In an international analysis, the social competence of preschool children was explored by Fernie, Davies, Kantor, and McMurray (1993). The researchers compared ethnographies of the Ohio State University preschool and two rural and two metropolitan preschools in Australia. The researchers found that children demonstrated their social competence in multiple ways: (a) their success in negotiating "distinctive social memberships as students, peers, and gendered persons within classroom contexts"; (b) their ability to "read" the social cues that dictated their participation in the classroom; and (c) their ability to "stretch situational boundaries to accomplish comfortable places for themselves and . . . to change the shape of events" (p. 107).

Roskos (1991) used ethnographic interviewing, nonparticipant observation, and the analysis of children's writings to study the pretend play episodes of eight preschoolers. Thirty-one of the forty-one observed episodes included reading- and writing-like behavior. Roskos concluded that young children seem to know a great deal about literacy and recommended the inclusion of "lifelike literacy situations with their accompanying activity patterns to tap and extend children's understanding of the forms and functions of literacy" (p. 50).

Kantor, Green, Bradley, and Lin (1992) investigated how three- and four-year-old children construct schooled discourse repertoires. The authors explored circle time, especially the component designed to assist children in learning to talk in a group. Their goal was to analyze how young children learn to be conversationally appropriate partners. They argue that "discourse patterns are always constructed in classrooms and that these patterns help to frame what is worth knowing, what it means to be a member of the particular group, and how to participate in the everyday life of the particular classroom" (p. 165).

Participant observation was used to study the social-communicative competence of thirteen preschool students with mild to profound handicaps (Salisbury, Britzman, & Kang, 1989). The study was conducted in a special education classroom located in a public elementary school. Three themes were identified: (1) each child consistently utilized individualized initiation strategies; (2) all students attempted to continue interactions through such strategies as redundant cueing; and (3) the children's initiation strategies served specific functions, such as getting attention and showing affection.

Peck, Hayden, Wandschneider, Peterson, and Richarz (1989) studied the resistance of parents, teachers, and administrators to the establishment of a federally funded preschool program designed to integrate handicapped and nonhandicapped children. The study was conducted in two concurrent phases. In Phase One, the researchers interviewed ten parents, ten teachers, and ten administrators by telephone. Phase Two consisted of participant observations at planning meetings in three rural communities. Three thematic concerns were identified: (1) preparation for teachers, parents, and children; (2) resources; and (3) conflicts arising in an integrated program.

In an effort to "show what's possible," Ayers (1989) collected the life stories of six excellent early childhood educators: an infant-toddler teacher, a family-home provider, a day care teacher, a public school pre-k teacher, a teacher of homeless young children, and a teacher in a private kindergarten. Using a narrative approach, Ayers utilized a variety of data collection tools for constructing the six stories, including interviewing, participant observation, written correspondence, and "autobiographical reflection." Across the group, the teachers are characterized by "the sense of urgency, of practicality, of present-orientation, of seeking primary rewards from children, . . . and [of] what it means to be grounded in a posture of caring and concern" (pp. 135–136).

Nelson (1990) studied the experience of family day care providers. Relying heavily on semistructured interviews, eighty-six day care providers, nineteen mothers, seven husbands, and others participated in the research. The study describes: the work of family day care providers, relationships with mothers, mothering others' children, relations within the providers' own families, and professional providers as "deviants." Nelson's work tells the providers' story from their point of view, revealing the complex struggles involved in balancing the needs of caregivers with those of the recipients of their care.

STUDIES AT THE KINDERGARTEN LEVEL

Hatch and Freeman studied the relationship between kindergarten educators' philosophies of early childhood education and their professional practices. Teachers, principals, and supervisors were interviewed, and curriculum materials and kindergarten report cards were collected from across the state of Ohio. The researchers described "philosophy-reality conflicts" (Hatch & Freeman, 1988a) that characterized the experience of more than half of the educators interviewed. Kindergartens were academic in nature for several reasons that educators saw as beyond their control (Hatch & Freeman, 1988b), which placed teachers with more child-centered philosophies in conflict; they were responsible for implementing programs that many thought were not in the best interest of children. In the same study, kindergarten report cards were analyzed as artifacts in an effort to reveal what schools expect young children to know and do (Freeman & Hatch, 1989).

The social construction of meanings of readiness for kindergarten was the topic of research by Graue (1993). Three demographically different school communities in the same district were studied using interviews with parents, teachers, and children; participant observation in kindergarten classes; and document analysis. Different constructions of readiness were discovered in each of the school-community settings. Graue summarized: "the meanings of readiness were locally developed and used. . . . [T]hey came out of ideas about how children grow and develop, out of the local purposes for the kindergarten, out of notions for what it means to be a good parent or teacher" (p. 248).

Kindergarten teachers' beliefs and practices related to readiness and retention were explored using clinical interviews with teachers, participant observation in classrooms, analysis of school documents, and interviews with parents (Smith & Shepard, 1988). Data were collected over a year's time in one school district. Forty kindergarten teachers were interviewed, and six schools were selected for observation. School documents examined included school retention policies, pamphlets on school readiness, and curriculum objectives for kindergarten. Parents were interviewed by telephone. Smith and Shepard found that teachers' beliefs about school readiness were based on nativism, that this belief accounted for their adherence to the practice of retention, and that the culture of the particular schools may have also influenced these beliefs and practices. Through the parent interviews, the researchers determined that the views of the teachers were not congruous with those of the parents.

Smith (1989) used clinical interviews as her primary source of data in investigating kindergarten teachers' beliefs about retention. She triangulated data from the interviews with data from classroom observations and documents such as the retention records of the various schools. She also cross-referenced the teachers' self-reports with data obtained from parent interviews. Smith found that all teachers endorsed retention as beneficial especially for those children seen as immature. Most of the teachers could not recall perceiving any negative effects on children who had been retained in kindergarten.

Using artistic criticism, Huenecke (1992) studied the aesthetics of *Writing to Read*, a computer-based literacy program. The researcher initiated the observation of a group of thirty kindergarten children in April as they began the *Writing to Read* program. Observations continued through December of their first-grade year when they completed the program. Two artistic criteria, balance and coherence, were used to analyze the observations of the computer class. Balance, in the form of individuality and opportunity for exploration, existed in the design of the program itself and in the activities provided. However, in an attempt to balance time and equipment, the teacher deterred creativity. Coherence, defined as "unity, cohesion, and consistency" (p. 56), was lacking due to the imposed time constraints and the failure of the teacher to integrate the activities of the computer lab with those in the regular classroom.

Dyson (1985) used participant observation to study literacy instruction in a kindergarten classroom. Three children, identified as typical of the other students, were observed for fourteen weeks during teacher-initiated beginning literacy activities. Audiotape recordings were made of the children's talk as they wrote, and the written products were analyzed. Through this study, Dyson questioned traditional beginning literacy activities such as copying text from the board. She determined that teachers cannot completely control the literacy curriculum because "children interpret school experiences in light of their own understandings" (p. 509). More specifically, this study demonstrated the "limitations of copying in helping children become composers" (p. 510).

Hatch has conducted a series of participant observation and interview studies of children's peer interactions in kindergarten settings. The theoretical framework for this work has been symbolic interactionism, and the goal has been to understand social behavior among peers from the perspectives of the children involved. Social phenomena examined by Hatch include: impression management (1987a); status and social power (1987b); secondary adjustments to school expectations (1989); and peer stigmatization (1988).

STUDIES AT THE PRIMARY LEVEL

Dorr-Bremme (1990) utilized videotapes to record a kindergarten/first grade teacher's use of contextualization cues. First circle, a whole group activity at the beginning of each day, was videotaped fourteen times across a two-year span. Dorr-Bremme analyzed eight of the episodes in detail, comparing this analysis with the remaining six tapes and with observational notes of other first circles. Dorr-Bremme also reviewed the tapes with the teacher, requesting her reactions and comments. Markers, "succinct behaviors routinely enacted by one participant as the context changes" (p. 388), were identified in the teacher's speech. These markers assisted the teacher in maintaining control and in expediting the events associated with first circle.

Through participant observation and interviewing, Schnorr (1990) determined that students defined their experience as first graders according to who their teacher was, where their physical classroom was located, the kinds of activities and materials they were expected to complete, and their classmates. Schnorr found that these criteria for belonging to the group served to exclude Peter, a part-time mainstreamed student, from being seen as a member of the class. This exclusion was at odds with the special education teacher's goal of socialization for Peter.

Coenen (1986), in an attempt to gain insight into "the processes of social meaning-constitution through corporeality" (p. 258), used participant observation and phenomenological-interpretive analysis to study deaf children aged 3 through 9 in a San Francisco-area school for the deaf. In his six-month study, Coenen identified two themes of interaction that he labeled as "incorporation" and "annexation." Incorporation involved the manner in which the deaf children drew others into social interaction. Annexation was the exclusion-inclusion process of interaction between some of the deaf students and the teachers of the nondeaf classrooms into which they were mainstreamed.

Bennett (1991) used a variety of interactive and non-interactive ethnographic methods to study reading instruction in an Appalachian first grade. The school was located in a low-SES Appalachian neighborhood within a large midwestern city. The interactive methods employed included participant observation and interviews. More than sixty reading group lessons were observed, and formal interviews were conducted with the teacher, her supervisor, and the principal. Observations were also made in Chapter I reading classes, faculty meetings, and student placement meetings. Many informal interviews were conducted with the school faculty and administration. Non-interactive methods included stream-of-behavior chronicles, audiotaped lessons, and artifacts such as student report cards and district curriculum guides. Bennett drew two major conclusions from the data collected in this study. First, she found disagreement between "the formal philosophy of the district at the macrolevel and the actual reading program which was provided to students at the microlevel of classroom reality" (p. 45). Second, the stratification of reading groups within the classroom contributed to the reading deficits of the Appalachian children.

Utilizing observation and interviewing as her data-gathering techniques, Bondy (1990) found first graders' definitions of reading varied according to their level of placement in reading groups. Low-group children defined reading as "saying words," "schoolwork," and "a source of status." High-group children defined it as a "way to learn things," "private pleasure," and "social activity" (p. 35). The author discussed the implications of these findings for teacher education programs.

Hatch and Bondy (1984) studied remedial reading instruction in two summer school primary classrooms. Reading instruction for students who had "failed" reading during the regular school year was characterized as: skill-based, product-oriented, reactive, disconnected, and materials-centered. The authors challenged the notion that children who are having difficulties with materials-centered instruction during the school year ought to be given a "double dose" of the same ineffective medicine during the summer.

Qualitative and quantitative methods were combined to study the perspectives of women who were mothers of young children as well as kindergarten or primary grade teachers (Claesson & Brice, 1989). The researchers interviewed participants and analyzed their responses. Participants generally believed their dual roles to be complimentary and mutually beneficial; expectations emanating from both roles were sometimes ambiguous and unrealistically high; and their experiences and commitment "provided them with opportunities to gain insight and learn strategies for coping with both roles" (p. 14).

Walsh, Baturka, and Smith (1991) collaborated with Nan Colter to conduct a case study of a teacher in transition. Colter, a first grade teacher in Virginia, was observed at least twice a week for an entire school year. The researchers interviewed her formally once a week and informally often over the course of the year. Nan was reluctant to define herself as changing from the outset of the study, even though her peers indicated that she had changed her teaching practices. The researchers attributed this reluctance to the complexity of Nan's definition of herself. She viewed the changes she had made in her classroom as merely a sign of the deliberate, continuous process she was undergoing both as a teacher and as a person.

METHODS AND ETHICS

As we searched the literature, we found relatively few examples of published work directed specifically at methodological or ethical issues related to early childhood qualitative research. Authors of the studies we reviewed cited a broad array of general methods books and articles to establish the methodological and ethical foundations of their studies, but included almost no references targeted to early childhood. (We have included an appendix listing the general qualitative research texts cited in the studies in this review.) In the remainder of this chapter, we review recently published work that addresses directly methodological and ethical concerns of qualitative researchers doing work in early childhood settings.

Parker (1984) discussed problems and promises in interviewing children. In a discussion of interviews with preschool-age children, he suggested that care should be taken to relax children and win their trust, perhaps through playing a game, at the outset of an interview. He recommended the use of visual aids, props, and pictures to stimulate children's participation. Parker also noted that the ways the interview context is structured have powerful effects on children's responses. He warned against the unethical practices of: (a) using adult status to coerce children into participating or responding; and (b) sharing information offered by children with others in ways that would not be done with adult informants.

A discussion by Tammivaara and Enright (1986) emphasized overcoming "adult-centrism" by adjusting ethnographic questions to fit the special situations created in interviews with young children. They recommended that adults "change their demeanor and ongoing relations with child informants so that perceptions of adults' status will also change" (p. 229). They identified two adult controlling behaviors as prohibited: (1) controlling the behavior of the child within the interview context; and (2) doing all the initiating within the interview. As a tool for getting children's perspectives, they recommended "playing dumb, by explicitly taking the role of an ignorant confused participant who requires the assistance of child insiders" (p. 231).

Hatch (1990) used his experiences interviewing young children to identify four problems that can threaten the quality of data obtained in interview contexts: (1) the adult-child problem (differential power and status relations are built into an interview between an adult researcher and child informant); (2) the right-answer problem (children often see the interview as a school-related recitation exercise); (3) the pre-operational thought problem (egocentrism, complexive thinking, and centering may limit young children's ability to respond in ways expected of older informants); and (4) the self-as-social-object problem (children may have difficulty thinking of themselves separately from the experience of being themselves). Emphasizing that they belong to the researcher and not the children, Hatch suggested four strategies for dealing with the "problems" identified: (1) take time to establish personal relationships with children; (2) emphasize informal rather than formal interviews; (3)

ask questions children can answer, expect them to answer, and accept their answers; and (4) provide concrete objects or pictures to elicit explanations of classroom phenomena.

Corsaro's (1985) description of the "reactive" field-entry methods used in his study of preschool peer culture is a guide to participant observation methods appropriate for early childhood settings. By being reactive (i.e., being available for interactions but allowing children to initiate contacts) and by spending considerable time gradually working his way into the fabric of life in the classroom, Corsaro reduced the impact of his physical size and perceived power. He described his participation as peripheral: "I entered an ecological area, moved when necessary, responded when addressed, and occasionally offered verbal contributions when they seemed appropriate" (p. 32). He recorded short summaries in a small notebook shortly after the end of episodes, then filled in and expanded his field notes at the end of each day. Corsaro's work offers a model for other qualitative researchers interested in classroom research.

Tobin and Davidson (1990) discussed the ethics of polyvocal ethnography as used in their "Preschool in Three Cultures" study (Tobin, Wu, & Davidson, 1989). Using their own methodological perspective, they addressed many ethical dilemmas that relate to other kinds of studies of young children and their teachers. They examined issues such as: teachers' vulnerability, informed consent, the uses of videotaped material, ethical ambiguities in cross-cultural research, video voyeurism, textualizing teachers, and authorial power. Tobin and Davidson concluded by inviting readers to become another voice in the research process, to contest their interpretations, and to compose alternative texts, "in their minds reworking, recasting, retelling our stories" (p. 282).

We hope this review gives readers a starting place for entering the literature on qualitative studies related to early childhood. The other chapters included in this collection provide another valuable source of references. We believe that early childhood qualitative research is an exciting new field of inquiry and that opportunities for contributing to both the substantive and methodological knowledge base are plentiful.

REFERENCES

Ayers, W. (1989). *The good preschool teacher: Six teachers reflect on their lives.* New York: Teachers College Press.

Bennett, K. (1991). Doing school in an urban Appalachian first grade. In C. Sleeter (Ed.), *Empowerment through multicultural education* (pp. 27–46). Albany: SUNY Press.

Bondy, E. (1990). See it their way: What children's definitions of reading tell us about improving teacher education. *Journal of Teacher Education, 41,* 33–45.

Budwig, N., Strage, A., & Bamberg, M. (1986). The construction of joint activities with an age-mate: The transition from caregiver-child to peer play. In J. Cook-Gumperz, W. Corsaro, & J. Streeck (Eds.), *Children's worlds and children's language* (pp. 83–108). Berlin: Mouton.

Claesson, M. A., & Brice, R. A. (1989). Teacher/mothers: Effects of a dual role. *American Education Research Journal, 26*, 1–23.

Coenen, H. (1986). A silent world of movements: Interactional processes among deaf children. In J. Cook-Gumperz, W. Corsaro, & J. Streeck (Eds.), *Children's worlds and children's language* (pp. 253–287). Berlin: Mouton.

Corsaro, W. A. (1985). *Friendship and peer culture in the early years*. Norwood, N.J.: Ablex.

Corsaro, W. A. (1988). Routines in the peer culture of American and Italian nursery school children. *Sociology of Education, 61*, 1–14.

Dorr-Bremme, D. W. (1990). Contextualization cues in the classroom: Discourse regulation and social control functions. *Language in Society, 19*, 379–402.

Dyson, A. H. (1985). Three emergent writers and the school curriculum: Copying and other myths. *The Elementary School Journal, 85*, 497–512.

Elgas, P. M., Klein, E., Kantor, R., & Fernie, D. E. (1988). Play and the peer culture: Play styles and object use. *Journal of Research in Childhood Education, 3*, 142–153.

Fernie, D. E., Davies, B., Kantor, R., & McMurray, P. (1993). Becoming a person in the preschool: Creating integrated gender, school culture, and peer culture positionings. *Qualitative Studies in Education, 6*, 95–110.

Freeman, E. B., & Hatch, J. A. (1989). What schools expect young children to know and do: An analysis of kindergarten report cards. *Elementary School Journal, 89*, 595–605.

Graue, M. E. (1993). *Ready for what? Constructing meanings of readiness for kindergarten*. Albany: SUNY Press.

Hatch, J. A. (1987a). Impression management in kindergarten classrooms: An analysis of children's face-work in peer interactions. *Anthropology and Education Quarterly, 18*, 100–115.

Hatch, J. A. (1987b). Status and social power in a kindergarten peer group. *Elementary School Journal, 88*, 79–92.

Hatch, J. A. (1988). Learning to be an outsider: Peer stigmatization in kindergarten. *Urban Review, 20*, 59–72.

Hatch, J. A. (1989). Alone in a crowd: Analysis of secondary adjustments in a kindergarten. *Early Child Development and Care, 44*, 39–49.

Hatch, J. A. (1990). Young children as informants in classroom studies. *Early Childhood Research Quarterly, 5*, 251–264.

Hatch, J. A., & Bondy, E. (1984). A double dose of the same medicine: Implications from a naturalistic study of summer school reading instruction. *Urban Education, 19*, 29–38.

Hatch, J. A., & Freeman, E. B. (1988a). Kindergarten philosophies and practices: Perspectives of teachers, principals, and supervisors. *Early Childhood Research Quarterly, 3*, 151–166.

Hatch, J. A., & Freeman, E. B. (1988b). Who's pushing whom? Stress and kindergarten. *Phi Delta Kappan, 70*, 145–148.

Heath, S. B. (1983). *Ways with words: Language, life, and work in communities and classrooms*. Cambridge: Cambridge University Press.

Heath, S. B. (1985). Narrative play in second-language learning. In L. Galda & A. D. Pellegrini (Eds.), *Play, language, and stories: The development of children's literate behavior*. Norwood, N.J.: Ablex.

Huenecke, D. (1992). An artistic criticism of a computer-based reading program. *Educational Technology, 32*, 53–57.

Johnson, L. G., & Hatch, J. A. (1990). A descriptive study of the creative and social behavior of four highly original young children. *Journal of Creative Behavior, 24*, 205–224.

Kantor, R., Elgas, P. M., & Fernie, D. E. (1993). Cultural knowledge and social competence within a preschool peer culture group. *Early Childhood Research Quarterly, 8*, 125–147.

Kantor, R., Green, J., Bradley, M., & Lin, L. (1992). The construction of schooled discourse repertoires: An interactional sociolinguistic perspective on learning to talk in preschool. *Linguistics and Education, 4*, 131–172.

Lubeck, S. (1985). *Sandbox society: Early education in black and white America*. London: Falmer Press.

Nelson, M. K. (1990). *Negotiated care: The experience of family day care providers*. Philadelphia: Temple University Press.

Parker, W. C. (1984). Interviewing children: Problems and promise. *Journal of Negro Education, 53* (1), 18–28.

Peck, C. A., Hayden, L., Wandschneider, M., Peterson, K., & Richarz, S. (1989). Development of integrated preschools: A qualitative inquiry into sources of resistance among parents, administrators, and teachers. *Journal of Early Intervention, 13*, 353–364.

Roskos, K. (1991). An inventory of literate behavior in the pretend play episodes of eight preschoolers. *Reading Research and Instruction, 30*, 39–52.

Salisbury, C. L., Britzman, D., & Kang, J. (1989). Using qualitative methods to assess the social-communicative competence of young handicapped children. *Journal of Early Intervention, 13*, 153–164.

Schnorr, R. F. (1990). "Peter? He comes and goes . . .": First-graders' perspective on a part-time mainstream student. *Journal of the Association for Persons with Severe Handicaps, 15*, 231–240.

Smith, M. L. (1989). Teachers' beliefs about retention. In L. A. Shepard & M. L. Smith (Eds.), *Flunking grades: Research and policies on retention* (pp. 132–150). London: Falmer Press.

Smith, M. L., & Shepard, L. A. (1988). Kindergarten readiness and retention: A qualitative study of teacher's beliefs and practices. *American Educational Research Journal, 25*, 307–333.

Tammivaara, J., & Enright, D. S. (1986). On eliciting information: Dialogues with child informants. *Anthropology & Education Quarterly, 17*, 218–238.

Tobin, J., & Davidson, D. (1990). The ethics of polyvocal ethnography: Empowering vs. textualizing children and teachers. *Qualitative Studies in Education, 3*, 271–283.

Tobin, J. J., Wu, D. Y., & Davidson, D. H. (1989). *Preschool in three cultures: Japan, China, and the United States*. New Haven: Yale University Press.

Walsh, D. J., Baturka, N. L., & Smith, M. E. (1991). Changing one's mind—Maintaining one's identity: A first-grade teacher's story. *Teachers College Record*, *93*, 73–86.

Woodhouse, L. (1988). The new dependencies of women. *Family Relations, 37*, 379–384.

APPENDIX: QUALITATIVE RESEARCH TEXTS CITED IN STUDIES REVIEWED

Agar, M. H. (1980). *The professional stranger: An informal introduction to ethnography*. New York: Academic Press.

Bernard, H. R. (1988). *Research methods in cultural anthropology*. Newbury Park, Calif.: Sage.

Blumer, H. (1969). *Symbolic interactionism: Perspective and method*. Englewood Cliffs, N.J.: Prentice-Hall.

Bogdan, R. C., & Biklen, S. K. (1982). *Qualitative research for education: An introduction to theory and methods*. New York: Allyn and Bacon.

Clifford, J. (1988). *The predicament of culture: Twentieth-century ethnography, literature, and art*. Cambridge, Mass.: Harvard University Press.

Denzin, N. K. (1978). *The Research act: A theoretical introduction to sociological methods*. Chicago: Aldine.

Dobbert, M. (1982). *Ethnographic research: Theory and application for modern schools and societies*. New York: Praeger.

Fetterman, D. M. (1989). *Ethnography: Step by step*. Newbury Park, Calif.: Sage.

Garfinkel, H. (1967). *Studies in ethnomethodology*. New York: Prentice-Hall.

Geertz, C. (1973). *The interpretation of cultures*. New York: Basic Books.

Geertz, C. (1988). *Works and lives: The anthropologist as author*. Stanford: Stanford University Press.

Glaser, B. G., & Strauss, A. L. (1967). *The discovery of grounded theory: Strategies for qualitative research*. New York: Aldine.

Goetz, J. P., & LeCompte, M. D. (1984). *Ethnography and qualitative design in educational research*. Orlando, Fla.: Academic Press.

Goffman, E. (1974). *Frame analysis*. New York: Harper & Row.

Hammersley, M., & Atkinson, P. (1989). *Ethnography: Principles in practice*. New York: Routledge.

Jackson, B. (1987). *Fieldwork*. Urbana: University of Illinois Press.

Kaplan, A. (1963). *Conduct of inquiry: Methodology for behavioral science*. New York: Harper & Row.

Lincoln, Y. S., & Guba, E. G. (1985). *Naturalistic inquiry*. Newbury Park, Calif.: Sage.

Lofland, J., & Lofland, L. (1984). *Analyzing social settings: A guide to qualitative observation and analysis (2nd ed.)*. Belmont, Calif.: Wadsworth.

Marcus, G., & Fischer, M. (1986). *Anthropology as cultural critique*. Chicago: University of Chicago Press.

Miles, M., & Huberman, A. (1984). *Qualitative data analysis*. Beverly Hills, Calif.: Sage.

Mishler, E. G. (1986). *Research interviewing: Context and narrative*. Cambridge, Mass.: Harvard University Press.

Patton, M. Q. (1980). *Qualitative methods in educational evaluation research*. Beverly Hills, Calif.: Sage.

Pelto, P., & Pelto, G. (1978). *Anthropological research: The structure of inquiry*. New York: Cambridge University Press.

Schwartz, H., & Jacobs, J. (1979). *Qualitative sociology*. New York: Free Press.

Spradley, J. P. (1979). *The ethnographic interview*. New York: Holt, Rinehart and Winston.

Spradley, J. P. (1980). *Participant observation*. New York: Holt, Rinehart & Winston.

Stainback, S. (1988). *Understanding and conducting qualitative research*. Dubuque, Iowa: Kendall Hunt.

Taylor, S. J., & Bogdan, R. (1984). *An introduction to qualitative research methods (2nd ed.)*. New York: Wiley.

Wax, R. (1971). *Doing fieldwork: Warnings and advice*. Chicago: University of Chicago Press.

Yin, R. K. (1989). *Case study research*. Newbury Park, Calif.: Sage.

Part II

Methods, Ethics, and Theory

Chapter 7

Studying Childhood as a Cultural Invention: A Rationale and Framework

J. Amos Hatch

Once each year I teach a graduate course entitled "Social Change and Its Effects on Young Children." As part of the course, I try to help students think in unfamiliar ways about the "nature of childhood" and our ways of learning about it. I always assign William Kessen's article, "The American Child and Other Cultural Inventions," as a way of challenging some of the students' assumptions about childhood and ways of doing research concerning children.

The original publication of the Kessen article was in a 1979 special issue of *American Psychologist* devoted to the topic of "Children and Their Development." This past semester, as part of the readings for the "Social Change" course, I required that the students read several articles from another *American Psychologist* special issue on the same topic, this one published ten years after the first. As we read about social change in the 1989 issue, it became clear that Kessen's call for richer perspectives on the study of childhood had not been heard, at least not by most of the researchers selected for inclusion in the more recent collection.

In this chapter, I will review Kessen's critique and argue that themes of child study that emerged in the nineteenth century continue to dominate our perspectives on doing research related to childhood. I will discuss the notion of childhood as a social construction and suggest a framework for thinking about, designing, and evaluating studies that take seriously the premise that childhood is a cultural invention.

CHILDHOOD AS A CULTURAL INVENTION

There is no permanent and essential nature of childhood. The idea of childhood is defined differently in every culture, in every time period, in every political climate, in every economic era, in every social context. Our everyday assumption that the childhood we "know" is and always has been *the* definition of childhood turns out to be false. Scholars from a variety of disciplines have carefully documented vastly different understandings of childhood across cultures, time, and political-economic circumstances (e.g., Aries, 1962; Lasch, 1978; Postman, 1982).

Kessen (1979, pp. 815–816) points out that what experts have said about the young, "from Locke to Skinner, from Rousseau to Piaget, from Comenius to Erikson—will expose as bewildering a taxonomy as the one provided by preachers, parents, and poets." Just as our shared understandings of what constitutes childhood are socially constructed, so are our understandings of what constitute appropriate ways of studying children, or anything else (see Kuhn, 1970).

Kessen makes the case that science follows culture, "but often at a discreet distance" (p. 819). He identifies three themes that have profoundly influenced child study since the end of the nineteenth century: the commitment to science and technology; the importance of mothers, early experiences, and personal responsibility; and the belief in the individual and self-contained child. He traces the roots of these themes and argues that each continues to constrain perspectives on childhood and child study.[1] I will briefly review Kessen's 1979 description of each theme, then argue that these themes continue to hold sway, using examples from the 1989 *American Psychologist* special issue to support my argument.

DOMINANT THEMES OF CHILD STUDY

Commitment to Science and Technology

In the late nineteenth century, psychology and other disciplines related to child study were energetic in their efforts to be recognized as "sciences" in a world that had been turned around by the successes of the physical sciences. The belief that all social and psychological problems could be solved with the careful application of science and technology became pervasive.

In the area of child study, "experts" were created, and it came to be assumed that parents and other lay individuals needed the guidance of these experts in order to guide the development of children successfully. Scientific statements took on the weight of ethical imperatives, and scientific descriptions became normative guidelines against which to measure individual growth and competence.

This emerging reliance on science and technology, coupled with a romantic view of the purity and perfectibility of the child, led to the perception that children are appropriate vehicles for solving problems in society. The notion was that if we can somehow intervene in the lives of children, then poverty, racism, crime, drug abuse, and any number of social ills can be erased. Children became instruments of society's need to improve itself, and childhood became a time during which social problems were either solved or determined to be unsolvable.

Importance of Mothers, Early Experience, and Personal Responsibility

A second theme that has dominated child study from its beginnings is the assumption that every child needs a home and a mother in order to develop successfully. The mother is seen as having primary responsibility for the upbringing of the child, and if problems occur, she is generally to blame.

The critical role of early experience is uncontested in this view. Normative standards have been established for what constitutes appropriate mothering and early development. It is understood that childhood is a critical period and that if certain milestones are not accomplished during this period, the chances for successful adjustments later on are slim.

Western culture's premium on individuality and the "scientific" need to identify causes combine to generate an ethic of personal responsibility that dominates analyses of social and psychological problems addressed by child study experts. When problems are identified, it is assumed that *someone* is responsible. Since childhood is considered a critical period, and since mothers are seen as the primary agents for supervising development in childhood, individual "someones" are typically mothers, who face a great deal of personal responsibility.

Belief in the Individual, Self-Contained Child

Underlying the first two themes is the taken-for-granted notion of the child as a freestanding, isolable entity who moves through his or her development as a self-contained and complete individual. Theories that have dominated the field are based on the premise of individual development, and research conducted within these theoretical perspectives assumes the primacy of the self-contained child.

It is easier to study the child alone, and this has become the accepted unit of analysis in child study. Those features of childhood that are determined to be important are taken to be contained within the child, including impulses, traits, thoughts, and attachments. Few serious attempts have been made to study childhood as if it were a social construction. Instead, perspectives and methods for studying children and childhood have been driven by what individual children can conveniently bring to the laboratories, test sites, and controlled research settings of child study researchers.

Child Study Themes Revisited.

Looking closely at the 1989 *American Psychologist* special issue on "Children and Their Development" reveals that the themes Kessen identified a decade earlier continue to strongly influence the field of child study.[2] That science and technology are appropriate tools for solving social and psychological problems is an unexamined assumption that undergirds virtually all the scholarship included in the special issue. Problems as wide-ranging as drug abuse, anti-social behavior, teen pregnancy, welfare participation, and unemployment are scientifically related to childhood experiences, and solutions are suggested in terms of behavioral technologies such as training experiences, interventions, therapies, and education programs. The assumed primacy of expert over lay knowledge is evident throughout but is especially salient in descriptions of appropriate parenting styles for working mothers, parents experiencing divorce and remarriage, and parents of children at risk for anti-social development.

Themes of mothers' importance, individual responsibility, and early experience continued to be influential in the 1989 issue. Although mothers are probably less central in studies of children's development, the critical nature of their influence continues to be assumed in research on the effects of day care and of maternal employment on children. The use of the term "maternal employment" to describe an important area of child study clearly signals the centrality of mothers' influence to the perspectives taken in the research. When mothers' importance is shared with others, such as fathers, preschool teachers, and day care providers, *someone* is still responsible for a variety of positive and negative outcomes associated with children's development. The role of early experience, the notion that childhood is a critical period during which children's futures are inexorably determined, continues to go unchallenged. Reviews of work done in the areas of marital transitions, day care effects, drug use and abuse, social development, child abuse, and preschool effects provide strong examples of the assumed critical importance of early experience on later development.

That the individual, self-contained child is the appropriate unit of analysis continued to hold sway in 1989. The constructs of interest, the dependent variables, *are in the child*. From studies of the effects of television viewing to examinations of mental health and behavioral disorders, the focus on an independent, freestanding, individual child remains in force. The continued reliance on "strange situation" laboratory procedures for determining the attachment of infants to their mothers and other caregivers is a powerful example of the perceived efficacy of studying very narrowly defined attributes of children in sterile contexts that are strange indeed.

STUDYING CHILDHOOD AS A CULTURAL INVENTION

The themes reviewed above reflect positivistic notions of childhood as an objective, definable entity that researchers can come to know if only they perfect their measuring tools and adequately control for interfering variables. In this section, I will present a framework for thinking about child study that provides researchers with an initial model for designing and evaluating studies that take as their starting point that childhood is a cultural invention.[3] I will organize my description around the following series of questions I believe researchers should ask: (a) What are my assumptions about childhood and appropriate ways to study it? (b) What questions are answerable given my assumptions? (c) In what contexts can my questions best be answered? (d) Who will be the participants in my study? (f) What data-gathering tools are best suited to answering my questions? (g) How will I analyze my data? and (h) How will I report my findings?

Assumptions

What are my assumptions about childhood and appropriate ways to study it? This elemental question is rarely asked as researchers contemplate studies related to children. The nature of assumptions is that they are not challenged, critiqued, reflected upon, unpacked—that is why they are called assumptions. However, as I have argued elsewhere (Hatch, 1985), unexamined assumptions can lead to research that lacks logical consistency at the least and is of questionable integrity at the worst.

The dominant paradigm in child study, as in virtually all scientific disciplines, continues to be positivist in nature. Positivism assumes an objective world that has order independent of human perception. The goal of positivist science is to discover the order built into the universe, constructing generalizations, theories, and laws that allow prediction across settings. Child study researchers who operate within a positivist paradigm assume that law-like relationships can be drawn among constructs they identify, operationalize, and measure. So, as in the examples from the 1989 *American Psychologist*, children are studied in controlled settings, variables are isolated, measured, and correlated with other variables, and predictions are made to populations represented by the samples being studied. These procedures are based on the assumption of a "componential world perceived as consisting of units that can be taken apart and put together again" (Keat & Urry, 1975, p. 72). It is not my goal here to argue against positivist assumptions, but to point out the pervasive and unexamined influence of the positivist view on child study and to note that research conceptualized within this view does not qualify as studying childhood as a cultural invention.

An alternative paradigm, which I will call constructivism,[4] begins by rejecting the positivist notion of a componential, externally verifiable universe that exists apart from our perceptions of it. Constructivist scientists argue that "knowledge is symbolically constructed and not objective; that understandings of the world are based on conventions, on perceptions held in community with others; that truth is, in fact, what we agree it is" (Hatch, 1985, p. 161). Research growing out of constructivist assumptions seeks to describe and analyze contextualized social phenomena. The effort is to understand how the world operates by studying that world through the perspectives of those participating in it. For constructivists studying the worlds of children, this means using research methods that are fundamentally different from those used in positivist studies. Instead of control, constructivists want naturally occurring social behavior; in place of isolated variables, they seek a contextualized, holistic examination of participant perspectives; instead of measuring, correlating, and predicting, constructivists describe and interpret. Research that claims to study childhood as a cultural invention shares several assumptions with a constructivist paradigm.

My view, building on Kuhn's (1970) description of paradigms, is that researchers who hold positivist assumptions concerning how the world is ordered are logically confined to the use of quantitative methods in their studies of children and childhood. Paradigms start with particular notions of how the world is ordered and, based on those notions, generate their own criteria for acceptable science, including methods, definitions of a problem-field, and standards of solution (Kuhn, 1970). The assumptions of positivism lead to methods, questions, and solutions that have been codified in the quantitative research tradition.

The same logic holds for constructivist researchers. Acceptance of constructivist assumptions concerning the nature of the world leads logically—and I argue exclusively—to the use of qualitative methods. This means that researchers interested in studying childhood as a cultural invention (rather than taking the positivist view that childhood exists and can be revealed, if only enough control and rigor can be applied) are logically bound to the use of qualitative methods designed to reveal how children and other participants in children's worlds are experiencing and constructing their realities.

Questions

What questions are answerable given my assumptions? It is not un-common for new researchers to be told to identify the questions they want to answer, then pick a methodology that best helps them answer their questions. This approach ignores the central importance of unpack-ing assumptions as researchers (experienced and novice) approach their work. Any question about research questions ought to start with an ex-amination of assumptions.

Child study researchers who hold constructivist assumptions are inter-ested in perspectives and processes, not prescriptions and products. They see children as active participants in the construction of their own cul-tures (Corsaro, 1985; Fernie, Davies, Kantor, & McMurray, 1993). Theirs are often open-ended, guiding questions designed to lead researchers into the understandings of their participants.

As a way of demonstrating the kinds of questions that guide qualitative studies, I will contrast these with questions that quantitative researchers might ask. Researchers from both paradigms are interested in similar so-cial phenomena; their questions and the methods used to answer them, however, are quite different. Three social phenomena that are of interest to both are anti-social development, drug abuse, and marital transitions. Quantitative questions extrapolated from the research reviews in the 1989 special issue of *American Psychologist* on these topics include: What parenting practices are determinants for childhood conduct disor-ders? What are environmental and intrapsychic factors that predict drug use and abuse among children? What is the relationship between the child's developmental status, sex, and temperament and the long-term effects of family reorganization?

In contrast to the emphasis on determinants, prediction, and statistical relationships, qualitative researchers interested in the three topic areas might generate questions such as the following: What are the processes through which children stigmatize others as outsiders in their play and work groups? What are children's definitions of drug use and abuse? What are children's experiences of family discord, divorce, and remarriage?

Research questions generated by researchers holding constructivist as-sumptions about the nature of the child's world establish a direction for the research and signal the expectation that the information of value in the study will come from the participants in the study, not from the hypotheses of the researcher. Children's worlds are constructed by chil-dren and the adults around them, and good research questions lead to studies that describe and interpret those worlds from the inside out.

Contexts

In what contexts can my questions best be answered? As with the discussion above, answers to this question are different depending on which paradigmatic circle one chooses to stand within. Researchers who see children as active participants in the construction of their own contexts view the question very differently from those who see research settings as places where, insofar as possible, everything should be held constant except the manipulation of key independent variables. On the one hand are researchers who want to keep research settings as natural as possible, while on the other are those who want to maintain as much control over the settings as possible.

From a qualitative research perspective, contexts always include the physical setting in which social action occurs, a set of participants and their relationships to one another, and the activities in which participants are involved (Bondy, 1983). Contexts do not, however, exist as static entities that can be understood by simply identifying settings, participants, and activities. Contexts are socially constructed phenomena that are created and maintained by individuals joined together in social exchange. The social meanings that participants construct together are constantly being redefined through the give-and-take of face-to-face interaction. It is the participants' shared understanding of the functions of a physical setting, their common perceptions of their relative status and role relationships, and their mutually constituted conceptions of the purposes and procedures of their activity that make a context (Erickson & Shultz, 1981; McDermott, 1976).

For child study researchers asking questions about children's perspectives, understanding children's constructions of contexts is central. How children construct meaning in natural contexts is the stuff of qualitative studies of childhood. The more natural the settings, the more likely it is that researchers will have access to social processes that reflect children's ways of understanding and constructing meaning.

Research on attachment provides an example of how differently positivist researchers define appropriate research settings from those in the constructivist camp. Ainsworth's Strange Situation (Ainsworth, Blehar, Waters, & Wall, 1978) is taken to be the standard assessment for children's attachment to their mothers (Clark-Stewart, 1989). The Strange Situation consists of a series of eight episodes "involving mother-infant separation and reunion in a novel environment where there are attractive toys and strange adults" (McGraw, 1987, p. 629). Observers score mother-child, child-stranger, and child-object interactions over a twenty-minute session. The Strange Situation is clearly an example of a research setting dominated by the need for standardization and control.

Constructivist researchers interested in attachment-related questions would be more likely to study the interactions of infants and their care-givers in natural surroundings such as maternity wards, homes, and day care centers. These researchers would not assume that certain child be-haviors such as approach or avoidance signaled the existence of a more or less fixed attachment or lack of it. They would seek to understand the shared meanings constructed by caregiver and infant. How these partic-ipants define physical space, construct their relationship with each other, and develop shared understandings of their mutually constituted activi-ties are the important elements of context in such a study. The best con-texts for research that takes seriously the study of childhood as a social construction are settings in which naturally occurring social behavior is observed in natural surroundings.

Participants

Who will be the participants in my study? Since participants construct the contexts of a qualitative study, this question is directly tied to the issues just discussed. Individuals who are unwilling or unable to share their perspectives in open-ended interviews or are unwilling or unable to act naturally while being closely observed do not make good partici-pants. An essential element in any study that attempts to get at participant perspectives is the development of trust and rapport between researcher and informant or participant (Spradley, 1980; Hatch & Bondy, 1986). Negotiating trust and rapport takes time and a certain receptiveness on the part of both researcher and informant (Ball, 1990). Selecting partic-ipants for qualitative studies involves careful consideration of the willing-ness and abilities of individuals to be exposed and available for long periods of time.

When children are participants in qualitative studies, special consid-erations need to be given to selection and the establishment of rapport. While it is my experience that children are very comfortable acting nat-urally in settings with which they are familiar, children are frequently uncomfortable and unnatural in unfamiliar settings such as interview con-texts that are frequently used by researchers (see Hatch, 1990). Because participant perspectives are the substance of studies of childhood as a social construction, careful communication and rapport building should be emphasized early in the selection process.

Quantitative researchers talk about samples and subjects, not partici-pants. The words and processes are different from qualitative emphases. Generally, selection of subjects for quantitative studies is better when: the number of subjects (n's) is high; samples are thought to represent a larger population; and samples allow for the control of extraneous vari-ables. In contrast, qualitative researchers argue that: no direct relation-ship exists between the number of participants and the quality of the findings—questions of number are answered in terms of research questions and levels of analysis; participant perspectives are not meant to generalize to larger populations—contexts are carefully described so that readers can make their own judgments concerning the importance of applying understandings gained in the study to contexts they know about; there are no extraneous variables—any element that is perceived to be important by participants *is* important. The criteria for selection of subjects or participants grow out of different assumptions and serve different ends.

Data Collection

What data-gathering tools are best suited for answering my questions? Questions that follow from constructivist conceptions of the research process lead to data collection tools that provide ways to capture participant perspectives. As Schwartz and Jacobs (1979, p. 7) have written: "We want to know what actors know, see what they see, understand what they understand. As a result our data attempt to describe their vocabularies, their ways of looking, their sense of the important and unimportant, and so on." Data of this nature are usually collected using tools such as observation, interviewing, and the collection of unobtrusive data.[5]

Quantitative child study researchers sometimes use observation, interviewing, and unobtrusive data in their work; but the ways these tools are utilized are very different from how qualitative researchers use them. Observation techniques in quantitative studies typically involve supplying observers with checklists of predetermined behaviors and a stopwatch. Their job is to record the frequency of occurrence of behaviors as defined on the checklists so that these frequencies can be tabulated and statistically related to other behaviors or measurable outcomes. Observers in qualitative studies spend extended periods of time acting as participant-observers in contexts they are studying. Participant-observers seek to acquire insiders' knowledge using the same cognitive processes that participants use to learn and make sense of the social contexts within which they are operating. In the words of Hood, McDermott, and Cole (1980, p. 158), "People learn about themselves and about each other by the work they do constructing environments for acting in the world, and this is how we (researchers) must come to know them as well." Participant-observers do not use checklists with predetermined categories, but typically make detailed records of conversations, behaviors, and contexts in the form of field notes.

Quantitative researchers usually conduct interviews with detailed interview schedules that include certain questions to be asked in certain language in certain order. Sometimes interview subjects are given choices from which to respond. Qualitative interviews are thought to be special social contexts constructed by the researcher and informant (Mishler, 1986). Researchers often have guiding questions in mind or an area they hope informants will discuss, but interviews are open-ended in that both parties participate in the construction of the interview and questions and discussions develop from the context of the interaction—interviews are not circumscribed by predetermined questions or forced choices.

Unobtrusive data refers to the products of "any measure of observation that directly removes the observer from the set of interactions or events being studied" (Denzin, 1978, p. 256). Examples of unobtrusive data that might be collected in studies of children include such items as: health records; children's school work; curriculum materials, representational maps, descriptions or photographs of day care facilities; letters to parents; and so on. Researchers from positivist perspectives might collect unobtrusive data that can be statistically expressed, for example, demographic data found in school records. Qualitative researchers are more likely to treat unobtrusive data as artifacts, using items such as the products of children's work and play as ways of learning more about children's understandings of the settings in which they are operating (Freeman & Hatch, 1989).

Data Analysis

How will I analyze my data? Data collection and analysis are closely connected in qualitative studies. Rather than a linear model (collect the complete data set, then analyze it), qualitative researchers are more likely to employ a recursive model (data are collected, then analyzed, then more data collection is done based on the analysis, and so on). Spradley's (1980) Developmental Research Sequence is an example of an anthropological research model that involves an ongoing cycle of data collection and analysis.

Data analysis in quantitative studies is virtually always accomplished through the application of sophisticated computer programs. Researchers or computer experts enter raw data into programs, and complex computational operations are performed on the data, producing printouts that summarize statistical relationships among variables fed into the programs. Although some computer programs have been developed for sorting qualitative data (see Tesch, 1990), qualitative analysis always involves an inductive, interpretive process that cannot be duplicated with a computer program. Interpretation always involves making subjective, inferential judgments regarding the meanings that participants ascribe to particular expressions, actions, or objects. Inferences are not arbitrary but are empirically bound to the data, using methods such as analytic induction (Denzin, 1978) or constant comparison (Glaser & Strauss, 1967). As Berger & Kellner (1981, p. 46) summarize: "Sociological interpretation is not a philosophical enterprise. It is always subject to testing by empirical evidence."

Again, the differences in analytical approaches between positivists and constructivists are clear. Deductive-statistical analytical models are well suited to the assumptions, questions, and data-collection techniques of quantitative researchers, while inductive-inferential models fit logically and practically within the qualitative tradition. Attempts to analyze qualitative data using statistical tools, or quantitative data using interpretive models, ignore ontological and epistemological underpinnings on which the collection of each kind of data is based. It follows that in studies that emphasize understanding childhood as a social invention, data analysis will necessarily be inductive and interpretive in nature.

Findings

How will I report my findings? Since qualitative child study researchers start with different assumptions, ask different questions, and use different methods, it should be no surprise that their findings look different and serve different purposes than the findings of quantitative scholars. In quantitative reports, findings are summaries of statistical relationships found in the analyses, frequently reported in tables with accompanying text. Qualitative reports are most often detailed narratives revealing participant perspectives through the use of data that let the reader "hear the voices" of participants in the text. Qualitative findings are generally longer and less easily reduced to tables and graphs.

Findings from different paradigms look different and read differently but, more important, they serve different ends. The purposes of positivist research are to predict and prescribe, while qualitative researchers seek to explain and describe. The logic of prediction in quantitative, particularly correlational, studies is evident in the following quote from a standard introduction to an educational research text:

When correlational analysis indicates some degree of relationship between two variables, we can use the information about one of them to make predictions about the other. For example, having found that intelligence and achievement are correlated we can make predictions about the future achievement of schoolchildren from the results of an intelligence test given at the beginning of the school year. (Ary, Jacobs, & Razavieh, 1979, p. 116)

Along with predictions, quantitative research findings generate normative expectations and prescriptions for meeting those expectations. A quick look at the reviews of research in the 1989 *American Psychologist* discussed in this chapter reveals the continued dominance of the normative and prescriptive in child study research.

Qualitative research seeks to describe *what is* rather than prescribe *what ought to be* (Hatch, 1988; Hinely & Ponder, 1979). It is better suited for giving individuals frameworks for thinking about social phenomena in new and enriched ways than for predicting the occurrence of one variable from the discovery of another. The assumption of a world that is a social construction or cultural invention precludes the possibilities of establishing predictive validity or normative expectations or the prescriptions that follow.

CONCLUSIONS

This chapter has outlined an initial framework for conceptualizing, designing, and evaluating studies of children and childhood in ways that challenge dominant notions of appropriate research practice. Kessen's (1979) formulation of childhood as a cultural invention and references to the 1989 *American Psychologist* special issue on children and their development have been used as devices to point out the efficacy of Kessen's notion for developing a much broader and richer child study discipline and to make the case that broader and richer perspectives continue to be left out of the child study mainstream.

Applying the framework described, that is, studying childhood as a cultural invention, has the power to dramatically change the themes Kessen identifies as dominating child study for the past century: science and technology; mothers, early experience, and personal responsibility; and the individual, self-contained child. With regard to the theme of science and technology, the constructivist paradigm challenges the very definitions of science that have dominated child study for the last hundred years. Qualitative assumptions, methods, and findings run directly counter to what has been considered scientific by many in the past. Beliefs that expertise from science and technology can solve social and psychological problems that ordinary lay individuals are incapable of resolving run counter to constructivist perspectives on the importance of participant perspectives and are directly contradicted by the emphasis in qualitative findings on describing and explaining using the voices of participants.

From a qualitative perspective, the importance of mothers, early experience, and personal responsibility are socially constructed concepts that are actively reconstructed and, therefore, different in every social setting, in every culture, in every time period, and in every social-political context. The importance of mothers is not taken for granted as questions related to children's development are generated, contexts for study negotiated, participants invited, or data are collected and analyzed. If participants operate under the belief that mothers are important to development, then understanding that belief is profoundly important to the research; but discovering that it is important to the participants is vastly different from assuming it is important to all mothers and infants. The same can be said for the role of early experience and for the importance of personal responsibility; these are culturally constructed concepts as well.

The positivist focus on the individual, self-contained child is challenged by constructivist perspectives and methods as well. Qualitative researchers study children and others who influence children in natural contexts, in interaction with other people and objects in their surroundings. Children are not reduced to a set of variables to be manipulated and correlated but are treated as active co-constructors of their own realities; they are studied as the products and producers of their own cultures. Qualitative child study researchers challenge the notion of a freestanding, self-contained child as the object of study. They see Kessen's 1979 evaluation as true today:

Most expert students of children continue to assert the truth of the positivistic dream—that we have not yet found the underlying structural simplicities that will reveal the child entire, that we have not yet cut nature at the joints—but it may be wise . . . to peer into the abyss of the positivistic nightmare—that the child is essentially and eternally a cultural invention and that the variety of the child's definition is not the removable error of an incomplete science. (p. 815)

By applying a constructivist perspective and utilizing qualitative research methods, that is, by studying children and childhood as cultural inventions, child study researchers can break free of the assumptions and methods that continue to constrain our understandings of children and the contexts in which they live. Indeed, confronting the positivistic nightmare described by Kessen may awaken the child study community to avenues that will enrich our understandings and our abilities to understand.[6]

NOTES

1. Kessen's frame of reference is "child psychology" as opposed to the broader term, "child study," which I have used throughout this essay. Although the two are not synonymous, it would be hard to argue that child psychology has not dominated child study for the last hundred years.

2. I acknowledge that the *American Psychologist* special issue offers a limited basis on which to critique the state of the field. Still, the articles included are selected to present syntheses of the most up-to-date research available in several important areas of child study.

3. The framework presented here is a set of "signposts" that researchers should be aware of as they journey into constructivist territory. It is not the trip, only a

series of important markers that provide an outline for planning and evaluating qualitative approaches to child study.

4. I take the term *constructivist* from Guba and Lincoln (Beld, 1994). I originally used the term *conventionalist* to describe this paradigm (Hatch, 1985); but conventionalism (that our understandings are mutually constructed conventions) is too easily confused with the idea of conventional as traditional or accepted (as in conventional practices, wisdom, etc.).

5. Several detailed descriptions of qualitative data collection and analysis procedures are available, including texts by Taylor and Bogdan (1984), Goetz and LeCompte (1984), Lincoln and Guba (1985), and Spradley (1980). For a list of texts used in courses for teaching qualitative methods, see Glesne and Webb (1993).

6. I recognize that I have painted with a broad brush, portraying extreme positions to emphasize differences between positivist and constructivist approaches. Qualitative approaches in early childhood research have received more attention in the years since the 1989 issue. Still, positivism continues to dominate; see, for example, the recent *Handbook of Research on the Education of Young Children* (Spodek, 1993) in which only one chapter among over thirty research syntheses is given to qualitative work.

REFERENCES

Ainsworth, M.D.S., Blehar, M. C., Waters, E., & Wall, S. (1978). *Patterns of attachment: A psychological study of the strange situation*. Hillsdale, N.J.: Lawrence Erlbaum.

American Psychological Association. (1989). Special issue—Children and their development: Knowledge base, research agenda, and social policy application. *American Psychologist, 44*, 95–490.

Aries, P. (1962). *Centuries of childhood: A social history of family life*. (R. Baldick, Trans.). New York: Knopf.

Ary, D., Jacobs, L. C., & Razavieh, A. (1979). *Introduction to research in education*. New York: Holt, Rinehart and Winston.

Ball, S. J. (1990). Self-doubt and soft data: Social and technical trajectories in ethnographic fieldwork. *International Journal of Qualitative Studies in Education, 3*, 157–172.

Beld, J. M. (1994). Constructing a collaboration: A conversation with Egon G. Guba and Yvonna S. Lincoln. *International Journal of Qualitative Studies in Education, 7*, 303–320.

Berger, P. L., & Kellner, H. (1981). *Sociology reinterpreted*. Garden City, N.Y.: Anchor.

Bondy, E. (1983). *Children's talk in and out of school: Contextual influences on oral language*. Unpublished paper, University of Florida.

Clark-Stewart, K. A. (1989). Infant day care: Maligned or malignant? *American Psychologist, 44*, 266–273.

Corsaro, W. A. (1985). *Friendship and peer culture in the early years*. Norwood, N.J.: Ablex.

Denzin, N. K. (1978). *The research act: A theoretical introduction to sociological methods*. New York: McGraw-Hill.

Erickson, F., & Shultz, J. (1981). When is a context? Some issues and methods in the analysis of social competence. In J. L. Green and C. Wallat (Eds.), *Ethnography and language in educational settings* (pp. 147–160). Norwood, N.J.: Ablex.

Fernie, D. E., Davies, B., Kantor, R., & McMurray, P. (1993). Becoming a person in the preschool: Creating integrated gender, school culture, and peer positionings. *International Journal of Qualitative Studies in Education, 6*, 95–110.

Freeman, E. B., & Hatch, J. A. (1989). What schools expect young children to know and do: An analysis of kindergarten report cards. *Elementary School Journal, 89*, 595–605.

Glaser, B. G., & Strauss, A. (1967). *The discovery of grounded theory: Strategies for qualitative research*. Chicago: Aldine.

Glesne, C., & Webb. R. (1993). Teaching qualitative research: Who does what? *International Journal of Qualitative Studies in Education, 6*, 253–266.

Goetz, J. P., & LeCompte, M. D. (1984). *Ethnography and qualitative design in educational research*. Orlando, Fla.: Academic Press.

Hatch, J. A. (1985). The quantoids versus the smooshes: Struggling with methodological rapprochement. *Issues in Education, 3*, 158–167.

Hatch, J. A. (1988). Peer evaluation and competence motivation in a kindergarten classroom. *Early Child Development and Care, 34*, 15–26.

Hatch, J. A. (1990). Young children as informants in classroom studies. *Early Childhood Research Quarterly, 5*, 251–264.

Hatch, J. A., & Bondy, E. (1986). The researcher-teacher relationship: Observations and implications from naturalistic studies in classrooms. *The Journal of Research and Development in Education, 19*, 48–56.

Hinely, R., & Ponder, G. (1979). Theory, practice, and classroom research. *Theory into Practice, 18*, 135–137.

Hood, L., McDermott, R., & Cole, M. (1980). 'Let's try to make it a good day'— Some not so simple ways. *Discourse Processes, 3*, 155–168.

Keat, R., & Urry, J. (1975). *Social theory as science*. London: Routledge and Kegan Paul.

Kessen, W. (1979). The American child and other cultural inventions. *American Psychologist, 34*, 815–820.

Kuhn, T. S. (1970). *The structure of scientific revolutions*. 2nd ed. Chicago: University of Chicago Press.

Lasch, C. (1978). *The culture of narcissism: American life in an age of diminished expectations*. New York: Norton.

Lincoln, Y. S., & Guba, E. G. (1985). *Naturalistic inquiry*. Beverly Hills, Calif.: Sage.

McDermott, R. P. (1976). Kids make sense: An ethnographic account of the interactional management of success and failure in one first grade classroom. Doctoral dissertation, Department of Anthropology, Stanford University.

McGraw, K. O. (1987). *Developmental psychology*. New York: Harcourt Brace Jovanovich.

Mishler, E. G. (1986). *Research interviewing: Context and narrative*. Cambridge, Mass.: Harvard University Press.

Postman, N. (1982). *The disappearance of childhood*. New York: Delacourte.

Schwartz, H., & Jacobs, J. (1979). *Qualitative sociology*. New York: Free Press.

Spodek, B. (Ed.). (1993). *Handbook of research on the education of young children*. New York: Macmillan.

Spradley, J. P. (1980). *Participant observation*. New York: Holt, Rinehart and Winston.

Taylor, S. J., & Bogdan, R. (1984). *Introduction to qualitative research methods: The search for meanings*, 2nd ed. New York: John Wiley & Sons.

Tesch, R. (1990). *Qualitative research: Analysis types and software tools*. London: Falmer.

Chapter 8

Children in Context: Interpreting the Here and Now of Children's Lives

M. Elizabeth Graue and
Daniel J. Walsh

In this chapter, we argue for the importance of research on young children that pursues "the meaning of human action in cultural context" (Gaskins, Miller, & Corsaro, 1992, p. 6). Although such work has been commonly termed *qualitative*, following Erickson (1986), we prefer *interpretive*, a term we find more inclusive and free of the non-quantitative connotations that qualitative has acquired.

We see the purpose of interpretive research in much the same light as Cronbach did for general social science research: "in each generation to pin down contemporary facts . . . [and] to realign culture's view of [people] with present realities" (1975, p. 126). The goal of interpretive research is not the development of grand acultural theory but richly detailed cultural descriptions that realign our present understandings of the realities of contemporary children's lives.

We begin by critiquing research approaches that have dominated the discourse on young children. We then argue for the utility of studies of children in context, describing how context frames not only the children we study but our positioning as researchers. Finally, we discuss briefly Vygotsky's concept of activity as a tool for thinking about children in context.

THE CHILD AS OBJECT

The literature of early childhood education is filled with reports of studies in which children have been the objects of inquiry. Given the amount of work focused on children, it is surprising how little we know about their lives. Little if any attention is paid to the contexts in which children live. Where are those young ones whose actions change so much from home to school to playground? Where is the understanding of, or even interest in, children's lived experiences? It is ironic that a field that takes great pride in its attention to young children has been dominated by research methodologies that are, in practice, quite distanced from children themselves.

It would be easy to blame this distanced view on the dominance of quantitative research. Although the prevailing quantitative approaches have certainly contributed to the problem, one must not forget that much of what we think we know about children stems from Piaget's markedly non-quantitative inquiry. In fact, as we argue below, the field has been particularly susceptible to the well-turned anecdote.

Instead, the distance stems from the dominance of a particular psychological perspective in which researchers see children as either windows onto universal psychological laws or as indicators of treatment effects. In both cases, the children themselves are simply instruments. The quest has not been to understand children but to pursue the lofty academic goals of the universal law and the ultimate treatment.

As windows to universal laws, children, most often examined in laboratories, become raw materials for the construction of theories of development and learning. Although we have come a long way from the recapitulationism of G. Stanley Hall, who believed that by listening carefully to children one could hear the distant call of our ancestors (Kliebard, 1986), the quest for universal laws remains alive and well, as is evidenced by the remarkable tenacity of Piagetian theory.

As indicators of treatment effects, children, most often in institutional settings, provide pre- and post-test results. These results are then used to justify or reject some new form of pedagogy or discipline, some new program for teaching math or social skills, or even some new parenting strategy. In this work, children are simply vehicles for measuring outcomes.

In neither case are real, living children of interest. Children may be used as exhibits to demonstrate the laws or the treatment effects, but who the specific children are, beyond coded demographic characteristics such as age, gender, or race, is immaterial. Their experiences in a particular program or classroom are certainly neither sought nor considered.

For the purposes of our critique, we have subdivided this dominant psychological perspective into three categories: Piagetian, quantitative, and anecdotal. The categories are constructed to facilitate our discussion; they are not intended to be definitive or mutually exclusive.

The Persistence of Piaget

Piagetian theory has had near hegemonic influence in early childhood education for the past three decades. It continues to exhibit remarkable persistence in the face of a growing body of disconfirming evidence. We will not present this evidence here. Effective critiques have been made elsewhere (e.g., Bruner & Haste, 1987; Bruner, 1986, 1990; Donaldson, 1978; Gelman, 1979; Gelman & Baillargeon, 1983; Hatano & Inagaki, 1982–83; Inagaki, 1992; Walsh, 1991). We note only that although the work of Piaget and colleagues has often been richly descriptive, it has been singularly inattentive to context or children's experience.

For the most part, Piagetian descriptions have been of children in laboratory settings doing "novel, nonsignificant problems . . . [requiring] formal-logically coherent justifications" (Hatano & Inagaki, 1982–83, p. 4). The Genevan school has ignored the influence of culture, as it has ignored the influence of what Donaldson (1978) called the child's "human sense," that meaningful understanding of the world the child has constructed through her culturally mediated experience with it. For the Genevans, the child has been a window onto universal laws, laws that operate independently of culture and context. For a perspective that has the reputation for taking an interactivist view of children, its conceptualization of the child is vacuum-like, disconnecting individuals from their heritages.

The Narrowness of Numbers

The bulk of published research on young children has been quantitative (thumb through, for example, the recent *Handbook of Research on the Education of Young Children* [Spodek, 1993]). In this country even Piagetians have tended to be quantitative. Focused as it is on instrumental measures of difference and outcome, quantitative research relies on entities that are amenable to measurement. As a result, researchers often reduce the complex realities of children's lives to scores on instruments and questionnaires, to counts of individual behaviors, or to behaviors in contrived settings. Readiness for school, for example, has been measured by such quantifiable factors as the number of teeth lost and the ability to identify shapes and colors.

The methodological focus in these studies is on the technical issues of measurement: how well the instruments capture the proxy for the characteristic of interest rather than on how well the proxy captures that characteristic. The theoretical link between the topic of interest and its measured representation often seems to fade into the background in the rush for technical elegance. This ignores the distinction between *precision* (how well can the operationalization be measured) and *accuracy* (how well is the actual phenomenon of interest being measured or described) (King, Keohane, & Verba, 1994). Instead, precision is presented as accuracy, when, more often than not, more precise measures are more likely to be inaccurate. For example, counting how many times children poke each other is relatively easy, but it will not give an accurate measure of aggression in children. Human life, in its complexity, simply cannot be pinned down so easily.

Consider the following operationalizations from one issue of *Early Childhood Research Quarterly*: A discussion of friendship defines peer contact as being "within 3 feet of a peer and at least engaged in parallel activity with mutual awareness" (Howes, 1988, p. 24); social problem-solving skills are assessed by showing children a series of pictures and inquiring about hypothetical situations (Holloway & Reichhart-Erickson, 1988); children's curiosity is analyzed in "four six-minute episodes in a semistructured setting," which were scored in ten-second intervals (Bradbard, Halperin, & Endsley, 1988, p. 95). We can learn something from such efforts, but what we learn is severely limited by the distance between the operationalization of the construct, which must be narrow to be technically defensible, and the construct as lived by children, which is inherently complex. The examples provide measures of something, but those somethings are tangential at best to children's friendships, their ability to interact socially, or their curiosity. Researchers rarely mention the limitations of their efforts, and they talk as though they have actually studied such complex entities as the phenomena in the examples.

Observing children and coming away with nothing but numbers (or worse, standardized numbers) has told us little about the day-to-day interactions of children. Worse, it has led us to believe that such interactions can be reduced to computations. Those aspects of children's lives that cannot be readily measured, but that must be *interpreted*, have been ignored or operationalized in ways that distort the experience of children.

The Appeal of the Anecdote

Couched as it is in the voice of expertise and experience and dating back to the time when the field was heavily dependent on psychoanalytic theory (where the clinical anecdote rules), the salient anecdote has long influenced discourse on young children. In fact, the prevalence of this pseudo-interpretive approach has been the bane of interpretive researchers working in early childhood education, who often see their labor-intensive, time-consuming work dismissed as "mere anecdote."

In anecdotal approaches, experts draw on their memories of working with children (generally in the distant past) and on the experience of observing in classrooms (occasionally and briefly) to analyze young children and their development. This analysis is inevitably couched in psychological theories of development, for the past few decades primarily Piagetian theory. The ancedotal approach dominates textbooks used for teacher training. It permeates much of the literature that is published by professional early childhood groups such as the National Association for the Education of Young Children. What is particularly troubling is that it creates the illusion that the writer has paid close attention to the children described. In fact, many of those who are most often listened to *about* young children have done precious little listening *to* young children themselves.

Summary

All three approaches described create the illusion that we know more about young children than we actually do. We have systematically, but narrowly, studied children in this country for more than a hundred years, dating back to Hall's 1883 publication, "The Content of Children's Minds." Hall himself concluded from his research that "[t]he guardians of the young should strive first of all to keep out of nature's way" (1901, p. 474). It is not clear that we have moved much beyond that prescription. But until we take seriously the charge to study children in context, our knowledge of children will continue to be severely limited. For the rest of this chapter, we address the issue of context.

CONTEXT

How does one study children in context? We are not going to use this chapter to develop a detailed discussion of the mechanics of interpretive fieldwork. There are a number of excellent general overviews (e.g., Delamont, 1992; Denzin, 1989; Erickson, 1986; Glesne & Peshkin, 1992), and we assume that the reader of this volume can access that literature. Instead, we focus our discussion in a way that is in some ways simple and commonsensical, yet as complex as everyday life.

To study children in context, we pay close and systematic attention to children where they are, be it the playground, school, backyard, or afterschool program. We attend to the "concrete particulars" (Erickson, 1986) of their lives in these contexts. And we record those particulars in painstaking detail.

In traditional research on children, the context in which the child and her activity occur is irrelevant beyond its specification as a variable in a research design. Indeed, the goal is to standardize the context as much as possible, thus the popularity of laboratory or laboratory-like rooms—

the contextless context. There, children are supposedly buffered from history and culture. Other less bufferable factors such as gender, social class, and intelligence are either ignored, as by Piaget, or are dealt with methodologically, for example, by partitioning variance.

The concern for standardization and objectivity has required researchers to maintain distance between themselves and children through strategies such as one-way mirrors and hidden checklists of behavior. Researchers even lie to children about what they are doing so that the data will remain pristine. It is assumed that child activity is exactly as it appears on the adult-perceived surface. No attention is paid to the meaning or underlying motive—the goal is to capture the behavior.

We propose that researchers think of children as living in *specific* settings, with *specific* experiences and life situations. We suggest that researchers spend less time attempting to develop grand theories and more time learning to portray the richness of children's lives across the many contexts in which children find themselves. In this "post-everything" world (Erickson, 1992), grand theories do not carry the weight they once did, or at the very least, fewer people are willing to carry that weight around.

There is a growing presence in the field of early childhood education of scholars whose work is interpretive (see, for example, Walsh, Tobin, & Graue's review, 1993) and who do look at children in context. This trend mirrors the larger educational community's effort to broaden its approaches to research. Nevertheless, the interpretive record of children's contextualized lives remains underdeveloped. There is not enough of it. It is too school-focused. As much as an improvement as interpretive work is over earlier scholarship, it is very often undercontextualized.

The majority of the interpretive studies on children have focused on school-related issues or have taken place in school environments. As a result, we have an incomplete record of vast portions of children's day-to-day experiences. Sociologists and anthropologists have studied children in little leagues and on playgrounds (see Fine & Sandstrom, 1988, for examples), but we know much more about children in schools or school-like settings than we do elsewhere.

Consider, for example, how many children in this society spend large portions of their lives in some form of child care. Many children spend 80 percent or more of their waking weekday lives in child care. For its pervasive presence in children's lives, try to find thick descriptive accounts of children's experiences when they leave home and enter the child care situation. There are amazingly few, and the descriptions that we know of are often painful to read (e.g., Leavitt, 1994; Wolf, 1993). We contend that the present discourse on child care would be dramatically changed if a body of interpretive studies of child care existed. In all areas of early childhood, the emerging body of interpretive research represents a significant improvement over much of the earlier research on children. We believe, however, that we still have much to learn about studying children in context.

What Is a Context?

Children's contexts have changed dramatically in recent years as social, cultural, and economic factors have modified the resources and experiences in their lives. Different relationships are available to children now as compared to previous generations—as varied as play-group peers to Barney the Dinosaur—and different knowledge is available to them, from computer savvy to thinking about AIDS. Children cannot remain untouched by their contexts. Just as their contexts are shaped by their presence, so are children shaped by their contexts; children and their contexts mutually constitute each other. To try to think about children without considering their life situations is to strip children and their actions of meaning. Why have we not attended closely to these experiences in very local contexts, in specific cultures, at single points in historical time?

To answer or even consider this question, we must think of children differently than we have in the previously dominant research paradigm. Rather than sampling subjects to represent a population, we must be fiercely interested in individuals, particular individuals. The focus of inquiry must become intensely local. The lens of research must zoom in to a shot of the situated child. Her context is more than an interchangeable backdrop—it is part of the picture, bringing life to the image portrayed by the researcher.

What is a context? *A context is a culturally and historically situated place and time, a specific here and now*. This definition is not particularly profound. We can only wonder how contexts have been so universally ignored or wished away. If we are not here and now, just where and when are we?

We differentiate between the local context, where one conducts one's research, and the larger context, in which the local context is embedded and by which one's research and, ultimately, one's interpretation are framed. A local context is right here, right now. It is a physical and social place, a yard or a park or a classroom, or more localized, a certain work table in a classroom or one climbing structure at a park. There is little point in arguing how large a local context can be before it ceases being local. The researcher chooses the context, whether a specific structure in a play area, the play area in the park, or the park itself. This decision is based on the researcher's interest and resources. But we will note that researchers who must look too widely risk losing the chance to look carefully.

The local context is embedded in many larger nested and overlapping contexts. The block area is nested within the day care room, which is nested within the center, which is nested within the local day care network, the larger discourse on day care, and a given culture. More important than the distinction between the local and the larger context is the relationship between the two. Data records are constructed in and of the local context, but those records cannot be interpreted without reference to their larger milieu. Our emphasis on attending to the specific refers to the process of doing research, to the systematic observing and listening that comprise fieldwork. Interpretation must be grounded in the data records constructed in this local process; otherwise it tends to be very thin.

This failure to connect to the local context, to the larger culture and history, is where much interpretive works falls short. Many case studies, in particular, seem to float in a world of their own. In these works, a researcher conducts a descriptive study of a single unit focusing on the individual case (a person, play group, etc.) in the same way psychological work conceptualizes the individual person. Where explanations were located within the individual child, the case study locates them within the individual site. No connection is made beyond the classroom or other walls, no exploration conducted of the relations among contemporaries, no links examined concerning community standards and ideals. The case stands alone, as if it existed in a vacuum.

Much of this undercontextualized work relies on the assumption that individual actions are explainable by an underlying set of beliefs. These beliefs are contained, formed, and framed within individual heads, untouched by others' ideas, by power relations, or by the cultural-historical forces that shape human thought and action. Although this work is a step beyond the descriptive analysis of behavior that has dominated much of the early childhood research community, it is small progress to move out of the context-free laboratory to the context-free "natural" setting.

Our understandings of children cannot be realigned by isolated studies that do not attend to the larger cultural-historical context; studies must be located. The process of doing interpretation within a cultural-historical framework requires attention to the fit between the local situation within which we have become immersed and the larger picture. A careful analysis is required of the relationship between the local and the larger societal contexts, of the "power/knowledge relations among whatever particular, regional, and contemporary circumstances happen to be present at any given moment" (Fendler & Popkewitz, 1993, p. 24).

Contexts as relational

Here and now, place and time, refer to much more than a bounded succession of moments and the intersection of coordinates in space. They are certainly that, but they cannot be reduced to that alone. Our here and now are best thought of as the complex web of personal and temporal interactions that make up everyday life.

A context does not merely contain the child and her actions; contexts are *relational*. They shape and are shaped by individuals, tools, resources, intentions, and ideas in a particular setting, within a particular time. Contexts are not static, waiting to be captured by a series of descriptive variables in a regression equation (Gaskins, Miller, & Corsaro, 1992). Instead, contexts are fluid and dynamic, constantly reconstructing themselves within activity. Contexts are inherently social, reflecting and framing interaction (Wertsch, 1985). The most important facet of any context is the other people who share a particular here and now. Mehan described the social aspect of context in this way:

Contexts are not to be equated with the physical surrounding of settings like classrooms, kitchens, and churches; they are constructed by the people present in varying combinations of participants and audience (Erickson & Schultz, 1977; McDermott & Roth, 1979). As McDermott and Roth have put it, contexts are constituted by what people are doing, as well as when and where they are doing it. That is, people in interaction serve as environments for each other. And, ultimately, social contexts consist of mutually ratified and constructed environments. (1980, p. 136)

The emphasis on the social is inherent in the contextual perspective taken here. This social view of children and context is in contrast to the traditional western psychological focus on the private self: "[The assumption is that] there is some inherently individualistic Self that develops, determined by the universal sense, this Self is assumed to be ineffable, private" (Bruner, 1986, p. 85). When we separate consideration of individuals from their contexts (and each other), we tend to look for explanations within individuals. Where else is there to look? A child is having problems in school? It must be the child. How would it be different if we looked within the context? How would we then define problems and construct responsibility?

CHILDREN IN CONTEXT

Contemporary Children

If it is important to study people in context, it is particularly important that we study children in context. More often than not children are placed into contexts over which they have little control—adults make most decisions for them, particularly in institutions like schools. Unlike adults, who can choose to avoid situations that they find uncomfortable or threatening, children are constantly challenged to develop competence in settings in which they have few options and no escape. A child who finds she does not like her kindergarten classroom cannot, like her older sister away at college, "change majors." Further, children are rarely allowed the luxury of refusing participation in research or most other adult-conducted activities; again, adults are the gatekeepers.

The nature of contemporary children's lives, as they become increasingly institutionalized at school and day care, is such that they are constantly under the watchful eye of adults. Children are rarely given private places to work and play. Teachers and caregivers are told that they must be able to see all the children all the time. The early childhood community has accepted unquestioningly the assumption that low teacher/student ratios are ideal and must be maintained at all times (see Tobin, 1992). The boundaries of children's experiences are patrolled by adults in a way that makes any researcher-child relationship a strange mix that must be reconciled explicitly within the data collection and analysis process.

This is not to say that children are powerless. Clearly they resist adult and other directives (e.g., Skinner, 1989). They are able to invent, within adult-created contexts, their own sub-contexts, which most often remain invisible to adults (Corsaro, 1985). Nevertheless, young children are more context-dependent and context-vulnerable than older children and adults.

RESEARCH IN CONTEXT

The Researcher

Just as children are situated within contexts, the research act exists in context as well. The researcher is culturally and historically situated. This situatedness provides perspectives on the way that the world works as well as relations with others that affect interactions in the field. This context frames all aspects of the research endeavor: the way the question is posed, the theoretical orientations (or their lack) used, the relations forged with participants, the technology employed to gather and analyze data, and the communities to which the studies are communicated. This context provides culturally and historically situated lenses that are as salient to the findings as the "data" themselves. Good interpretive research addresses the gaps between the researcher's perspective and those of a study's participants and should be reflexive about the history of the researcher's viewpoint.

Issues of power and representation are just two aspects of the relationship between research and participants that must be negotiated in context. In a world where compliant children are good children, where answering adult questions is rarely a matter of choice, studying children is an exercise in power that presents complex ethical and methodological conundrums. Contemplation of interpretive research with children must include consideration of ways that adult power and authority become part of the context that frames child activity and shape the information generated in research situations.

The Children

Studying children in context makes an already problematic endeavor even more so. No matter how we position ourselves, how close our relationships, how good our intentions, we remain outsiders. The physical, social, cognitive, and political differences and distances between the adult and child make their relationship inherently different from relationships among adults. Regardless of the rapport between researcher and child, the researcher is NOT a child. The adult remains an adult, an outsider, an "other." The relationship between adult and child is asymmetrical and can never be bridged by taking what some have called a "least adult role" (Mandell, 1988). Acting like a child is not enough. Just taking into account the physical difference between the grown-up and the child, it is impossible to imagine we could enter the child's world unnoticed:

While there is some disagreement among scholars as to how easy it is for adults to gain access to the world of children (Wacksler, 1986), the assumptions and values of these two social categories [adults and children] inevitably differ. . . . Like the white researcher in black society, the male researcher studying women, or the ethnologist observing a distant tribal culture, the adult participant observer who attempts to understand a children's culture cannot pass unnoticed as a member of that group. (Fine & Sandstrom, 1988, pp. 10–13)

Fieldwork in Context

Even more than other types of interpretive research, fieldwork with young children depends on the quality of the relationships developed between researcher and participants. Sensitivity to individual children's needs and ideas develops over time. What is surprising is how frequently adult researchers barge into the lives of young children with observation forms and interview protocols to gather data, barely taking the time to introduce themselves to the children, much less to negotiate a relationship. Ignoring the development of shared context between adult and child results in shallow perspectives on children's lives, informed more by the adult's assumptions about children than by anything happening in the setting.

To gain understanding of children's lives in context, researchers must invest long periods of time with children on the children's terms. Long periods mean more than hours to desensitize children to adult presence—the goal should be to help children incorporate the researcher into their worlds.

Gaining access to the child's world cannot be achieved unless the researchers make clear in their own minds, as well as the minds of participants, who they are in that context. In Graue's (1992) work on meanings of readiness, she took the role of teacher aide in fieldwork and, as a result, interacted with children in the role of an educator. This role put very specific limits on her interactions with the children in the classroom—she was a supervisor and manager of children rather than a collaborator or pseudo-peer. The role made sense because her primary focus was the teachers' understandings of children.

In contrast, Corsaro's (1985) work on peer socialization took him into the play groups of preschoolers. There he took what he called a "reactive" role, letting the children take the lead in interactions, making it clear that he knew that he was on their turf. A supervisory role would not make sense for Corsaro's study because the focus was the children's construction of peer culture. Therefore, the researcher needed to be someone who would not intervene or control activities.

In both cases, these researchers gathered interesting information from and about children, but the nature of the information was quite different and the relationships between adult and child, researcher and participant, were also quite different. The role was defined and negotiated in relation to the research questions pursued and within the local research context.

Interviewing

The problems of participant observation with young children are magnified when one considers doing formal interviews. The younger the child, the greater the challenge. Adult researchers tend to make two mistakes when they interview children, based on very different assumptions. The first mistake is to assume that children are too developmentally immature to be able to think conceptually or to have the language necessary to be able to express their ideas. They then restrict their interrogations (and interchanges in interviews with young children are typically more like interrogations than conversations) to simple, concrete questions about objects and observable activity.

This tactic is boring for most children and shows a surprising lack of respect for children's considerable knowledge of their own world. These dumbed-down interviews resemble a verbally administered survey instrument. What they miss is the key to good interviewing technique: relying on the child to teach the interviewer the questions most important to ask. As Spradley (1979) noted, the purpose of a good interview is to discover what questions to ask. Why is this important? Because the context shapes what the child knows and thinks, interview interactions cannot be scripted by even the wisest adult. Leaving room for children to teach us what we need to know, while providing them with questions to spur them to do just that, is the essence of good interviewing.

The second mistake adults make is to assume that children perceive the interview situation as adults do, with a similar balance of power and rules for interaction. Children do not see interviews as speech events (Mishler, 1986) with particular rules. Children tend to view the interview situation as one of three categories of adult-child question-asking occasions. The first is the kindly coercive question, such as "Wouldn't you like to go outside now?" The second kind of question children typically hear from adults is the pseudo-test, in which the adult already knows the answer: "What color is a carrot?" The final kind of question is procedural or mechanical, designed to elicit concrete information: "Where did you put your coat?!" With experience with these kinds of questions, the child sees the interview as a search for the right answer, that is, the one that will satisfy the adult. Using their ideas of what adult-child conversation typically entails, children define the interview in terms of interrogation. The speech event ends up having very closed rules with little true conversation.

One way to avoid these kinds of staccato exchanges is to change the context to one that is more amenable to a real conversation. The most comfortable strategy we have found is one used by D'Amato (1986) and Baturka and Walsh (1991), which involves interviewing children in pairs or small groups. Rather than worrying about children influencing each other's answers, these authors found that kindergarten, first, and second graders were much more relaxed when they were asked questions with a friend.

We can think of several reasons for the success of group interviewing with young children. First, it relies on a format that children know and are comfortable with—talking with other kids. Children know the rules for that kind of interaction, and they are rules over which children have more power. They tend to keep each other on track and truthful. D'Amato described how when one child would begin to embellish a tale, the other child would respond, "You lie! You lie!" (personal communication).

Second, group interviews capitalize on social interaction, using it as a context to generate information for the researcher. Children's worlds are social worlds, and their communication for peers is much more real than for adults in one-on-one interviews. Baturka and Walsh (1991) found that the richest parts of interviews came from discussions between children as they responded to questions. This is in contrast to their direct answers, which often appeared to be attempts to find what they thought was the right answer.

Finally, group interviews allow children more room to set both the level and content of the discussion. This helps children guide researchers to the best questions by showing them what is most important at that particular point in time for those specific children. Baturka's work showed that discussion allowed children to change the question to one that was more to their liking, which they would then answer.

Doing research with young children is as complex, rewarding, and messy as living and working with them. It takes concerted attention to their needs rather than to the needs of the research project. It requires attention to the special circumstances that allow children to show us their worlds. In addition, it necessitates employment of theoretical frameworks that provide a structure for examining children's lived experience. The use of theory helps researchers move beyond the local intricacies of a set of data, allowing them to see connections between lives in the here and now and their cultural and historical contexts. In the next section, we describe a theoretical framework that we have found particularly useful in understanding children in context. Derived from Vygotskian theory, activity theory provides a tool for connecting present experience with broader social and historical contexts.

ACTIVITY THEORY

The goal of interpretive research is to understand the meaning that children construct in their everyday *situated actions*, that is, actions "situated in a cultural setting, and in the mutually interacting intentional states of the participants" (Bruner, 1990, p. 19). Much of the work in the early childhood literature has focused on behavior. A key distinction we would make is between *action* and *behavior*. Action is located within specific cultural and historical practices and time. It is populated by meaning and intentions and is tethered to particular communities and individuals. In contrast, behavior is action stripped of these local characteristics; it is mechanical description without narration. To develop thick descriptions of children's actions, we must go beyond simply detailing what people are doing. Going beyond involves exploring meaning and intention.

A problem that has plagued much research has been the practice of using as one's explanatory factor the very thing that one is trying to explain. Vygotsky (in Kozulin, 1986) was the first to criticize psychology for doing just that—mentalists trying to explain mental activity by mental activity, behaviorists, behavior by behavior. In contrast, Vygotsky argued that psychology should be about explaining human intention by human activity, an idea that later became known as activity theory. In activity theory, one begins with "a unit of analysis that includes both the individual and his/her culturally defined environment" (Wertsch, 1979,

p. viii). Researchers consider not only the actions of individuals but also the culturally defined context that serves as the origin for these behaviors. These contexts, called "activity settings," are seen as:

social institutionally defined settings . . . grounded in a set of assumptions about appropriate roles, goals, and means used by the participants in that setting . . . one could say that an activity setting guides the selection of actions and the operational composition of actions, and it determines the functional significance of these actions. (Wertsch, 1985, p. 212)

Individual action is generated out of social interactions and the meanings they create. It is enabled and constrained by the tools and resources (including other individuals) that comprise the context. Leont'ev argued forcefully for a perspective on individual action that respected its contextualized nature:

[I]f we removed human activity from the system of social relationships and social life, it would not exist and would have no structure. With all its varied forms, the human individual's activity is a system in a system of social relations. It does not exist without these relations. . . . It turns out that the activity of separate individuals depends on their place in society, on the conditions that fall to their lot, and on idiosyncratic, individual factors. (Wertsch, 1985, p. 47)

For the activity theorist, intention or motive is central. Individuals are motivated to do some things and not others. In much work on children, motivation has either been ignored in favor of developmental bounds or is reduced to external factors such as reward and punishment.

A pair of examples will help to clarify the notion of motive. A kindergarten classroom that Graue observed (1992) had a strong emphasis on writing. The teacher prided herself on the use of what she called "writing process," in which children learned to write by writing. In theory, written expression was not limited by knowledge of spelling words; instead, children were encouraged to write their ideas using any notational system they could develop. Over time, children should move into traditional spelling and punctuation as their awareness of print grows. While she encouraged open expression and invented spelling in a supportive atmosphere, her students focused almost exclusively on spelling words correctly. Attending to surface behavior only, one would conclude that these children were not ready to write. Graue found, however, that the students were using the criteria applied to classroom phonics worksheets to shape their orientation to writing. Rather than being motivated to express themselves in writing, the children wanted to get their writing right, just like the worksheets.

This example illustrates how important it is to pay careful attention to young children's actions and ideas. If the teacher's meaning for writing had been taken as that of the children, their meaning would not have been heard or understood. Although there were shared meanings for activities in this classroom, children constructed their own meanings of particular roles and activities in the context of demands and criteria held for different tasks.

This example can be further contextualized by placing it in the larger conflict between the writing process approach to literacy, whole language approaches to reading, and the pervasive efficiency orientation increasingly permeating our schools. Thus one has journals alongside worksheets. This larger contradiction, which affects teachers, parents, and children, is played out each day in classrooms. Children are caught in the crossfire between these very different theories and practices as adults try to sort out their ideas about how literacy works and how we should measure its development.

A cross-cultural example illustrates how adult motives shape the resources available to children. Gaskins (in Gaskins, Miller, & Corsaro, 1992) found that Mayan infants rarely engaged in complex exploratory play because their parents regarded it as unimportant. According to Gaskins, the motivation for encouraging only certain types of play was culturally formed and provided the children with certain types of resources for their development. Here we have a vivid example of local parent-child interactions being culturally and historically contextualized.

Getting at intention and motive is not a simple, straightforward task. As anthropologists are fond of noting—get it indirectly or get very little. Conklin, for example, discovered that the Hanunoo knew the names of fourteen hundred different plants (1954). He did not learn this all at once by asking people how many plants they could name. Motives are tacit to actors and therefore are not accessible for conscious reflection (Wertsch, 1985). Asking children why they are doing things, explanations they do not give in their normal interactions, is like asking a fish about water. First, you need to explain what water is and remind the fish that it is there. What the fish then has to say about water may be interesting, but it has as much to do with your question and its setup as it does with the fish's experience with water. To get a sense of motives, it is important to watch children's interactions closely, to listen to children's explanations of their actions, and to be respectful of their voices. It requires the basic methods of interpretive research, plus attention to the connections between the local context and the broader culture and history.

CONCLUSION

In this chapter, we have argued the need for studies that locate children's experience in specific cultural and historical contexts. This approach provides a locally grounded perspective on the experiences of particular individuals that can then be linked to other descriptions. The results of this perspective can be a rich narrative that is at once general and particularistic, broadly focused while thickly descriptive.

If interpretive researchers are to take seriously the issue of context, then a number of implications are obvious. First, we need to attend to the larger world of research, including quantitative research. In addition to using work that has been done before, we can, as Walsh, Tobin, and Graue noted, go beyond it:

Interpretive research has often been relegated to pilot study status, as though interpretive researchers were merely doing advanced scout work for their positivist colleagues. We argue to the contrary that interpretive inquiry has the potential to allow access to the contextual issues that give meaning to research findings and, in so doing, can provide understandings that allow us to make sense of existing positivist work. (1993, p. 465)

Second, we are going to need to take theory more seriously. This statement may sound contradictory to our earlier criticism of research aimed at developing grand acultural theory, but our point is that one does not go into the field as though one knows nothing about children. Post-Piagetian perspectives (e.g., Inagaki, 1992; Walsh, 1992, 1993), for example, stress the importance of culture that is very useful for interpretive early childhood research. For our purposes, activity theory has been particularly helpful as we have worked to explore children's lives in context.

We also need to explore the socially constructed positionings that serve as contexts for children's relations with others; among the most important are racial and ethnic identities, gender, and socioeconomic status. These markers are used by others to frame their interactions with children in ways that construct who the child is across the local contexts. Thinking about these characteristics as contexts for children's experience could help us understand more about the process of their growth and development and could move us away from their reification as determinants of certain outcomes.

Third, individual research studies need to be seen as part of larger research programs, both by the individual researcher and by researchers at large. Connecting individual pieces of interpretive scholarship to the broader scope of inquiry is more than the traditional bow to our ancestors in a literature review. They must be linked theoretically, a complex task that requires deep knowledge of the local context and its data, the terrain of extant research, and a good grasp of the theories used to frame inquiry. Rather than struggling to outline the particular contribution of a single slice of work, researchers should highlight how their works add to a growing mosaic of understanding. We need far more collaborative work, not only with those we study, as the word collaborative has lately come to mean, but with other researchers. Others include researchers from other disciplines and research methodologies, including those "quantitative" in nature. In connecting our work to that of others, we bring the idea of context full circle. Just as our view of children must be more contextualized, we recognize that, as researchers, we too work in context. The rich descriptions that are the hallmark of good interpretive research must be connected to those contexts in which they are embedded: the child within her setting, the setting within a larger community, researchers within their scholarly cultures, and ideas within theoretical frameworks. No one piece stands alone if we are to hope for a perspective on children that begins to capture the complexities of their lives.

REFERENCES

Baturka, N. L., & Walsh, D. J. (1991, April). *"In the Guinness Book of World Records it says that a girl stayed in kindergarten until she was 13": First graders who have been retained make sense of their world.* Paper presented at the Annual Meeting of the American Educational Research Association, Chicago.

Bradbard, M. R., Halperin, S. M., & Endsley, R. C. (1988). The curiosity of abused preschool children in mother-present, teacher-present, and stranger-present situations. *Early Childhood Research Quarterly, 3,* 91–105.

Bruner, J. (1986). *Actual minds, possible worlds.* Cambridge, Mass.: Harvard University Press.

Bruner, J. (1990). *Acts of meaning.* Cambridge, Mass.: Harvard University Press.

Bruner, J., & Haste, H. (1987). *Making sense: The child's construction of reality.* New York: Methuen.

Conklin, H. C. (1954). *The relationship of Hanunoo culture to the plant world.* Ann Arbor, Mich.: University Microfilms.

Corsaro, W. (1985). *Friendship and peer culture in the early years.* Norwood, N.J.: Ablex.

Cronbach, L. J. (1975). Beyond the two disciplines of scientific inquiry. *American Psychologist, 30,* 116–127.

D'Amato, J. (1986). *"We cool, tha's why": A study of personhood and place in Hawaiian second graders.* Unpublished doctoral dissertation, University of Hawaii.

Delamont, S. (1992). *Fieldwork in educational settings: Methods, pitfalls, and perspectives.* London: Falmer.

Denzin, N. K. (1989). *Interpretive interactionism.* Newbury Park, Calif.: Sage.

Donaldson, M. (1978). *Children's minds.* New York: W. W. Norton.

Erickson, F. (1986). Qualitative methods in research on teaching. In M. C. Wittrock (Ed.), *Handbook of research on teaching,* 3rd ed. (pp. 119–161). New York: Macmillan.

Erickson, F. (1992, April). *Post-everything: The word of the moment and how we got here*. Paper delivered at the Annual Meeting of the American Educational Research Association, San Francisco.

Fendler, L., & Popkewitz, T. S. (1993). (Re)constituting critical traditions. *Educational researcher, 22* (6), 24–26.

Fine, G. A., & Sandstrom, K. L. (1988). *Knowing children: Participant observation with minors*. Newbury Park, Calif.: Sage.

Gaskins, S., Miller, P. J., & Corsaro, W. A. (1992). Theoretical and methodological perspectives in the interpretive study of children. In W. A. Corsaro & P. J. Miller (Eds.), *New directions in child development, no. 58*, Winter 1992, pp. 5–23. San Francisco: Jossey-Bass.

Gelman, R. (1979). Preschool thought. *American Psychologist, 34*, 900–905.

Gelman, R., & Baillargeon, R. (1983). A review of some Piagetian concepts. In P. H. Mussen (Ed.), *Handbook of child psychology, vol. 3: Cognitive development* [J. Flavell & E. M. Markham, vol. eds.] (pp. 167–230). New York: Wiley.

Glesne, C., & Peshkin, A. (1992). *Becoming qualitative researchers: An introduction*. White Plains, N.Y.: Longman.

Graue, M. E. (1992). *Ready for what? Constructing meanings of readiness for kindergarten*. Albany: SUNY.

Hall, G. S. (1883). The content of children's minds. *Princeton Review, 2*, 249–272.

Hall, G. S. (1901). Ideal school based on child study. *Journal of Proceedings and Addresses of the National Education Association*, pp. 474–488.

Hatano, G., & Inagaki, K. (1982–83). Two courses of expertise. Sapporo, Japan: Research and Clinical Center for Child Development.

Holloway, S. D., & Reichhart-Erickson, M. (1988). The relationship of day care quality to children's free-play behavior and social problem solving skills. *Early Childhood Research Quarterly, 3*, 39–53.

Howes, C. (1988). Same- and cross-sex friends: Implications for interaction and social skills. *Early Childhood Research Quarterly, 3*, 21–37.

Inagaki, K. (1992). Piagetian and post-Piagetian conceptions of development and their implications for science education in early childhood. *Early Childhood Research Quarterly, 7*, 115–133.

King, G., Keohane, R. O., & Verba, S. (1994). *Scientific inference in qualitative research*. Princeton, N.J.: Princeton University Press.

Kliebard, H. (1986). *The struggle for the American curriculum 1893–1958*. Boston: Routledge & Kegan Paul.

Kozulin, A. (1986). The concept of activity in Soviet psychology: Vygotsky, his disciples and critics. *American Psychologist, 41* (3), 264–274.

Leavitt, R. (1994). *Power and emotion in infant-toddler day care*. Albany: SUNY Press.

Mendell, N. (1988). The least-adult role in studying children. *Journal of Contemporary Ethnography, 16*, 433–467.

Mehan, H. (1980). The competent student. *Anthropology and Education Quarterly, 11* (3), 131–152.

Mishler, E. G. (1986). *Research interviewing: Context and narrative*. Cambridge, Mass.: Harvard University Press.

Skinner, D. (1989, November). *Nepali children's formation of social selves*. Paper presented at the Annual Meeting of the American Anthropological Association, Phoenix.

Spodek, B. (Ed.) (1993). *Handbook of research on the education of young children*. New York: Macmillan.

Spradley, J. P. (1979). *The ethnographic interview*. New York: Holt, Rinehart & Winston.

Tobin, J. (1992). Early childhood education and the public schools: Obstacles to reconstructing the relationship. *Early Education and Development, 3* (2), 196–200.

Wacksler, F. C. (1986). Studying children: Phenomenological insights. *Human Studies, 9,* 71–92.

Walsh, D. J. (1991). Reconstructing the discourse on development appropriateness: A developmental perspective. *Early Education and Development, 2,* 109–119.

Walsh, D. J. (1992, December). *Implications of a post-Piagetian perspective for early childhood education: Helping children make sense*. Invited paper: Taipei Municipal Teachers College Conference on Early Childhood Education, Taipei, Taiwan.

Walsh, D. J. (1993, April). *Time to move on: A few thoughts on a post-Piagtian/cultural psychology*. Paper presented at the Annual Meeting of the American Education Research Association, Atlanta.

Walsh, D. J., Tobin, J. J., and Graue, M. E. (1993). The interpretive voice: Qualitative research in early childhood education. In B. Spodek (Ed.), *Handbook of research on the education of young children* (pp. 464–476). New York: Free Press.

Wertsch, J. (1979). Introduction. In J. V. Wertsch (Ed.), *Culture, communication, and cognition*. New York: Cambridge University Press.

Wolf, J. (1993). *Doing day care*. Unpublished doctoral dissertation, University of Illinois at Urbana-Champaign.

Chapter 9

Learning from Classroom Ethnographies: Same Places, Different Times

DAVID E. FERNIE, REBECCA KANTOR, AND
KIMBERLEE L. Whaley

INTRODUCTION

In this chapter, we explicate, extend, and demonstrate the utility of apply-ing a peer culture research perspective, drawing on findings from two pro-grams of ethnographic research conducted within the side-by-side classrooms of the A. Sophie Rogers Laboratory School at The Ohio State University. The infant-toddler classroom, serving children six weeks through three years of age, is the setting for the child care program and re-search group headed by Kim Whaley, while the adjacent preschool class-room of three- and four-year-olds has been the setting for the preschool ethnography of Rebecca Kantor, David Fernie, and their colleagues. What we have to say in this chapter is the yield of a continuing dialogue and a convergence of interests among these three researchers.

Below, two topical strands are interwoven. The first is related to con-tent. Drawing across both programs of research, we present and interpret selected research findings from both classrooms to inform theory about peer culture and practical knowledge of children's play and peer culture in early childhood settings. More specifically, our content goals focus on: (a) how social dynamics and cultural elements are related across young children's peer cultures; (b) how aspects of infants' and toddlers' play may be reasonably interpreted in peer culture terms; and, (c) how an awareness of peer culture informs teachers' practices and influences everyday life in these two closely related classrooms.

The second topical strand concerns an issue of context. We discuss how our findings, interpretations, and a productive discourse among researchers have been catalyzed by this distinctive arrangement of side-by-side classrooms studied ethnographically and collaboratively over multiple years. We will argue that such an arrangement provides a distinctive purview, purchase, and set of opportunities framing what we can address across these programs of research. We begin with a brief history of the two programs of research and a description of the institutional configuration of the research context.

A Brief History

The program of ethnographic research begun in 1987 in the preschool room at the lab school was strongly influenced by the sociocultural work of both Judith Green and William Corsaro as departure points and orienting perspectives. While most of Green's work has focused on teaching and learning in elementary and secondary classrooms (Green & Harker, 1982; Green & Wallat, 1981), Corsaro's (1985) benchmark study described the rich social world that preschool children created through their classroom play. Specifically, Corsaro found that three- and four-year-old children "constructed and shared a peer culture of behaviors, routines, rituals, artifacts, and values" (1985, p. 171). A peer culture perspective gives us a lens through which to view the play of children from an emic perspective, and thus poses a powerful qualitative alternative or complement to the prevailing positivist/psychological perspective often seen as early education's root discipline.

In his writings, Corsaro provides salient and vivid examples of how peer culture elements are related to the social dynamics they serve. For example, he interprets "gatekeeping" routines as more than simple exclusion and rejection of those left at the gate; such routines serve to protect the fragile "interactive space" that young peers have created and are striving to maintain (Corsaro, 1985).

In order to explore both the unique and common aspects of peer culture across cultures, Corsaro has extended his ethnographic work to Italian preschoolers (Corsaro, 1988; Corsaro & Emiliani, 1992; Corsaro & Molinari, 1990). This work documents unique Italian peer culture elements reflecting the larger Italian culture (e.g., *discussione*, a form of friendly argument or discussion), routines reminiscent of American preschoolers (e.g., children's covert use of forbidden objects in school), and peer culture routines of toddlers. Yet perhaps because "peer culture" is a newly articulated construct, only a few aspects of peer culture have been plumbed in the available research.

With a departure point in the above-mentioned work, the research programs at the A. Sophie Rogers Lab School extend this perspective in some new directions. The preschool ethnography employs a set of linked, mutually informing analyses to enhance our understanding of daily life within this classroom. One heuristic that has proved helpful to us in explaining this classroom and our research program is to conceptualize this classroom as two overlapping or intersecting domains: a distinctive peer culture domain and a parallel school culture domain, the latter reflecting the academic purposes and community/group nature of classroom life. Analyses primarily focused on the peer culture include how a regular affinity group of players constructed distinctive object use (Elgas, Klein, Kantor, & Fernie, 1988) and a complex of cultural knowledge (Kantor, Elgas, & Fernie, 1993) to serve their play and to maintain their group, as well as how individuals positioned themselves either successfully or unsuccessfully in relation to this group (Fernie, Davies, Kantor, & MacMurray, 1993). Analyses emphasizing school culture explore how children's abilities to conduct small group collaboration (Williams, 1988) and large group conversation (Kantor, Elgas, & Fernie, 1993) develop over time and through guided participation. Still others explore the intersection of school culture and peer culture in such phenomena as the construction of literacy (Miller, 1991) and of social "outsiders" (Scott, 1991), phenomena we have found to be evident across both peer culture and school culture domains of this classroom.

The program of research begun by Kim Whaley in 1990 extends the peer culture perspective to the social world of an infant-toddler child care setting. The general focus of this work is on the peer relations and friendships of these youngest participants in educational settings. Much of the extant literature on this topic deals with older children, employing interview methods and observation within controlled experimental settings for relatively short periods of time. As a result, for very young children in everyday group care, their friendship possibilities and abilities are the topic of little research, are poorly understood, and are probably underestimated.

Reflecting a naturalistic, qualitative orientation from the outset, Whaley's program of research has evolved toward a sociocultural interpretive framework, convergent with both the program of research in the preschool room and with the recent explorations of toddler relations in Corsaro's work. Now into a fourth year of data collection for various studies, Whaley and her graduate student colleagues have documented the impressive synchrony and similarity in the first friendships that infants and toddlers construct over time in a supportive early childhood setting (Whaley & Rubenstein, 1994). While analyses related to early friendship continue, other analyses of this data have turned toward those activities that comprise the peer culture of this classroom.

The Distinctiveness of the Research Context

Over the past several years, the convergence of the two programs of research has been enhanced through participation in various higher education activities. These include informal collegial dialogue and the discussion of data collected, shared papers and presentations, joint membership on doctoral committees, guest lecturing in each other's classes, and the development of a shared doctoral program across two departments in different colleges. At times, some of these activities involve two of the authors, while at others all three are involved. Elsewhere we described the unity across higher education activities possible within collaborative, ethnographic programs of research (Fernie & Kantor, 1994). Here we focus on a major impetus to this continuing exchange among researchers: the closely linked nature of these two classrooms.

While it is a truism to note that the nature of a research context frames what can be found there, we believe that the conduct of ethnographic analyses in side-by-side classrooms across multiple years creates a unique opportunity when compared to other types and programs of research. Traditional programs of educational and psychological research often build a body of findings through successive studies conducted in different physical locations. Inherent variations in both physical setting and classroom culture are typically underplayed as an influence, both in individual studies and in the interpretation of cumulative findings. When successive studies are conducted within the same setting (e.g., a psych lab setting within a university), sets of data examined in different studies are often treated as relatively unrelated, either because they are conducted by different researchers with different orientations, or because they address substantially different questions within a program of research.

In contrast, setting and culture are central to comparative ethnographic work (sometimes called ethnology), and many ethnographers purposefully select contrasting cultures to investigate both variation and commonality in the conduct of everyday life across institutions (e.g., Lubeck's 1985 comparison of a middle-class white preschool with a working-class black Head Start program), communities (Heath's 1983 study of literacy in Trackton and Roadville), or countries (e.g., Corsaro's 1988 ethnology of American and Italian preschoolers). The programs of research described in this chapter have evolved toward a common, ethnographic methodological orientation, but one focused on the comparison of two closely connected classroom settings. The staffs in the two classrooms have arrived at a shared social constructionist philosophy, one forged in the interplay of theory, research, and practice. These connections are strengthened by the fact that children often "graduate" from the infant-toddler group to the preschool classroom, and teachers in one of the classrooms may shift assignment to the other. Lab school teachers are

involved in masters/doctoral coursework centered around these two programs of research, and are themselves instructors of preservice courses
and practica. Thus the lab school teachers' practices and the formal curricular formats have evolved slowly and self-consciously within these two
classrooms, and with considerable consensus and continuity across the
two classrooms. Put differently, the school cultures of the two classrooms
reflect a high degree of consensus and continuity and are relatively stable
from year to year.

On the other hand, the peer culture elements that children construct
have looked quite different from year to year, reflecting the new cohort,
their personalities, and changing events in the world and media beyond
the classroom. This creates the opportunity to reflect on the changing
versions of peer culture we have seen carried out over multiple years in
these two closely aligned settings and to interpret what we believe to be
common enduring social dynamics underlying these distinctive instantiations of peer cultures.

In what follows, we use data-based examples from both classrooms to
show how the social dynamics of affiliation and inclusion-exclusion endure across settings and cohorts and are reconstructed in diverse peer
culture elements. Across both programs of research, we have found it
helpful to distinguish among whole group, small group, and individual-
within-group frameworks for interpreting classroom phenomena. Here
we demonstrate this approach, first detailing how the social dynamic of
affiliation is manifested at the whole group level and, second, showing
how the social dynamic of inclusion-exclusion is manifested at the small
group level. As we describe each dynamic, we highlight (a) theoretical
issues of social construction and peer culture evident as we have seen
each dynamic recur over successive years; (b) developmental implications
emerging from studying the infant-toddler years through the preschool
years; and (c) implications for early childhood classroom practice.

PEER CULTURE SOCIAL DYNAMICS:
TWO EXTENDED EXAMPLES

Affiliation with the Whole Group

In this section, we introduce several aspects of peer culture and show
how they are manifested in each of the two rooms. The first aspect of
peer culture, and perhaps the most salient, is what we have termed "peer
culture affiliation." We interpret this social dynamic as children's need
or desire to signal "we-ness," that is, their solidarity and group identity.
Its saliency is related to the *whole group* nature of this peer culture dynamic—a social dynamic constructed among many of the children in the

classroom, independent of particular friendships and basically available to all of the children.

We first became aware of this dynamic during the first year of the pre-school ethnography. During the first week of school, Bob brought to the classroom his interest in sticks. He would find a small branch on the playground and put it in his belt or down his shirt. As he became involved with other children, stick collecting became a common and expected activity for a peer group of five or six children. Soon the sticks became props for a variety of shared sociodramatic activities evident in excerpts from the researchers' field notes:

Outdoors . . . Bob, from the top of the climber, points sticks and shoots at Don: "I am half man half spider. . . . I'm Spiderman (repeats this 5 times). Spiderman will get you."

Because teachers were concerned with the jagged edge of the sticks, they asked children to store them in their cubbies but supported the children's interest in sticks in other ways. For example, they negotiated with the children to encourage their use of smooth, red, rhythm sticks from the music shelves during free play. Soon these sticks were seen everywhere. In an extensive analysis reported elsewhere (Elgas, 1988), a detailing of the social uses of these objects revealed their function as a marker of affiliation. Children "wore" collections of the sticks in their belt loops, down their shirt backs (as He-man apparently wore his sword), and stashed them in corners near their play. Piles of sticks were carried in pockets to circle time and small group time and could be seen in children's cubbies. Importantly, the overt uses of sticks observed in roles or themes within play episodes were less frequent than their use as a "badge" of affiliation. In other words, the sticks were not often used as conventional objects in sociodramatic play, but as a socially constructed signal of membership in a social network. Also important was the fact that while the sticks first emerged in the peer group of the boy who introduced them from the playground, they soon were seen in the hands and beltloops of children who played with other groups and even in the possession of those who typically chose to play alone or with teachers. Thus we characterize this social phenomenon as a whole group dynamic.

Over time, within and across several years of life in this classroom, we have seen other evidence of this affiliation dynamic constructed within peer culture life. For example, one group of girls established a routine of wearing bathing suits to school under their clothes so that they could strip down to them during playtime, even though their play was not related to swimming. This routine spread beyond this particular group of friends to most of the girls in the classroom. Other examples of affiliation-marking vehicles come from artifacts and routines related to mass media, for example: wearing Ninja Turtle masks; playing with toy replicas of media figures; calling each other superhero names like He-man and Batman; and, more recently, using face paints to transform themselves into Pongo and Perdita from *101 Dalmatians*.

The affiliation aspect of peer culture has also been found in the infant-toddler room. During the course of a data analysis related to friendship, it became obvious that this group of children had created routines that the majority of the children participated in, routines that were repeated on a regular basis throughout the course of the study. Just as in the preschool, these routines seemed to serve as a way for the older babies and toddlers to indicate that they were a group. While the toddlers also used objects as markers of their affiliation, these objects were frequently integrated into ritualized play activities. Thus, while the preschool children used objects as markers, the toddlers used *both* the object and the play routine itself as their marker of affiliation.

The majority of the affiliation routines we have noted in the infant-toddler setting involve some sort of motor activity paired with the use of the objects. For example, the "balls" routine began when one child started throwing a ball into the air while shouting and laughing. Soon many of the other children in the room were participating, balls flying through the air and shouts and laughter filling the room. This routine not only occurred with actual balls but also with pom poms, cotton balls, balloons, and any other item that resembled a ball. Further, the routine had specific rules which the children often prompted each other to remember: throwing the ball, yelling and laughing with glee as the action was performed, and always using whatever ball you started with rather than whichever ball landed closest to you. This routine, like many others we have seen, began with one or two children and quickly spread to others in the classroom.

One of the routines that we have seen in two "generations" of the infant-toddler room involves the use of small chairs that are present in the room. The children regularly used these chairs to create cars, trains, and other structures for play, not unlike the peer culture routine reported by Corsaro and Emiliani (1992) in the *asilo nido* (infant-toddler program) of Italy. In our setting, this routine began when one child would drag a chair to the middle of the room. This was followed by other children getting chairs and lining them up in a straight line across the room. The game that originally accompanied this was pretending to take a train ride, but this quickly switched to a car ride, complete with steering wheels and other props. Further, as the excerpt below documents, the "chairs" routine was then brought by the children into the school culture routines of the day:

Eve, the teacher, has already announced that it is clean-up time, and all the children are busy putting toys on the shelves. Before Eve begins to sing the song that signals the start of circle time, Harry (25 months) drags one of the small blue chairs to the circle area and places it on one of the spaces marking the circle on the floor. One by one, all except the two youngest children in the room bring a chair and place it around the circle.

This use of the chairs in circle time provides a nice example of how school culture and peer culture can intersect in complementary ways. Now, watching the third "generation" of children in the toddler program, once again the "chairs" routine is a part of circle time. This new group of children, only three of whom were in the room during the first year of data collection, perform this routine in the same way their earlier counterparts did.

Theoretical Implications

Across both classrooms and across multiple years, we have examined these and many other examples of affiliation markers for the characteristics they might have in common. One underlying commonality is that they are easily shared by many, either because they are a plentiful resource like the sticks, an easily gotten resource like the bathing suits, or are linked to widely known information like the media examples. Furthermore, these markers are all easily displayed—an important feature for signaling "groupness." In the toddlers' first experience with being a part of a group, these affiliation routines are also accessible because children with a variety of developmental skills are able to accomplish or approximate them. Knowledge of each cohort of children helps us to understand why particular objects, rituals, routines, roles, or language were constructed as socially important by that cohort. For example, in the "year of the sticks," the group personality was characterized by rich sociodramatic play and inventions of unique ways to use objects in the classroom, particularly by the peer culture leaders. On the other other hand, during a period we call the "year of bad words," the peer culture was particularly oppositional and given to displays of power, disruption of school events, and other forms of what the teachers jokingly called "peer culture mutinies."

Objects and rituals contain multiple meanings within the group, commonly signaling affiliation as well as other social characteristics particular to each year's peer culture. These affiliation markers very much exemplify Corsaro's (1985, p. 51) descriptions of peer culture in that children "do not always share the same view of the world" as adults. Thus the activities and objects chosen by the children seem foreign to the concerns and perspectives of adults. Instead, they mark the "childish" nature of an early childhood peer culture; in other words, those things that are valuable to children both bind them together and separate them from adults.

Methodological Implications

Working collaboratively across rooms and over time allowed us to realize that activities that appeared disparate on the surface were actually different instantiations of the same enduring dynamic: affiliation. When we first interpreted the unique social purposes of the sticks, this example became a topic of conversation within both classrooms of the lab. As a result, researchers in both classrooms were alerted to this affiliation dynamic and to the possibility that other cultural constructions might serve such a purpose. This anticipation made good sense given each classroom's relatively stable ecology (teaching philosophy, classroom physical arrangement, time allocation, child demographics, etc.) across years. As we noticed an emergent pattern of different affiliation examples in subsequent years and in both classrooms, these too became topics of conversation among researchers, classroom teachers, and university students.

Such insights gained from an ethnographic perspective and constructed through researchers' dialogue, then, are a result of collaborative activity in closely connected settings, and have become a part of the researchers' ongoing vision about life in these classrooms. Further, the opportunity to compare and contrast particular cohorts across years allowed us to view these activities from multiple perspectives and to see the multiple meanings of these activities within children's daily lives. For example, whereas prior examinations of toddlers' common activities would cast them as person-to-person imitation or parallel play, taking a whole group perspective reinterprets such behavior as signaling young children's awareness and construction of a beginning group life in peer culture. Over time, these affiliation routines spread from one child to another, to small groups of children, and ultimately to almost all classroom participants. Children even imported them into school culture activities initiated by adults. Thus these routines were used to mark affiliation broadly and frequently within the daily life of the infant and toddler classroom. With its focus on everyday life, the ethnographic lens allowed us to reinterpret this dynamic as a continuing one, within and across multiple peer cultures over multiple years.

Practical implications

It is no coincidence that these same activities which are so foreign to adults are viewed as common irritants by them. Imagine the conversation between the child and her parent when the child seems desperate to wear a bathing suit in the middle of the winter with no prospect of swimming! These are not concerns or desires that are understandable within adult worlds. As a result, teachers frequently attempt to stop these sorts of behaviors in classroom settings. For example, few teachers feel comfortable with an entire classroom of toddlers running around throwing balls and screaming. Likewise, many teachers prohibit activities such as stripping down to your bathing suit, moving chairs, and carrying sticks in your shirt. On a practical level, this suggests that those activities children often use to create and sustain a peer culture might be thwarted by a school culture that is uncomfortable with these types of activities. Teachers must develop an understanding of the idea of peer culture and the importance of it in young children's lives before they can begin to see these routines as something other than a disturbance in the classroom. Further, they must learn how to support them within the needs and values of their own school culture perspective (e.g., the smooth wooden sticks versus the jagged outdoor sticks).

Inclusion-Exclusion in Subgroups

In this section, the notion of peer culture social dynamics is again explored across the two rooms and across multiple years, but this time with a lens focused on small groups of children. Specifically, we examine the tendency of children to include some peers while excluding others. Corsaro (1985) described the "gatekeeping" used by groups of players as their desire to protect their "interactive space" from the intrusions of others (p. 125). His perspective provided a more positive slant on a dynamic that is often seen as the simple, and somehow heartless, rejection of peers. Corsaro described this phenomenon as one that occurs broadly across *changing* groups of players. In contrast, it has been our experience, across both classrooms, that each year's peer culture contains several *stable* and enduring friendship groups and that the inclusion-exclusion dynamic is a routinized feature of these particular groups (Elgas, 1988; Elgas, Klein, Kantor, & Fernie 1988; Whaley & Rubenstein, 1994). In the course of their play, children in subgroups constructed and shared rituals, routines, themes, language, and artifacts that served the inclusion-exclusion dynamic.

The first example of inclusion-exclusion we present is from an analysis of one such "affinity group" (so called because of the members' mutual attraction) within the peer culture of the preschool classroom (Elgas et al., 1988). Although there were several stable friendship groups in this classroom that year, this group was dubbed the "core" group because it had great cohesion and social salience within the wider peer culture of the room. Their "leader" was Bob, the same child who introduced the sticks into the classroom. The extent to which these sticks became social "currency" in the classroom reflects the influence of this subgroup on the wider peer culture in the room. While sticks served the affiliation dynamic, other objects, such as superhero capes, seemed to function as "entry vehicles"—ways to get in (or be kept out of) the group's play. These objects, endowed with social value by the core group, were hoarded and protected by its members. While many children coveted and gained access to the sticks, only a few non-core group members were able to possess these "entry vehicle" objects, and only for short periods of time (Elgas, 1988).

Across groups in the preschool, we have seen this inclusion-exclusion dynamic manifested in other ways. For example, LaMonte (1988) described what she called a "dominant" group of players in another study in the preschool. This group controlled the block area, always a favorite area of the room. LaMonte saw their social control of the block area being accomplished in three ways: through control of time (i.e., by being the first ones to leave snack and the first to arrive in the block area); through control of space and materials (i.e., by scooping up all the favorite materials and building the same large structure each day in the center of the block area); and through "gatekeeping" (e.g, building the structure with only enough seats for the group, then telling intruders that "you have to have a seat to play!"). This latter example is what Corsaro called "justification with reference to space or number of people" (1985, p. 130). In these diverse ways, inclusion-exclusion routines were a defining activity around which this group coalesced.

The toddlers, in subgroups of two or three friends, also constructed inclusion-exclusion rituals and routines, such as the "shopping cart" game. In this routine, toddlers were frequently observed pushing a shopping cart following each other around. While two children in particular, Jed and Beth, were often observed engaged in this type of activity, other children frequently used the carts when they were not in Beth and Jed's possession. Because the teachers observed the great interest in these carts, and because we were beginning to understand affiliation routines in this classroom, the teachers put more small shopping carts in the room to allow more of the children to participate. To our surprise, Beth and Jed stopped using the carts almost immediately and switched to pushing around the only two baby strollers in the room. This suggested to us that this shopping cart routine might "belong" to Jed and Beth and their particular friendship (Whaley & Rubenstein, 1994). This understanding was strengthened when we removed the extra shopping carts and Jed and Beth returned to using them on a regular basis. As we saw in the "chairs" routine for affiliation, this "shopping cart" routine has reappeared over each of the successive three years since the start of the study. Further, it is the routine most commonly used across "generations" by dyads of children identified as friends (Whaley & Rubenstein, 1994).

In a second routine observed between three older toddlers, the inclusion-exclusion dynamic was more obvious because it was verbal, and more easily identified because we had seen the earlier inclusion-exclusion routine. The start of this routine was signaled when one of the toddlers began spreading blankets on the floor of the small space between the cribs in the back of the room. They then moved rocking chairs and soft blocks to close off this space they called their "fort." From the field note record:

Carly tells Jed to wait while she carefully spreads the receiving blankets across the floor between two of the cribs in the back of the room. She shakes each blanket to smooth it out, then spreads it out on the floor. This action is repeated with six different blankets before she tells Jed to get in. He walks into the space and Carly pulls first one, then the other, small rocking chair in front of the "fort" they have made. They talk briefly, then Carly cups her hand to her mouth and yells, "No one can come in here! Nobody can get in." They lie down on the floor and begin to play.

Once again, our across-time look at the setting revealed that this "fort" routine has reappeared among later cohorts. Most recently, two of the oldest children in the room were observed creating their fort in a big easy chair, again using many blankets, soft blocks, and pillows.

Theoretical Implications

Looking across these examples of inclusion-exclusion, our analysis suggests an underlying commonality across the diverse ways this social dynamic was carried out. In each case—the capes, the block area, the forts, and the shopping carts—the resource was "controllable." Whether it was objects, time and space, or routines, children chose things that were available in only limited supply or created places and ways to limit access. This is in direct counterpoint to the characteristics of objects used for affiliation with the whole group, that is, abundance, easy access, and display.

These examples of inclusion-exclusion show us how differently the same dynamic can function within peer culture small groups. For some, like the toddlers and the block players, inclusion-exclusion served to create the "glue" for their group of friends. In other words, these players experienced themselves as friends through regular routines and rituals focused on keeping others out. For others, such as the core group, inclusion-exclusion seemed to be more about protecting interactive space as described by Corsaro (1985), so that they could get on with their sociodramatic play and other activities. Thus, looking across time and different groups of friends informs our understanding of how subgroups fit into the larger peer culture of each classroom, how the same social dynamic has a somewhat different meaning within each subgroup, and how it is created through different cultural elements.

Methodological implications

As was the case in examining affiliation routines, our across-setting, across-time view has revealed to us that actions that look vastly different on the surface can represent the same social dynamic, in this case the inclusion-exclusion dynamic. The juxtaposition of data sets across the two rooms also gave us an interpretive lens for understanding the more subtle, nonverbal inclusion-exclusion dynamic seen among toddlers. Continuing observation of the setting and children's interactions allowed us to interpret and reinterpret the meaning of children's ongoing play. For example, the provision of additional shopping carts by the teachers, and Jed and Beth's reactions to them, helped us to understand better that inclusion-exclusion and affiliation were distinct social dynamics. Lastly, our unique interactions as colleagues working in side-by-side settings have allowed us to speculate about the developmental course of these routines. In particular, we see that these activities occur first in small groups of two or three children in the toddler setting, and eventually become part of larger core groups of children in the preschool.

Practical implications

Teachers and researchers have a tendency to worry about classroom activities that exclude some children from participating. Certainly the extensive literature on rejected and excluded children supports this concern. Teachers fear that children who are excluded in preschool will always be excluded from the play of their peers. As a result, when teachers see inclusion-exclusion routines, their reaction is to attempt to control them with rules ("We have to share with all our friends" or "Everybody can play"). Our work in both rooms suggests that as soon as teachers ban one inclusion-exclusion routine, children find a way to create another.

As adults we tend to impose our adult meanings on children's activities. Our methodology, one which allows us to see children across both time and settings, indicates that rather than staying in one position, always included or always excluded, children move in and out of social positions. In a two-year ethnographic piece, Massoulos (1988) described a child who was rejected within a peer group in his first year in this preschool. In the second year, however, he was very successful with a different group of peers. This analysis, as well as our own, leaves us with the conviction that groups such as these are dynamic entities and that children are in a period of rapid development and growth. Thus the group norms may change over time, children may become more socially adept, and the configurations of peers may change, together producing more accessible dynamics for individual children.

DISCUSSION

We have used the examples of affiliation and inclusion-exclusion to illustrate what we have seen from a sociocultural perspective within a unique research context, one that stimulates a long-term, continuing dialogue about two closely related classrooms. Further examples could be discussed. Taking an individual-within-group look, for example, we could demonstrate how individual children have established leadership in unique ways across the various preschool cohorts. We could then explore whether leadership or its roots are evident among infant and toddler peers.

Other peer culture topics pique our interest but remain to be explored over time and across the classrooms. We have noticed, for example, that certain peer culture routines move up to the preschool with the toddler graduates, while others do not; other routines begin in the preschool and seem to spread down to the infant-toddler room; still others remain or even reappear in the same classroom long after those who initiated them have moved on. It would be interesting to explore why and how these peer culture phenomena happen.

Further, we have seen that at least one or two salient affinity groups develop each year, but each has a distinctive tone and character. Some groups construct bad words and disruption of teacher-led events to mark their peer culture, while others center their affinity around positive sociodramatic play. Despite a fairly stable and supportive school culture, then, some peer cultures are more oppositional in their values and practices than others. Why? The varied tone and character of the peer cultures seen over the years in the preschool room have disabused us of the notion, held when we began the preschool ethnography, that having a supportive school culture would produce a positive tone in the peer culture. Informed by the across-years look, the assertion that a supportive school culture tends to encourage a strong and vibrant peer culture seems a more informed interpretation or generalization. Yet depending on the participants, a robust peer culture may either be the linchpin of a vibrant and positive classroom or resemble something closer to *Mutiny on the Bounty*.

Much remains to be learned about children's peer culture. The methodological approach we have discussed here is one that allows us to explore and reveal the worlds created by young children within their everyday group life. The findings we have discussed add to an evolving peer culture theory and contrast with some of the widely accepted traditional literature, such as the research of Parten (1932) and Piaget (1952) that often guides early educational practice (e.g., Bredekamp, 1987).

What are the implications of this work for a theory of peer culture? Our analysis depicts aspects of the distinctive peer cultures found across two closely linked settings observed across multiple years, and interprets relationships between children's social dynamics and the cultural elements that serve and sustain them. Using the resources of the settings, changing cohorts of children reinvented a broad array of ways to show affiliation, signaling their status as a whole group of peers and marking what Corsaro (1985, p. 272) calls their "communal sharing." While Corsaro links such shared participation to children's resultant awareness of both peer culture and friendship, our suggestion is that these affiliation routines, rituals, and artifacts make their own unique contribution to children's establishment of themselves as a group with a distinctive status, that is, as children and peers.

In yearly reconstructions of inclusion-exclusion, in contrast, children always constructed and used more restricted resources to create and to control small group membership and participation. The centrality of using limited and controllable resources to monitor peer group play was made clear in the toddler teachers' well-intentioned but failed attempt to provide more shopping carts. Thus we saw diverse cultural elements serving two distinctive social dynamics, one manifested primarily at the whole group level and the other primarily at the small group level. Over time, each social dynamic came to be viewed as recurrent in both classrooms, though this was not immediately apparent to us, perhaps because the changing instantiations of each dynamic often looked so different (e.g., sticks in belts vs. throwing balls in the air, or wearing capes vs. creating forts). In terms of informing developmental aspects of peer culture theory, we saw that infants and toddlers evidence these same dynamics, but in ways reflecting their unique developmental status. The resources of newly developed sensorimotor schemes (e.g., throwing balls in the air), fascinating objects (e.g., shopping carts), and spaces small like themselves (e.g., forts) become the grounds for the formation of a nascent peer culture. Corsaro (1985) argued that the ongoing group nature of preschool life made it a likely venue for children's initial peer culture. Findings such as ours, as well as recent work in Italian infant-toddler centers (Corsaro & Emiliani, 1992; Corsaro & Molinari, 1990) extend the logic to argue that children may experience an even earlier first peer culture.

The research context of our work frames and makes possible these interpretations. The continuing involvement of the researchers over several years provided the opportunity to see multiple peer cultures constructed and reconstructed in two stable settings and to continue to interpret and reinterpret these peer cultures as our understandings evolved. The close relationship between the two classrooms allows for a developmental view of peer culture: peer culture can be studied longitudinally, as children move from one setting to the other, and cross-sectionally, as differently aged classes of children are compared at particular points in time.

Having seen these recurrent social dynamics and their early develop-ment in settings that are closely linked and consistent across years, we wonder whether these findings are specific to our settings or are more generally a part of children's peer culture in other early childhood set-tings. While a complete review of the relative correspondence across peer culture studies is beyond the scope of this chapter, we note that several ethnographic studies of early childhood settings (including our own) de-scribe certain peer culture phenomena in similar ways, for example, the construction of "outsiders" (Hatch, 1988; Massoulos, 1988; Scott, 1992), children's gatekeeping during play (Corsaro, 1985; LaMonte, 1988), and the sensorimotor/peer culture routines of Italian and American toddlers (Corsaro & Emiliani, 1992; Whaley & Rubenstein, 1994).

More broadly, the growing body of peer culture findings provides a dis-tinctive lens and research knowledge-base to help us understand early childhood classrooms—one that complements and, at times, challenges traditional early childhood literatures. The general compatibility and use-fulness of a sociocultural perspective to understanding group educational settings is argued and demonstrated elsewhere (e.g., Marshall, 1992; Fer-nie & Kantor, 1994). Here we can illustrate this point specifically by revis-iting the examples we have discussed. In one of the whole group affiliation examples, preschoolers wore and carried red rhythm sticks as markers of their shared status with others. In the traditional literature, such object use is valued for the practice in making symbolic transformations and for the cognitive flexibility provided when children pretend that sticks are fire hoses or even a horse to ride (Piaget, 1952; Vygotsky, 1978). Yet it was the frequent absence of observable symbolic use of the sticks that clued Elgas (1988) to the social uses of these objects. The toddler examples of throw-ing balls up in the air and pushing shopping carts would be valued for the development of sensorimotor schemes and a developing knowledge of how the object world operates. Yet viewing such behavior through a pri-marily cognitive lens may obscure its social aspects and the meanings of such shared constructions and routines for children.

A peer culture perspective also offers a purview different from that of much of the extant social literature. For example, the toddler activities would be seen as parallel play, a form of play that is fairly asocial, in Parten's (1932) classic descriptions of social participation. In her work, it is not until associative and cooperative play typical of four- and five-year-olds is observed that the group nature of children's play is recog-nized. The paucity of socially focused, naturalistic research in everyday group settings for very young children reinforces this prevailing view. We interpret our examples of affiliation and inclusion-exclusion in toddler play as showing a much more sophisticated ability to signal and sustain both whole group and small group membership than is indicated in Par-ten's work.

By contrasting these two classic perspectives with our findings, we are not implying that they are wrong and we are right. The point is that these traditional lenses not only describe but delimit what we look for and what we see as children play. The implication is that only a multiple perspective can give us the broader view of the richness, complexity, and diverse meanings of children's play.

While the importance of understanding peer culture is clear to us, it is equally clear that much more about it needs to be understood. Understanding children's worlds, as they construct and interpret them, helps teachers and other adults to accomplish more appropriate responses and stances toward peer culture—to know which actions to support, which to stay out of, what to acknowledge, and what to leave alone. Within this research context, over time, across settings and ages, and through dialogue, our understanding of children's play and peer culture is coming into clearer focus, helping us to see the complexities of young children's social worlds and the multiple meanings of their behavior within them.

REFERENCES

Bredekamp, S. (1987). *Developmentally appropriate practice in early childhood programs serving children from birth through age 8*. Washington, D.C.: National Association for the Education of Young Children.

Corsaro, W. A. (1985). *Friendship and peer culture in the early years*. Norwood, N.J.: Ablex.

Corsaro, W. A. (1988). Routines in the peer culture of American and Italian nursery school children. *Sociology of Education, 61*, 1–14.

Corsaro, W. A., & Molinari, L. (1990). From *seggiolini* to *discussione*: The generation and extension of peer culture among Italian preschool children. *Qualitative Studies in Education, 3* (3), 213–230.

Corsaro, W. A., & Emiliani, F. (1992). Child care, early education, and children's peer culture in Italy. In M. Lamb, K. Sternberg, C.-P. Hwang, & A. Broberg, (Eds.), *Child care in context* (pp. 81–115). Hillsdale, N.J.: Erlbaum.

Elgas, P. M. (1988). *The construction of preschool peer culture: The role of objects and play styles*. Unpublished doctoral dissertation, Ohio State University, Columbus.

Elgas, P., Klein, E., Kantor, R., & Fernie, D. (1988). Play and the peer culture: Play styles and object use. *Journal of Research in Childhood Education, 3*, 142–153.

Fernie, D., Davies, B., Kantor, R., & MacMurray, P. (1993). Learning to be a person in the preschool: Creating integrated gender, school culture, and peer culture positionings. *Qualitative Studies in Education, 6* (2), 95–110.

Fernie, D., & Kantor, R. (1994). Viewed through a prism: The enterprise of early childhood in education. In S. Goffin & D. Day (Eds.), *New perspectives on early childhood teacher education* (pp. 156–166). New York: Teachers College Press.

Green, J., & Harker, J. (1982). Gaining access to learning: Conversational, social, and cognitive demands of group participation. In L. Cherry-Wilkinson (Ed.), *Communication in classrooms*. New York: Academic Press.

Green, J., & Wallat, C. (Eds.) (1981). *Ethnography and language in educational settings*. Norwood, N.J.: Ablex.

Hatch, J. A. (1988). Learning to be an outsider: Peer stigmatization in kindergarten. *Urban Review, 20* (1), 59–72.

Heath, S. B. (1983). *Ways with words*. Cambridge: Cambridge University Press.

Kantor, R., Elgas, P., & Fernie, D. (1989). First the look and then the sound: Creating conversation at circle time. *Early Childhood Research Quarterly, 4* (4), 443–448.

Kantor, R., Elgas, P., & Fernie, D. (1993). Cultural knowledge and social competence within a preschool peer culture group. *Early Childhood Research Quarterly, 8*, 125–147.

LaMonte, A. (1988). *Understanding block play within children's social worlds*. Unpublished masters thesis, Ohio State University, Columbus.

Lubeck, S. (1985). *Sandbox society*. London: Falmer Press.

Marshall, H. H. (1992). *Redefining student learning*. Norwood, N.J.: Ablex.

Massoulos, C. G. (1988). *Acceptance and rejection of friendships in peer culture within an early childhood setting: An observational study approach*. Unpublished doctoral dissertation, Ohio State University, Columbus.

Miller, S. (1991). *Distinctive pathways to literacy in a preschool*. Unpublished doctoral dissertation, Ohio State University, Columbus.

Parten, M. (1932). Social participation among preschool children. *Journal of Abnormal and Social Psychology, 27*, 243–269.

Piaget, J. (1952). *The language and thought of the child*. London: Routledge and Kegan Paul.

Scott, J. (1991). *The social construction of "outsiders" status in preschool*. Unpublished doctoral dissertation, Ohio State University, Columbus.

Vygotsky, L. (1978). *Mind in society*. Cambridge, Mass.: Harvard University Press.

Whaley, K., & Rubenstein, T. S. (1994). How toddlers "do" friendship: A descriptive analysis of naturally occurring friendships in a group child care setting. *Journal of Social and Personal Relationships, 11*, 383–400.

Williams, D. (1988). *The complexities of small group process for beginning preschoolers*. Unpublished masters thesis, Ohio State University, Columbus.

Chapter 10 ───────────────────────

Toward a Stronger Teacher Voice in Research: A Collaborative Study of Antibias Early Education

Beth Blue Swadener and
Monica Miller Marsh

INTRODUCTION

> Much of qualitative research has reproduced, if contradiction-filled,
> a colonizing discourse of the "Other."
>
> —Michelle Fine (1994)

In this chapter, we draw from our work in antibias curriculum as a vehicle
for examining a number of issues in collaborative action research, an
approach to qualitative inquiry being increasingly utilized in early childhood research. We argue that among the groups often "othered" by early
childhood research, ironically, are both children and teachers. We believe
that authentically co-constructed research, in which early childhood educators collaborate directly in each step of the research process, is one
way to move the teacher's voice, and often the children's, from the margins to the center (hooks, 1984) of qualitative research.

Following a brief review of the literature on collaborative research in
early childhood settings and a framing of the contexts for antibias pedagogy in early childhood, we share individual stories and dialogue, drawing from our collaborative research experiences. Much of the chapter
unfolds through our stories about how the collaboration evolved, ways
in which we have benefited from this ongoing project, and barriers to
both antibias pedagogy and teacher research in early childhood settings,

including public schools. Finally, we raise a number of issues and make recommendations concerning both antibias approaches in early childhood and qualitative research methodologies that attempt to put early childhood educators at the center of the research process.

In terms of the theoretical framework and praxis of our work, we have been influenced by the work of such teacher-researchers and collaborative writers as Janet Miller (1990), Marilyn Cochran-Smith (1991), Vivian Gussin Paley (1984, 1989), Bill Ayers (1989, 1992, 1993), Mara Sapon-Shevin (1992, 1994), Mary Lou Holly (1989), Gloria Ladson-Billings (1990), Ken Zeichner (1991), and Michelle Fine (1990, 1994). We have also been influenced by the "literacy for empowerment" work of Lisa Delpit (1986, 1988), Concha Delgato-Gaitan (1990, 1993), Betsy Quintero (1994), and Denny Taylor (1989, 1991), and by Peter Reason's (1994) recent summary of qualitative approaches to participative and cooperative inquiry. This collective work, which has begun to move teachers and teacher-researchers' voices to the foreground of the scholarly discourse, draws from interpretive theory, phenomenology, life history and autobiographical work, culture centric and social reconstructionist conceptual frameworks, and provides examples of many ways in which early childhood educators are collaborating for empowerment and struggling for curricular and pedagogical transformation.

As Bill Ayers (1992) writes: "Recovering the voice of the teacher—usually a woman, increasingly a person of color, often a member of the working poor—is an essential part of reconceptualizing the field of early childhood education" (p. 266). We share the view that *authentic* collaboration with teachers and listening to what early childhood teachers, parents, and other caregivers have to tell us are essential in the enactment of an antibias, culturally inclusive early education (Swadener, Cahill, Marsh, & Arnold, 1994).

It is equally vital to recover, and listen to, the voice and perspective of children—particularly children who are not members of the dominant culture, as Lisa Delpit's (1986, 1988) discussion of the culture of power and emergent literacy analyzes. For several years at the annual meeting of the American Anthropological Association, sessions entitled "Through Children's Eyes and in Children's Voices" have sought to present ethnographic research on children in various cultural contexts, formal and informal education settings, and in family and community interactions. This body of work has served to expand the methodological and interpretive frame of early childhood research. Papers and participatory sessions at the annual "Reconceptualizing Research, Theory, and Practice in Early Childhood Education" conferences (of 1991–94) and the edited volume *Reconceptualizing the Early Childhood Curriculum: Beginning the Dialogue* (Kessler & Swadener, 1992) have served to broaden the dialogue and include more voices and perspectives of early childhood researchers, including teacher-researchers.

Our collaborative work is part of a growing reconceptualization of research in early childhood education, in that it is situated in contemporary theoretical frameworks (phenomenological, feminist, and interpretive) struggling to find a greater voice in the early childhood literature. Additionally, given the focus of this collaborative case study on antibias pedagogy and curriculum, our work falls within the framework described by Sleeter and Grant (1987) as education that is multicultural and social reconstructionist, an area which is beginning to gain momentum in early childhood theory and practice.

NEED FOR ANTIBIAS EARLY EDUCATION

According to census information and demographic predictions, by the year 2000, one out of three Americans will be a person of color, and at least fifty-three U.S. cities will be predominantly non-white (*Education Week*, May, 1986). Immigration is now the major source of population growth in the United States, with over fourteen million foreign-born people living in the United States in the early 1980s, and between eleven million and thirteen million added for the decade (Carrol and Schensul, 1990). By the end of the 1990s, many schools will have a majority of students of color; however, the percentage of teachers of color has not kept pace with increasing student diversity.

These statistics call for a reconceptualization of the educational process in U.S. schools (Marsh, 1992). In order for educators to meet the challenges of the 1990s and beyond, they need to acknowledge that racism, sexism, ableism, classism, and heterosexism exist in their lives and schools. We share the view that these issues need to be confronted by early childhood educators on both a personal and professional level, and that all students need to be engaged in activities that inform them about these social issues in authentic and developmentally appropriate ways. We believe students should be empowered to discuss, explore, and take action to make lasting social changes. Failure to meet the needs of all students could cause serious societal repercussions, including an increase in the high incidence of school dropouts and "push outs" (Fine, 1990), the miseducation of many poor children, children of color, and privileged children (Arnold & Swadener, 1993), and the creation of a generation of adults who will not be adequately prepared to compete in our rapidly changing society. Inequities in funding and curriculum (Kozol, 1991) add to the number of people in the United States who are living on the margins of dominant society and "in the shadows of democracy" (Polakow, 1992, 1993).

One comprehensive approach to curriculum that addresses the diverse needs of America's school-age children is antibias pedagogy and curriculum. Antibias curriculum is an integrated approach that attempts to be culturally inclusive and proactive in examining, in developmentally appropriate ways, forms of bias, stereotyping, and misinformation that contribute to a climate of oppression. It is based on children's developmental tasks children use to construct identity and attitudes about themselves and others. Antibias curriculum not only addresses the race and ethnicity of a child, but includes the dimensions of gender, language, religious diversity, sexual orientation, physical and mental ableness, and class. Antibias curriculum challenges existing prejudices, stereotypes, and discriminatory behavior and attitudes in young children's development and interactions, just at a time when they are being internalized. Not unlike multicultural education, which grew out of the multicultural and ethnic studies movements of the 1960s and 1970s, antibias curriculum incorporates lessons and activities that directly address cultural diversity.

Although many early childhood educators and child and family advocates have embraced multicultural education (Ramsey & Derman-Sparks, 1992) and have struggled to create more culturally compatible and inclusive programs for children from diverse backgrounds, it has only been within the past decade that a concerted effort to promote antibias education in early childhood (i.e., preschool through primary) has been initiated. Antibias education extends earlier work in human relations and multicultural education which often took an additive or "tourist" approach, focusing on holidays, festivals, foods, distant cultures, and customs (Derman-Sparks, 1989). The danger of becoming a "tourist" curriculum (Derman-Sparks, 1989) is lessened as antibias activities are infused into all units of study. Antibias curriculum goals are to "enable every child to construct a knowledgeable, confident self identity; to develop a comfortable, empathetic and just interaction with diversity; and to develop critical thinking and the skills for standing up for oneself in the face of injustice" (Derman-Sparks, 1989, p. ix).

Following the publication of *Anti-Bias Curriculum: Tools for Empowering Young Children* (Derman-Sparks, 1989), a small but growing network of early childhood educators committed to implementing antibias curriculum with young children has been organized. During the past decade, several early childhood research studies, employing qualitative methodologies and including the research described in this chapter, have been conducted (e.g., Ayers, 1989; Jones & Derman-Sparks, 1992; Marsh, 1992; Paley, 1984; Ramsey, 1987; Romero, 1991; Swadener, 1988; Swadener, Cahill, Marsh, & Arnold, 1994; Whaley & Swadener, 1990).

In order to understand better the strengths and limitations of implementing antibias curriculum with kindergarten children (ages 4–6 years), our collaborative action research study was undertaken. This study systematically analyzed the nature and quality of antibias activities which were planned and implemented in the classroom. Additionally, we examined the many ways in which young children raised antibias issues in their informal play, discussions, and interactions.

OUR EVOLVING COLLABORATION

In this section, we utilize a dialogue format to discuss how our research collaboration evolved and describe more fully the study we completed during the first year that Monica implemented an antibias curriculum in her urban/suburban kindergarten classroom. This section will raise issues to be considered in conducting teacher research and collaborative case studies in early childhood settings. Monica describes our evolving collaboration first, followed by Beth's interpretation.

Monica: During the summer of 1990, I had many things on my mind. In addition to planning an October wedding, I was making a job transition. In the fall I would be teaching in a new school district and making the switch from fifth grade to kindergarten. As if that wasn't enough, I was contemplating the number of ways I could fulfill the requirements for a master's thesis.

I had first heard of Dr. Swadener from a friend and fellow graduate student, Julie. Julie shared a copy of the *Anti-Bias Curriculum: Tools for Empowering Young Children* (Derman-Sparks, 1989), which was being used in her class, with me. We would often discuss the topics that were being discussed in Dr. Swadener's class. Since I was interested in both early childhood and multicultural education, I decided to seek out Dr. Swadener and ask if she would be my thesis adviser.

Upon our initial meeting, Beth expressed how she had been looking for a collaborative teacher-researcher. She explained that she had just completed several projects which had evolved from a four-year collaboration with a Friends School teacher from Pennsylvania. Her work had included a two-year ethnographic study, the production of a videotape, as well as presentations and collaboratively written papers. Beth also explained that she had been in Ohio for less than one year. One of the major reasons for the move to a more urban area was to study attempts to implement education that is multicultural in culturally diverse public school settings.

The idea of collaborating with Beth sounded very enticing. However, I reiterated that I was looking for ideas for my master's thesis research and wanted to finish working on the thesis before I moved on to another project. Beth assured me that the thesis could be a collaborative venture. We agreed upon a one-year collaborative action research study that would focus on implementing antibias curriculum in my kindergarten classroom.

Beth: When I first met Monica in June 1990, I also had many things on my mind. I had been looking for a potential collaborating teacher-researcher. I had just completed several projects which had evolved from a four-year collaboration with another early childhood teacher. That work had underscored the importance of documenting examples of positive/exemplary practice in the areas of human relations, conflict mediation, and education that is multicultural.

My research and teacher education interests were also continuing to evolve, emphasizing antibias, anti-oppression work; and by this time, several women colleagues and I had started an Institute for Education that is Multicultural, focusing on staff development and school change in five Cleveland and Akron public elementary and middle schools. When Monica came to me looking for ideas for her master's research, and explained that she was particularly interested in exploring early childhood multicultural education approaches, I was delighted at the possibilities of collaboration. Monica's evolving interests in implementing an antibias curriculum in her kindergarten, combined with her willingness to be an active researcher during the coming academic year, were exciting. I was delighted at the possibilities of collaborating with her during her first year of teaching kindergarten. I have also been interested in ways in which curricula are created, contested, and enacted, and have taught courses and done research on the hidden or implicit curriculum in early childhood settings. Thus the idea of working with a teacher who was creating a year-long antibias curriculum was an appealing possibility indeed.

During that initial meeting, we discussed methods of documenting the first year of Monica's efforts to implement an antibias curriculum with her kindergarten children and their families. Monica decided to keep a daily journal of her personal and professional observations (based in many ways on the approach to teacher research recommended in Holly's 1989 book, *Writing to Grow: Keeping a Personal-Professional Journal*). Other sources of data would include the children's work, particularly journal entries and illustrations, videotaped highlights of free play and centers, and Beth's observations, which we intended would be both representative and "targeted" to times in which antibias topics would be likely to be discussed by the children, including some activities involving parents. Monica describes her responsibilities and emerging research questions next.

Monica: As the teacher-researcher, I would be responsible for keeping a professional journal. I would begin my journal on the first day of school and make daily entries. The journal entries would highlight children's reactions to and interactions during formal and spontaneous antibias lessons and activities. I would also raise questions, issues, and reflections to discuss with Beth.

As the university collaborator, Beth would be responsible for observing my teaching of selected antibias activities and recording the responses and interactions between the children and me. We established that, during her biweekly visits, she would serve as a participant observer, both working directly with the children and taking as many field notes as possible. The children generated another critical source of data as they illustrated and responded to selected antibias activities in their journals, through art work, and through both group discussion and informal interviews.

Observations would be made at various times throughout the school day (e.g., during learning centers and large-group activities, on the playground, and at snack). Additionally, some activities involving parents (e.g., alternative Thanksgiving potluck, play, picnic at end of the school year, etc.) would be observed. Data from the multiple sources would be collected and analyzed. We would look for recurring themes and begin making grounded inferences or posing further questions, based on our ongoing analysis of the data.

As the teacher-researcher, I formulated three basic questions which guided our study: (1) How do children from ethnically and racially diverse backgrounds respond to formal and spontaneous antibias curriculum? (2) What are ways in which children enact the antibias curriculum in their play, questions, interactions, and conversations? and (3) What are the experiences of the teacher who designs and implements antibias activities?

My ideas for antibias activities and lessons came from two major sources, the *Anti-Bias Curriculum: Tools for Empowering Young Children* (Derman-Sparks, 1989), and the children. The children generated many questions which led me to create and/or search for more activities that would meet their specific needs. Lessons and activities were designed around seventeen units of study, which were adapted according to the interests and needs of the children throughout the year. The units of study taught this first year, in order of presentation, were Getting Acquainted, I Am Special, Safety Is Important, Pioneers, Native Americans, Immigration, Friends from around the World, Knights and Castles, Resolutions, Cooperation and Peace, Tools and Simple Machines, Inventions, Careers, Space, Our Planet Earth, Plants, and Animals.

Beth: Over the course of the first year, we developed a workable pattern of meeting immediately after my classroom visits to discuss my notes, observations, Monica's journal entries from the previous week, and to brainstorm together future activities or extensions of activities consistent with an antibias approach. Looking back, our only regret about these frequent meetings was that we did not taperecord them. Since this time, as we have collaborated on three writing projects, we have taped and transcribed discussions and found these tapes to be quite valuable in capturing the spirit of our distinct voices and perspectives. Next, Monica discusses her perceptions of the research process.

Monica: I would anticipate Beth's scheduled observation time. We would meet immediately after her observations to discuss and clarify field notes. During this time we would brainstorm future activities or extensions of activities, share information related to the classroom, and plan for the next observation. I used Beth as a sounding board. I felt comfortable sharing the way the children were reacting to activities, as well as sharing the personal growth that I was experiencing as I challenged some of my own beliefs and confronted some of my misconceptions. Being new to the district, I often felt isolated, and I thrived on our conversations.

Journaling also served as an outlet for the frustration and isolation I often felt. As Holly (1989) describes, through keeping a journal, I watched myself grow. At first the entries consisted mainly of my fears and apprehensions about teaching antibias lessons and activities for the first time. As I grew more confident, I focused on the reactions and contributions of the children. Through making the daily journal entries, I was able to watch the children grow and mature. Patterns in their behavior and thinking began to emerge on paper that I never would have connected without the documentation to review and analyze.

Children's dictated journal entries proved to be invaluable to me. Through serving as a scribe for the entries and viewing the illustrations, I had insights into what was meaningful to the students. For example, many students had intense feelings about the war in the Persian Gulf and included comments about the war in their journals. The following excerpt was taken from Anna's journal. She dictated this entry to me on January 17, 1991:

On Tuesday night I went to a program at a church in honor of Martin Luther King's birthday. It was a very long program, and I got tired and hungry. There were lots of speakers talking about peace and why there should never again be war. There was beautiful singing by the choir. They sang "We Shall Overcome," and my mother cried. There was one song I knew, it was "Glory, Glory Hallelujah." The next morning I woke up and found out the war had started. I felt very sad because over there are mothers, fathers, and grandmas and grandpas getting killed by the bombs.

This information helped me to gauge what experiences, information, and perceptions the children were processing, as well as how they were interpreting these experiences.

Throughout the year, data from multiple sources were collected and analyzed. The information fell into five primary areas: (1) race and ethnicity, (2) gender and sexual orientation, (3) holidays and religious diversity, (4) individual differences, and (5) socioeconomic status. The data we had collected was categorized using these broad themes, grouped into information that would address each of the three broad questions guiding the study, and coded accordingly.

Several recurring themes began to emerge through a content analysis of my journal, the children's journal entries and drawings, Beth's field notes, and our discussions. These themes included: the children's high level of awareness and interest in antibias activities; their generation of spontaneous discussions and activities; the unconditional acceptance, on the whole, of one another, and the apprehension that I felt as I presented antibias materials and facilitated related activities for the first time.

SUCCESS AND CHALLENGES IN OUR COLLABORATIVE WORK

As we have reflected on the dynamics, successes, and challenges of our collaborative research, a number of themes of potential relevance to other early childhood teacher-researchers and university collaborators emerged. In this section we discuss some of the strengths and supportive aspects of our collaborative research, followed by some of the major challenges, barriers, and frustrations. These lead directly to our shared recommendations for others pursuing collaborative research or action research in early childhood settings.

The support of Monica's kindergarten parents and her principal was one of the greatest assets to the implementation of the antibias curriculum. Parents actively participated in activities such as a family tree/ethnic roots sharing; an alternative Thanksgiving potluck that focused on the diversity of families in the room and in the United States; and volunteering to be guest speakers to talk about their work, some of which represented non-traditional careers. Since a large number of students in Monica's classroom came from Jewish backgrounds, which were not completely familiar to her, Monica relied on parents to educate her about their religious practice and customs.

Monica's principal, who was African-American, was also very supportive of an antibias curriculum. She was willing to discuss ideas and make changes in policy when Monica presented evidence from the children. For example, the kindergarten classes were excluded from an assembly which was to be a tribute to Dr. Martin Luther King, Jr. The principal felt that the simulation of bus boycotts and sit-ins by older children would be "too advanced for kindergarten children to understand." After Monica shared some of the children's journal entries and pictures pertaining to class discussions and activities concerning the civil rights movement, her principal agreed that these children did have an understanding of social justice. The kindergarten teachers were then given the option to attend the assembly. As the year progressed, Monica's principal became an advocate of the antibias approach and encouraged antibias activities throughout the school.

Children were a source of many spontaneous or informal antibias activities and discussions. During the Getting Acquainted unit, for example, each child had a "superstar day." On their superstar day, they acquired the position of line leader, brought in some of their favorite things to share, and provided snacks for the rest of the children. The following excerpt is taken from Monica's journal, dated September 15, 1990:

Jack, who brought in a snack for his superstar day, told the class that he had brought in bagels. I heard the following conversation.

Jack: "Bagels are a Jewish snack. I brought them in to celebrate Rosh Hashanah."

Sean: "What?"

Larry: "I've had bagels before."

Meredith: "I've eaten bagels before, and I'm not Jewish."

We briefly discussed ethnic foods and the fact that many of the foods that we eat originated in other countries. They seem to be very interested.

As collaborators, our roles, relationship, and "power lines" evolved from a professor/adviser and graduate student relationship to one of *full colleagueship*. As we have continued our collaborative growth, we have presented together at both national and international conferences, we have co-authored papers, and Monica has published a book chapter drawn from her master's thesis. Monica has guest lectured in Beth's social studies methods course, and we have co-facilitated workshops for primary teachers, as part of a larger project to help teachers identify exceptional potential in underrepresented populations. We have traveled together to a number of conferences, including participating together in two early childhood collaborative training seminars in Nairobi, Kenya, and plan to continue our work together in the foreseeaable future. Thus our relationship is a committed and trusting one, and we have become strong allies.

Our struggle to transcend some unequal power relations (e.g., mentor/student) relates to our shared concern that teachers' stories, reflections, action research, and other professional and scholarly work need a greater voice and enhanced visibility. The fact that this research began as Monica's master's thesis project was one way to help ensure her ownership and authorship of the research. Beth, as a university researcher, had moved from the center of the project, or the "principal investigator" role, to the background, as a consulting collaborator.

One of the greatest strengths of authentic collaborative partnerships is the reciprocal nature of the work. As mentioned earlier, Monica was a frequent guest speaker for preservice teachers. Her classroom served, in some ways, as a "laboratory" for activities and curriculum theories that Beth was advocating and teaching about in early childhood methods courses. Beth served as a sounding board, and also a source of journal references, conference papers, and other information which Monica was interested in, but had less time to pursue. We have also engaged in ongoing self-examination, as part of our work on unlearning oppression and interrogating white privilege and other equity issues (e.g., Swadener, Cahill, Marsh, & Arnold, 1994).

In summary, Monica's communication with parents, her principal, and her university collaborator all served to break down the isolation so typical in teaching in a self-contained classroom or program. This processing of events, issues, and challenges provided needed *structures of support* for doing research.

In terms of the challenges, shortcomings, and concerns we faced in this project, a major challenge was the lack of materials and other curricular resources for creating antibias education with young children. Time was also a major pressure on both of us. Monica needed time to create and plan for the activities she would infuse into the existing curriculum, involve parents and other community resources, make daily journal entries, meet with Beth, and complete her thesis. Zeichner (1990) and others have discussed some of the internal contradictions of many so-called "teacher empowerment" strategies (e.g., site-based management, Professional Development School initiatives, etc.). These often hidden barriers include the increased time demands without a release from other demands, or "load building." Having less time often accompanies an increase in genuine decision making or power.

Other barriers or concerns that we, and particularly Monica, faced included the lack of support, particularly financial, for the dissemination of Monica's research. For example, her district allotted $11.00 for her share of the gas on a round-trip from Kent, Ohio to Philadelphia to present a paper at a national research meeting. Colleagues and some administrators seemed to have trouble understanding why she would want to engage in research as a classroom teacher. This lack of professional understanding, encouragement, and support may be even greater in preprimary settings such as child care centers and preschools, where funds are typically extremely tight, with paid planning time or encouragement of teacher research rare.

Another issue that we identified as a limitation of our collaborative work was that, although we differed in age and background experiences, we were both European-American, middle-class women, which in itself biased our perspectives and influenced our ability to interrogate and interpret our shared data. In fact, when we were asked to write a book chapter examining some of the issues that our work on antibias curriculum addressed, we expanded the "writing team" to include a woman of color. In terms of looking at different classroom situations from multiple perspectives, this more inclusive collaborative effort definitely took our work to a deeper level of cultural meaning and self-interrogation. Monica's assistant teacher is African-American, and her interpretation of many of the events and conversations in the classroom was also invaluable to our collaboration.

Other issues that proved problematic to Monica's research included the isolation she faced as a teacher in one of only two "special" self-contained classrooms in her school. These two classrooms also happened to be isolated in one wing of an "open school" building. Monica's kindergarten class was referred to as the "enriched kindergarten." Participation in this program was based, in part, on children's demonstrated intellectual potential. Each child must score 2 standard deviations above the mean on a standardized assessment to qualify. Since the district provided only half-day services for kindergarten children, parents in the enriched kindergarten paid tuition for afternoon services.

Teachers choosing to implement antibias curriculum, as well as teachers engaged in any action research project, need opportunities to discuss ideas and concerns with one another. Monica describes the feeling of professional isolation she felt as the children from one of the other kindergarten classes in her school went running down the hall in their freshly made "Indian" headbands making "whooping" noises: "I had just spent the entire week helping my class unlearn these stereotypes about Native Americans." It would be less frustrating and mutually beneficial for teachers implementing antibias curriculum within the same school to identify themselves and meet on a regular basis. These meetings would allow teachers to share thoughts and concerns, brainstorm and revise the curriculum, and provide support for one another. Similar to the movement toward "peer supervision" and "teacher empowerment," such a support system might also provide ways for teachers to observe each other's antibias lessons and activities, and provide each other with the kind of feedback Beth was able to provide Monica.

As described earlier, writing in her journal also served as an outlet for the frustration and isolation that Monica often felt. Again, however, time and other pressures need to be recognized and addressed. While Monica was collecting data for her thesis, the purpose of making daily journal entries was more "apparent." In the second year of our collaboration, and of her use of the antibias curriculum, her journal entries became more intermittent. As we discussed this, the analogy of an exercise program seemed appropriate. It is often hard to begin and maintain a new exercise regimen without a partner. Similarly, having a "committed listener," genuinely interested in your research and classroom dilemmas and successes, is one way to maintain enthusiasm and follow-through with classroom research.

Once committed to antibias curriculum, Monica found that most of her time was spent searching for and planning activities. Monica learned on the job which types of antibias activities worked best with her students. Monica argues elsewhere (Marsh, 1992) that preservice coursework and field experiences in antibias education should be required for teachers so that educators would feel more confident teaching an antibias, culturally inclusive curriculum, and would have more accurate information readily available. We advocate the development of a clearinghouse similar to the national data bases for bilingual and migrant education which would make it less difficult for educators to access antibias materials and curricular ideas.

The teacher who chooses to implement antibias curriculum is a risk-taker on both a professional and personal level. Personal limitations include admitting that there is much we still needed to learn in order to present accurate information and authentic experiences. To fully implement antibias pedagogy with any age level, one must be willing to examine long-held assumptions about diverse cultures, and to acknowledge ways in which we can all stand in the shoes of both the victim and the oppressor. For us, an interrogation of white privilege and class background, a deepened understanding of the Afrocentric curriculum movement, research on religious practices including holiday observances, and a closer listening to parents and children were all essential to our shared exploration of antibias education.

Our research findings indicated that the young children in Monica's class were very aware of differences in color, gender, religious orientation, physical ableness, and socioeconomic status. The knowledge they possessed seemed to have been transmitted largely through the media and the beliefs and values of their immediate families (Marsh, 1992). The children's level of awareness and interest in certain issues led to the spontaneous generation of many discussions and activities. This evidence indicated that young children are indeed "ready" for antibias curriculum, if this curriculum is facilitated in developmentally appropriate as well as authentic ways.

RECOMMENDATIONS FOR COLLABORATIVE RESEARCH IN EARLY CHILDHOOD SETTINGS

In this final section, we make a number of recommendations concerning ways in which early childhood teachers can find a stronger voice in the research literature and can be empowered to conduct collaborative action research. In this section, we take a brief, "developmental" look at ways to encourage and support teacher research.

Increasingly, preservice teacher education courses require students to keep journals, and some programs have moved toward an integrated journal (across subject matter areas and field experiences). Long used in student teaching, the early encouragement of personal-professional journal keeping is a way to increase the likelihood that new teachers will be interested in conducting research such as that described in this chapter. In early childhood education, an excellent example of the role of both daily journal entries and frequent audiotaping is found in the work of master teacher Vivian Gussin Paley (1984, 1989).

An additional approach that may encourage an interest in teacher research is found in the growing number of programs that require a senior thesis, individual investigation, or other action research project during student teaching or final teaching internships. Another example, from the Alternative Teacher Education Program at Kent State University, is a "Learning To Teach Autobiography." Some programs, such as the field-based Interdisciplinary M.Ed. program at National-Louis University and the M.A.T. programs at Kent State University, build in a sequence of curriculum and teacher research courses and related experiences, culminating in teachers carrying out an action research project in their classrooms. Such programs involve a relatively small cohort of inservice teachers who serve as each other's support system over the duration of one to two years. Another example of a group of teachers who came together in the context of their graduate work and have continued to meet for over five years can be found in the work of Janet Miller, *Creating Spaces, Finding Voices: Teachers Collaborating for Change* (1990).

Early childhood educators and their supervisors or administrators need to make action research a priority. Observing the interactions and listening to the verbal exchanges that take place between children is a "natural" role of the early childhood teacher, whether in a lab school setting or a public school. Documenting and sharing this information with other educators, administrators, researchers, and future teachers encourages professional dialogue. Through dialogue teachers can identify similar problems and begin to generate workable solutions. Teachers are empowered as they take ownership of their concerns and work together to help one another. In order for this type of research and professional development to take place, teachers must be given the time and encouragement to carry out their research, observe each other's classrooms, and meet with one another.

Additionally, teachers should be made aware of the outlets for early education scholarship and be actively involved in writing and submitting presentation proposals at regional and national conferences. If the reconceptualization of research in early childhood education is to avoid reproducing patterns of marginalizing the perspectives, experiences, and voices of early childhood educators, as much of the previous research has done, active efforts must be directed to the "full inclusion" of teachers and caregivers in the conceptualization and interpretation of research. Collaboration with university or other researchers and writers is one vehicle for helping to ensure greater participation of early childhood educators in the research and policy discourse.

Our collaborative study also suggests a number of avenues for future research. There has been a paucity of research in the area of using the antibias approach with young learners. There is a need for further research, particularly in the primary grades. Collaborative research is one way in which teacher researchers and university collaborators can work together to identify and analyze critical incidents and classroom data (Cochran-Smith & Lytle, 1988; Cochran-Smith, 1991; Swadener & Piekielek, 1992).

A second direction that research might take is to investigate how children from both ethnically and racially diverse backgrounds respond to antibias activities in a more typical kindergarten class. The antibias lessons and activities should be investigated at multiple sites in heterogeneous as well as homogeneous settings. The children in Monica's kindergarten classroom were assessed and admitted to the enriched kindergarten program based on their intellectual potential. Characteristics such as advanced understanding, exceptional use if knowledge, and a high level of concern regarding social justice were also exhibited by Monica's children throughout the year. Thus the children's responses to antibias curriculum may not be representative of a more typical kindergarten population and must be viewed in the context of this program.

Finally, there is a need for further exploration of how one's life history affects the way antibias curriculum is approached. Research needs to be conducted addressing how specific characteristics and qualities, gender, socioeconomic status, and cultural background impact the way antibias curriculum is taught by an individual. Findings from this type of study would help educators to define certain areas of focus that might be more meaningful for them. Teachers could benefit from sharing life experiences and perspectives. In terms of antibias and culturally sensitive early education, it would seem logical that as many life experiences and perspectives as possible should be included in the debate and discussion of research in early childhood education. Such full inclusion of diverse teacher and parent voices, not to mention children's voices, will enrich our understanding of the multiple contexts of early childhood education in ways we can only begin to imagine.

REFERENCES

Arnold, M. S., & Swadener, B. B. (1993). *Savage inequalities* and the discourse of risk: What of the white children who have so much green grass? *The Review of Education, 15,* 261–272.

Ayers, W. (1989). *The good preschool teacher: Six teachers reflect on their lives*. New York: Teachers College Press.

Ayers, W. (1992). Disturbances from the field: Recovering the voice of the early childhood teacher. In S. A. Kessler & B. B. Swadener (Eds.), *Reconceptualizing the early childhood curriculum: Beginning the dialogue* (pp. 256–266). New York: Teachers College Press.

Ayers, W. (1993). *To teach: The journey of a teacher*. New York: Teachers College Press.

Bloch, M. N. (1991). Critical science and the history of child development's influence on early education research. *Early Education and Development, 2* (2), 95–108.

Carroll, T., & Schensul, J. (1990). Visions in America in the 1990s and beyond: Negotiating cultural diversity and educational change. *Education and Urban Society, 22* (4), 339–345.

Cochran-Smith, M. (1991). Learning to teach against the grain. *Harvard Educational Review, 61* (3), 279–309.

Cochran-Smith, M., & Lytle, S. (1988, February). *Teacher research: Contrasting perspectives on collaboration and critique*. Paper presented at the Ethnography and Education Research Forum, Philadelphia.

Delgato-Gaitan, C. (1990). *Literacy for empowerment: The role of parents in children's education*. New York: Falmer Press.

Delgato-Gaitan, C. (1993). Researching change, changing the researcher. *Harvard Educational Review, 63* (4), 389–411.

Delpit, L. (1986). Skills and other dilemmas of a progressive black educator. *Harvard Educational Review, 56* (4), 379–385.

Delpit, L. (1988). Power and pedagogy in educating other people's children. *Harvard Educational Review, 58* (1), 54–84.

Derman-Sparks, L. (1989). *Anti-bias curriculum: Tools for empowering young children*. Washington, D.C.: National Association for the Education of Young Children.

Education Week. (1986, May). Today's numbers, tomorrow's nation, p. 14.

Fine, M. (1990). *Framing dropouts: Notes on the politics of an urban high school*. Albany: State University of New York Press.

Fine, M. (1994). Working the hyphens: Reinventing self and other in qualitative research. In N. K. Denzin & Y. S. Lincoln (Eds.), *Handbook of qualitative research*. Thousand Oaks, Calif.: Sage.

Holly, M. L. (1989). *Writing to grow: Keeping a personal-professional journal*. Portsmouth, N.H.: Heinemann.

hooks, b. (1984). *Feminist theory: From margin to center*. Boston: South End Press.

Jacob, E. (1989, November). *Children creating culture: Cooperative learning in a multiethnic elementary school*. Paper presented at the annual meeting of the American Anthropological Association, Washington, D.C.

Jones, E., & Derman-Sparks, L. (1992). Meeting the challenge of diversity. *Young Children, 47* (2), 12–18.

Kessler, S. A., & Swadener, B. B. (Eds.) (1992). *Reconceptualizing the early childhood curriculum: Beginning the dialogue*. New York: Teachers College Press.

Kozol, J. (1991). *Savage inequalities: Children in America's schools*. New York: Crown.

Ladson-Billings, G. (1990, April). *Making a little magic: Teachers' talk about successful teaching strategies for black children*. Paper presented at the annual meeting of the American Educational Research Association, Boston.

Marsh, M. M. (1992). Implementing anti-bias curriculum in the kindergarten classroom. In S. A. Kessler & B. B. Swadener (Eds.), *Reconceptualizing the early childhood curriculum: Beginning the dialogue* (pp. 267–288). New York: Teachers College Press.

Miller, J. (1990). *Creating spaces, finding voices: Teachers collaborating for change*. Albany: State University of New York Press.

Paley, V. G. (1984). *Boys and girls: Superheroes in the doll corner*. Chicago: University of Chicago Press.

Paley, V. G. (1989). *White teacher*. Cambridge, Mass.: Harvard University Press.

Polakow, V. (1992). Deconstructing the discourse of care: Young children in the shadows of democracy. In S. A. Kessler & B. B. Swadener (Eds.), *Reconceptualizing the early childhood curriculum: Beginning the dialogue* (pp. 123–148). New York: Teachers College Press.

Polakow, V. (1993). *Lives on the edge: Single mothers and their children in the other America*. Chicago: University of Chicago Press.

Quintero, E., & Rummel, M. K. (1994). Voice unaltered: Marginalized young writers speak. In B. B. Swadener & S. Lubeck (Eds.), *Children and families "at promise": Reconstructing the discourse of risk*. Albany: State University of New York Press.

Ramsey, P. (1987). *Teaching and learning in a diverse world*. New York: Teachers College Press.

Ramsey, P., & Derman-Sparks, L. (1992). Multicultural education reaffirmed. *Young Children, 47* (2), 10–11.

Reason, P. (1994). Three approaches to participative inquiry. In N. Denzin & Y. Lincoln (Eds.), *Handbook of qualitative research* (pp. 324–339). Thousand Oaks, Calif.: Sage.

Romero, M. (1991). Work and play in the nursery school. In L. Weis et al. (Eds.), *Critical perspectives on early childhood education* (pp. 119–138). Albany: State University of New York Press.

Sapon-Shevin, M. (1992). Celebrating diversity, creating community: Curriculum that honors and builds on difference. In S. Stainback & B. Stainback (Eds.), *Adapting the regular classroom curriculum: Enhancing student success in inclusive classrooms*. Baltimore, Md.: Paul H. Brooklee.

Sapon-Shevin, M. (1994). *Playing favorites: Gifted education and the disruption of community*. Albany: State University of New York Press.

Sleeter, C., & Grant, C. (1987). An analysis of multicultural education in the United States. *Harvard Educational Review, 57* (4), 421–444.

Swadener, E. B. (1988). Implementing education that is multicultural in early childhood settings: A case study of two day care programs. *Urban Review, 2* (1), 8–27.

Swadener, B. B., & Piekielek, D. (1992). Beyond democracy to consensus: Reflections on a Friends school collaborative ethnography. In S. A. Kessler & B. B.

Swadener (Eds.), *Reconceptualizing the early childhood curriculum: Beginning the dialogue* (pp. 227–255). New York: Teachers College Press.

Swadener, B. B., Cahill, B., Marsh, M. M., & Arnold, M. S. (1994). Cultural and gender identity in early childhood: Anti-bias, culturally inclusive pedagogy with young learners. In C. A. Grant (Ed.), *In praise of diversity: A resource book for multicultural education.* New York: Allyn & Bacon.

Taylor, D. (1991). *Learning denied.* Portsmouth, N.H.: Heinemann.

Taylor, D., & Dorsey-Gaines, C. (1989). *Growing up literate: Learning from inner city families.* Portsmouth, N.H.: Heinemann.

Whaley, K., & Swadener, E. B. (1990). Multicultural education in infant and toddler settings. *Childhood Education, 66* (4), 48–50.

Witherell, C., & Noddings, N. (Eds.) (1991). *Stories lives tell: Narrative and dialogue in education.* New York: Teachers College Press.

Zeichner, K. (1990, April). *Contradictions in the professionalization of teaching and the democratization of schools.* Paper presented at the annual meeting of the American Educational Research Association, Boston.

Chapter 11

Multiple Voices, Contexts, and Methods: Making Choices in Qualitative Evaluation in Early Childhood Education Settings

Mary Jo McGee-Brown

> *Interviewer*: So what did you like best?
> *Child*: My mouth is tired.
> *Interviewer*: Your mouth is tired?
> *Child*: Yeah.
> *Interviewer*: You don't want to talk any more?
> *Child*: Nah.
> —excerpt from graduate student interview with five-year-old, 1989

INTRODUCTION: THE NATURE OF EVALUATION

Qualitative evaluation in early childhood education settings can provide systematic and rigorous data to answer questions about effectiveness or efficiency of new or existing programs, projects, resources, personnel, curricula, social groupings, or policy. The nature and contexts of early childhood education are changing. Programs are concerned with performance, social interaction and development, social construction of meaning, the importance of the family in the educational process, and the multicultural composition of groups. Children are being educated (formally and informally) at younger ages outside the home due to the changing structure and work patterns of the family. Qualitative evaluation, with roots in phenomenology and ethnography, is systematic inquiry in naturalistic settings which is consistent with these early childhood education concerns.

Evaluation has been defined as a planned systematic determination of the merit or worth of something by someone either internal or external to the things being evaluated (Scriven, 1993). Patton (1990, p. 11) defines evaluation "quite broadly to include any effort to increase human effectiveness through systematic data-based inquiry." Evaluation will result in specific evaluative conclusions. Qualitative evaluation is generally understood to be evaluation based in interpretivism. It is conducted in naturalistic settings and uses data collection methods of participant observation, individual or focus group interviews, open-ended questionnaires, and participant writings and document collection (Brown, 1994; Greene, 1994; Pitman & Maxwell, 1992). The qualitative evaluator is the instrument of data collection, interpretation, and analysis in the evaluation setting. Therefore, evaluator subjectivity and biases will affect the evaluation, and they need to be offset, to the degree possible, with methodological tools such as triangulation, member checks, negative case sampling, and establishing an audit trail. Because qualitative evaluators spend a great deal of time with participants in the context, establishing a trust relationship, building rapport, and determining reciprocity are key parts of the evaluation process. Evaluative conclusions in qualitative evaluation are based on contextually or situationally grounded data.

Evaluation Models

There are many models of evaluation, including multiple models in qualitative evaluation (Greene, 1994; Guba & Lincoln, 1989; Patton, 1990; Payne, 1994; Pietrzak, Ramler, Renner, Ford, & Gilbert, 1990; Pitman & Maxwell, 1992). In objectives-based evaluation (Payne, 1994), the evaluator uses predetermined program or project goals and evaluation objectives against which to judge program effectiveness. Goal-free evaluation (Scriven, 1973) focuses on identification of actual program effects and their importance in the context, rather than intended effects alone. The goal of responsive evaluation (Stake, 1975) is to discover and address program stakeholders' concerns to enhance program effects in a particular setting.

During the 1970s and 1980s the qualitative-quantitative debate about methods dominated research and evaluation literature. The nature of the debate was multifaceted, reflecting arguments from philosophy (Howe, 1988; Smith & Heshusius, 1986), research paradigms (Guba, 1978; Patton, 1986), characteristics of data collection methods, and evaluation questions (Howe, 1988; Reichardt & Cook, 1979). Reichardt and Cook (1979) assert that the debate unnecessarily polarized qualitative and quantitative methods. They suggest that evaluators should be trained in both approaches and draw from their expertise to use whatever "best fits the demands of the research problem at hand" (p. 19), including using a combination of qualitative and quantitative methods in a single evaluation. Smith and Heshusius (1986) and Guba (1987) argue that evaluators' alignment with a particular research paradigm, rather than the focus of research questions, dictates and limits the choice of data collection methods. Howe (1988), arguing from a pragmatist philosophical position, poses an argument similar to that of Reichardt and Cook (1979), calling for "methodological compatibilism," or using whatever methods work. Eisner's (1985) "educational criticism" model reflects an artistic approach in which specific data collection and analysis methods are purposely not delineated. Guba and Lincoln (1989) suggest that the meaning of evaluation is ever-changing due to social interaction and construction of meaning among evaluator and stakeholders (individuals who have a vested interest in the outcomes of the evaluation) in each unique setting. Guba and Lincoln's (1989) fourth generation evaluation model is based on a constructivist paradigm; the evaluator moves purposefully through hermeneutic dialectic circles of stakeholders to construct meaning interactively about the program being evaluated. While Greene (1994) argues that the paradigm debate led to a legitimization and acceptance of qualitative evaluation methodologies among many evaluation theorists and methodologists, in practice, many clients, sponsors, and program validators still require "hard data" to support positive evaluative claims about programs (Brown, 1993; Walberg & Niemiec, 1993; Zimiles, 1993).

Evaluation Goals: Formative and Summative

There are two major evaluation goals, formative and summative (Herman, Morris, & Fritz-Gibbon, 1987; Patton, 1990; Payne, 1994; Scriven, 1967). The distinction between the two purposes centers on context and generalizability and, in conjunction with evaluation questions, affects evaluation methods selection. Qualitative evaluation methods can and should be used in both approaches, but Patton (1990) and others suggest that qualitative methods are best suited to formative evaluation. When both approaches are used in the same evaluation, evaluator triangulation (one qualitative and one quantitative evaluator working together) is particularly effective. Beer and Bloomer (1986) assert that the formative-summative paradigm unnecessarily separates qualitative and quantitative methods and does not differentiate among various types of formative evaluation. They propose levels of evaluation where each level includes aspects of formative and summative evaluations and where mixed methods address evaluation questions.

Clarity on the purpose of evaluation is important. The primary goal of formative evaluation is to refine, revise, and improve a program, project, or policy within a specific context. The sample is generally small, and evaluation findings are rarely generalized or used for decision making beyond a single context. Summative evaluations provide an overall judgment of program, project, or policy effectiveness. The goal in summative evaluation is to provide findings based on sufficient data so that generalizations about effectiveness can inform decisions about dissemination. The sample size is generally large.

CONDUCTING QUALITATIVE EVALUATION IN EARLY CHILDHOOD SETTINGS

Essential Preliminary Negotiations

Comprehensive initial negotiations between the qualitative evaluator and stakeholders are essential in the evaluation process. Clarifying the evaluation task, establishing rapport, and building trust with stakeholders are critical preliminary steps in qualitative evaluation. Stakeholders in the early childhood setting might include program sponsors, children, parents, teachers, caregivers, day care administrators, and the early childhood education community. Some sponsors, unfamiliar with the nature of qualitative evaluation, feel betrayed when, at the end of the evaluation, they do not have definitive generalizable evaluative conclusions based on "hard data." A clear description of the qualitative approach provided to stakeholders *prior* to beginning the evaluation should detail the narrative nature of qualitative data; specify evaluator's role(s) at the site(s); emphasize the importance of understanding participants' constructions relative to effectiveness; define the process for translating raw data into findings and evaluative conclusions; indicate the large amount of time necessary for data collection, analysis, and interpretation; stress ethical concerns about interactions in the setting and use of data; and explain the open and flexible nature of qualitative evaluation designs.

It is important for stakeholders to understand that findings from early data will often guide topic and participant sampling as the evaluation progresses. For example, in a qualitative evaluation I conducted of a preschool program for at-risk children (Brown, 1992), after interviewing parents I identified the school bus ride as an educational time for children that needed to be investigated to understand the full impact of the program on children's learning. I had not planned to spent time collecting data in that context, thus I had to change the evaluation design to include that context and one person I had not anticipated in the sample, the bus driver. Finally, it is important to the qualitative evaluator and all stakeholders to define clearly at the beginning of the evaluation the expected report format, who will receive reports, and under what circumstances and with whom findings will be shared.

Eight basic components interact to help shape qualitative evaluation in early childhood education contexts: (1) identification of the desired outcomes stakeholders associate with the social program, project, or policy being evaluated; (2) the evaluator's understanding of all stakeholders' interests; (3) theoretical and philosophical perspectives of the evaluator; (4) the evaluator's ideological views about the purpose of social inquiry in program and policy decision making at the early childhood level; (5) ethical considerations relative to children, parents, and teachers; (6) the targeted evaluation questions; (7) the evaluator's knowledge of and biases about various evaluation methods; and (8) contextual, situational, and resource (financial, temporal and personnel) constraints on the proposed evaluation design.

Evaluation Questions

The first critical task in conducting qualitative evaluation after preliminary negotiations is to review evaluation questions that will be addressed. Insights gained during the negotiation period with stakeholders often provide direction for refining evaluation questions. Constraints of time, resources, personnel, and accessibility of program participants will interact with stakeholders' interests to narrow the evaluation questions. Time constraints and travel distance may limit evaluation questions or data collection methods. Qualitative data collection requires a great deal of time. Difficulty of contacting and interviewing parents of young children can often add significantly to unanticipated time and financial costs of the evaluation. Understanding the goal of the evaluation (formative, summative, or both) will also help provide a framework within which to develop clear evaluation questions.

Identification of unit(s) of analysis is essential in establishing clear evaluation questions and helping to determine the evaluation sample. Patton (1990, p. 168) describes the process of defining units of analysis as deciding "what it is you want to be able to say something about" at the end of the evaluation. Do you need findings which say something about individual children, teachers, parents, children and parents together, diverse groups of children, or some combination of these? Do you need to describe children's actions, interactions, verbalizations, body language, or something else? Do stakeholders need information about the program in an individual class, across classes, or across sites? If stakeholders want to know whether a program is effective or efficient, how do they define the two concepts within the program and with the participating sites, classes, or individuals? These are examples of questions used in determining the appropriate units of analysis in a qualitative evaluation.

Qualitative methods are useful in answering a variety of evaluation questions in early childhood education. Erickson (1986) suggests that interpretive methods are best for answering questions about social action in particular settings, participant meanings for actions in specific contexts, relations between social actions in a particular setting and those of other system levels inside and outside the setting, and comparative social organization of a particular setting with that of other settings in other places and times. In qualitative evaluation, each focus would be framed by the characteristics and intended outcomes of the program being evaluated.

Naturalistic Evaluation

Qualitative evaluation takes place in naturalistic settings rather than controlled artificial environments. For early childhood education, this means qualitative evaluation could be ongoing in preschools, community centers, homes, day care centers, playgrounds, churches, or anywhere else young children are being educated. Qualitative evaluators consider and note all characteristics of the natural contexts, both environmental and human. Unanticipated events, actions, interactions, or environmental details that impact the program implementation either positively or negatively are carefully documented.

There is no attempt to control variables because qualitative evaluation occurs in natural settings. Further, it is difficult to have control groups in naturalistic situations. It is not uncommon, however, to conduct comparative analyses of multiple case studies, either of the same program with dissimilar groups at different sites or different programs with similar groups at different sites. What is happening at the site relative to the program or project is integral to the evaluation, but data should also explain what is *not* happening, who is *not* interacting, components of the program that are *not* being implemented, and why. Further, evaluators document their expectations of the impact of the program on targeted participants in the context and throughout the evaluation attempt to generate support as well as disconfirming evidence for their expectations.

The focus of understanding learning and learning processes in young children has moved from the individual child to meaning making in social interactions with other children and adults in a social system (Bowman, 1993; Rogoff, 1990; Sameroff & Chandler, 1975). The implication for evaluation in early childhood education is that qualitative evaluators must examine overlapping social boundaries of children and teachers to determine the interaction of home, neighborhood, and school cultures as they impact learning experiences. Also, evaluators are more aware of marginal positions of persons in educational settings and seek to understand the impact of programs on those persons.

Cultural Context in Qualitative Evaluation

Human beings act, interact, and construct meaning within cultural contexts. In 1871 Edward Tylor (Kroeber & Kluckhohn, 1952, p. 81) defined culture as "that complex whole which includes knowledge, belief, art, law, morals, custom, and any other capabilities and habits acquired by man as a member of society." That definition, or variations of it, is useful in defining the culture of schooling today. A common theme in the qualitative literature on education (Erickson, 1984; Spindler, 1982, 1987; Trueba & Delgado-Gaitan, 1988; Webb & Sherman, 1989) is that social units such as classrooms, schools, and educational systems have cultures. Further, diversity resulting from multiple cultural identities of individuals makes the classroom and the school culture more complex. What a child must "know" to be able to function effectively in one classroom culture will differ from that needed in another. The cultural knowledge that a teacher must have to function well in one school is different from that needed at another.

The introduction of a new program, policy, social grouping, or curriculum in an early childhood setting results in culture change (adaptation to fit existing culture or total adoption) or program rejection. Partial adoption or rejection is common because programs frequently include language, beliefs, values, or world views that differ from those that already exist in the context. Traditional evaluation studies rarely investigate existing cultural and social restrictions to program implementation. The report of one study of teachers' efforts to implement curriculum in a pilot prekindergarten program exemplifies inquiry into the conflict between existing classroom culture and an innovative curriculum which teachers did not understand and which they felt did not meet their students' needs (Walsh, Smith, Alexander, & Ellwein, 1993):

it should be noted that for the pilot programme it was presented to the teachers as a comprehensive curriculum, specifying daily schedule, room arrangement, teaching methods and content—a complete package. . . . The overwhelmingly dominant theme in our interviews with teachers was frustration. . . . They named two primary sources of their frustration: their limited knowledge of the curriculum, and a feeling of being constrained by the curriculum. . . . We find it interesting that when Kathleen described what she liked about the curriculum, she used the language of the curriculum, words that had been assigned to her, for example, "cognitively oriented", "key concepts". When she described what she did not like, she used her own voice, her own words. (pp. 321–324)

Programs such as the one described which are developed outside of the targeted culture and without expert input from members of that culture are often met with member frustration, resentment, and rejection.

As new vocabulary unique to an innovative program is introduced, that which is adopted or adapted by participants carries with it changes in associated beliefs and values. The result is culture change to some degree. The goal for qualitative evaluators is to define the degree of change and specify what has changed and why relative to program goals. A study by Walsh, Smith, Alexander, and Ellwein (1993) illustrates this point as they describe teachers' views of innovative curriculum for at-risk four-year-olds as mysterious and constraining within their context limited implementation.

Culture is shared unequally in social groups (Trueba, 1991). The different roles people assume in a classroom or school culture affect individual interpretations of the culture as a whole; various phenomena and social interactions within it; and effectiveness and efficiency of programs, projects, or policy piloted within that culture. It is important to include perspectives and actions of persons across roles in evaluation data so that how the program is being unequally experienced by different groups of individuals can be assessed.

Outside Funding and Early Educational Evaluation

Qualitative researchers pay particular attention to changes in the economic base (the dollar amount of program support) as part of the cultural context in an evaluation report. This information informs stakeholders' decision making relative to program continuation and/or expansion. Further, it provides readers a basis for making informed decisions about the feasibility of program adoption.

A common change in the culture of schooling which accompanies piloting of innovative programs, projects, curriculum, or social structure is the allocation of short-term financial support through some type of external grant. I have asserted elsewhere (Brown & Dukes, 1993) that evaluations of innovative programs for young children often result in positive findings which do not continue because a short-term influx of funds through grants allows for structural, resource, and//or personnel changes that are impossible to continue beyond the developmental phase within existing local district financial constraints.

Generally, evaluation data are not provided which detail evolution of programs after certification or validation. Support for qualitative and/or quantitative evaluation generally exists only during the pilot phase of programs, and evaluative conclusions on which decisions are made about program retention, expansion, or dissemination reflect this resource-rich environment. Continuation of qualitative evaluation during the post-pilot implementation of lower budget, bastardized versions of programs is rarely included in the evaluation plan. The discrepancy between initial positive evaluative conclusions and perceptions of inadequacy of an implemented program is due in part to the fact that when funding for programs terminates, programs are generally implemented and expanded in very different, and often less effective, ways than originally envisioned by developers. Program changes generally include reduced teacher planning and staff development, classroom resources, personnel, and space.

QUALITATIVE EVALUATION DATA COLLECTION METHODS

There is no simple pattern qualitative evaluators can use to plan early childhood evaluations. A rich variety of data collection methods are available to the qualitative evaluator, and selection depends on goals in data collection, characteristics of participants, contextual constraints, and evaluation questions being answered. Common methods of qualitative data collection include participant observation, interviewing, open-ended questionnaires, and document collection. Qualitative evaluation is labor- and time-intensive. Evaluators strive for unobtrusiveness as they engage in inductive data collection. A common strategy to help ensure rigor and enhance validity is triangulation, or multiple methods. Triangulation approaches include multiple evaluators, data collection methods, data sources (persons, places, times), and explanatory theories (Denzin, 1989). Resulting narrative data can be coded and categorized to determine emerging themes of project participants. Findings can often be translated into frequencies which reveal representativeness of responses.

Participant Observation in Early Childhood
Education Evaluation

Participant observation is a method for monitoring the ongoing impact of a project or program within a specific context. A participant observer participates in and observes as much of the social interaction relative to the program as possible. Observation is generally unstructured, holistic, and frequent. Evaluators assume a role in the social setting which falls on a continuum from total researcher to total participant (Gold, 1958). Gaining entry, establishing a trust relationship, negotiating reciprocity, finding a relatively unobtrusive niche, and meeting different levels of persons in the program are important steps for successful participant observation in evaluation.

Participant observation is based on the underlying premise that humans are social beings who construct meaning in social contexts. As a participant observer, the qualitative evaluator is one member of the social group in which meaning is being constructed, and therefore must continually assess her own impact on the participants' verbalizations, actions, and interactions. That human thought is based in social interaction, that groups construct meaning as they interact, and that individuals interpret social interactions and situations (often referred to as reality) differently are underlying assumptions in qualitative research and evaluation (Geertz, 1973, 1983; Mehan, 1980). Many studies, for example, Graue's (1993) work on the local meaning of readiness for kindergarten children, suggest that understanding the nature and substance of social constructions of meaning is critical to understanding early childhood education programs.

Understanding the process of the social construction of meaning in early childhood educational contexts requires four things of the qualitative evaluator: (1) capturing the "said" of the negotiation of meaning; (2) identifying roles and relationships of persons involved in the negotiation; (3) describing the environmental and social context in which the negotiation takes place; and (4) determining whether the meaning generated is due to the evaluator's presence. Victor Turner cautions (in Bruner, 1984, p. 7) that "There may be a correspondence between a life as lived, a life as experienced, and a life as told, but the anthropologist should never assume the correspondence nor fail to make the distinction." A qualitative evaluator can never know directly what children or parents are experiencing, feeling, or thinking without interviewing them or listening to verbal interactions as a participant observer. What program participants say about their experiences of a program may differ distinctly from what the qualitative evaluator observes in the setting. The reactivity of the evaluator in the setting must be taken into account when interpreting data. A goal in qualitative evaluation is to generate data to help explain other data discrepancies.

Interviewing Young Children, Parents, and Educators

The purpose of interviewing in qualitative evaluation is to find out how participants are experiencing the program. Interview formats can vary on a continuum from highly structured, evaluator-directed question and response guides to informal conversations whose focus and direction are controlled by participants (Brown, 1994). The selection of interview format is determined by the type of information desired, the amount of time available to the evaluator, and the desired level of comparability of findings. Less structured interview formats (conversational interviews) require more time, and data are less comparable, but the interview focus becomes participants' concerns and issues.

Interviews can be with individuals or small groups of participants. Focus group interviewing is a form of qualitative data collection in which the evaluator functions as discussion facilitator for a small group of participants (between six and eight persons) and relies on interaction within the group to provide insights about topics proposed by the evaluator. Morgan (1988), in comparing advantages and disadvantages of focus group interviews, suggests that focus groups are relatively easy to conduct, they require less time than multiple individual interviews, and they provide the opportunity to collect data from group interaction around researcher-generated topics. Primary weaknesses of focus groups are that they are not conducted in naturalistic settings; it is impossible to discern individuals' perspectives; and the level of impact on individuals' responses and interactions of the evaluator, other participants, and recording equipment cannot be determined. Evaluators must carefully consider the tradeoffs relative to evaluation data needed when selecting interview formats.

Ethical considerations in interviewing are paramount in qualitative evaluation. The initial concern when interviewing young children, parents, and educators in early childhood education settings is identifying and following informed consent procedures. Evaluators should exercise precautions to protect the rights of all persons involved in the evaluation, especially children. When interviewing, a primary issue is how interview data will be recorded and when and how any taped (audio or video) data will be used and destroyed. A related issue is whether and how data will remain anonymous or confidential. Confidentiality can be achieved by using codes rather than names in transcribed data. A third issue is whether individuals might be identified locally by descriptions or quotations included in evaluation reports. The unit of analysis determines how data will be presented; if the unit of analysis is a group or class, individual identities can be masked more easily than if the unit of analysis is the individual child and her parents.

Interviewing Children

As the opening interview excerpt in this article suggests, interviewing young children is often frustrating—to the child as well as the adult interviewer. Young children have their own strategies for controlling an interview situation that may be uninteresting, nonsensical, or threatening to them. One strategy is simply not to respond. Another is to talk about something of interest which is totally unrelated to the focus of the interview. The attention span of young children is short, and rarely can adults keep a child engaged in an interview long enough to get "all the information" they want. Interviewing young children is problematic because of their limited verbal capabilities, level of conceptual development, restricted visual and motor response capabilities, and limited information-processing skills (Martin, 1988). Young children often confuse fact with wishful thinking. Young children have difficulty comparing and contrasting events and distinguishing levels of affect toward experiences. Young children confuse the order of events and have difficulty verbalizing temporal comparisons about themselves (Chafel, 1990). Evaluators encounter other problems when interviewing young children, such as limited verbal capability and inability to respond equally to different question formats (Allerton, 1993).

Triangulation of data collection methods and data sources is particularly useful in balancing the limitations of interviewing young children. For example, qualitative evaluators can use data from direct observations in different places and interviews with multiple children, parents, and educators to help clarify confusing interview data from young children and expand understanding of a program. It is important to note, however, that the use of triangulation does not always result in verification of findings (Mathison, 1988), but most frequently leads to multiple interpretations and even competing or inconsistent interpretations from different persons or the same person at different times or contexts.

Interviewing Parents

Parental involvement components have become commonplace in early childhood education programs and projects to address family and societal problems related to children's learning (Bloom, 1992; Powell, 1988, 1991; Weiss & Jacobs, 1988). Interviews with parents are frequently used in early childhood evaluation (Brown, 1991; Cooke, 1992; Harding, 1991) to gain parents' perspectives of program impacts on children, quality of resources, changes in parent attitudes or behaviors, concerns about the program, and other related issues. If the qualitative evaluator has infrequent contact with groups of parents at the educational setting, focus group interviews work particularly well because parents are more likely to interact with and respond to each other. It tends to be a more relaxed and less threatening interview environment than individual participant interviews with an unfamiliar external evaluator. If both evaluator and parents are in the educational context frequently with children, individual or small group informal conversational interviews become a natural part of social interaction and provide rich data that might not be obtained in formal focus group interviews. Qualitative evaluators should consider the value of using both interview approaches.

Some programs focus on changes in parent-child interaction and educational resources in the home. Interviews with parents in the home environment provide an opportunity for the evaluator to gain perspectives of parents while observing aspects of the environment to determine whether particular changes have occurred. The Home Observation for Measurement of the Environment (HOME) instrument (Caldwell & Bradley, 1984) is frequently used by teachers and qualitative evaluators as a guide for home interviews and observations in early childhood programs.

Evaluator-Generated Open-Ended Questionnaires

The goal of using carefully constructed open-ended questionnaires is the same as interviews: to get inside the heads of participants to understand their perspectives of the program or project. Major advantages of questionnaires over interviews are that data can be collected from larger numbers of participants, participants are all responding to exactly the same questions in the same order, and data collection takes less time. Questionnaire data are more comparable than those from conversational interviews, and therefore analysis is simplified. Disadvantages of questionnaires are that participants must be able to read and write, responses are limited to a certain amount of space, issues of most interest to participants might not be addressed, and there is generally a low return rate if questionnaires are mailed to participants.

The most effective open-ended questionnaires are short, include clearly written questions in language familiar to program participants, provide sufficient space for responses, and provide a final non-directed question (e.g., "Other Comments or Concerns" or "What concerns or issues would you like to discuss that have not been addressed on this questionnaire?") which allows participants to share things of interest to them relative to the program.

Obviously, written open-ended questionnaires would be of no use with young children because they do not have the necessary language and writing skills. They are, however, quite useful in many contexts with parents and teachers. Literacy skills of parents must be taken into account when decisions about use of parent questionnaires are being made. Ethical concerns relative to questionnaire use include confidentiality and anonymity of responses, particularly where there are power differences within the group which might lead some participants to feel threatened if others come to know their responses. In the latter instance, validity of data might be challenged because participants may alter genuine responses in order to provide information which they feel would not create problems for themselves.

QUALITATIVE DATA ANALYSIS

Qualitative data analysis is an ongoing cyclical process that consists of synthesizing information across data sources and data collection methods. Most qualitative data are in narrative form, but frequently qualitative evaluators will generate numerical data that help describe the setting. Examples of numerical data in qualitative evaluations might be proportions of different categories of children participating in a program, proportions of time different groups of children engage in specific activities on a daily basis, group sizes, or number of parent sessions attended by participants. Stakeholders want to know how representative evaluative claims are, but this is not a sufficient argument to transform rich narrative qualitative data into simple frequency counts. Numerical frequencies to support claims of representativeness can be used in conjunction with narrative category analysis to provide a clearer understanding of program effect.

The goal in qualitative data analysis in evaluation is to generate meaning and understandings from the data which will inform evaluative conclusions relative to program effectiveness. The first step in simultaneous data collection and analysis is to determine whether there are data to answer all evaluation questions and decide which data answer which questions. A common diversion from the evaluation focus is recording data on interesting interactions and activities at the site which have nothing to do with the evaluation questions. Additionally, in conversational interviews, it is common for participants to offer information on phenomena which are not relevant to the program evaluation. The best way to avoid this time-consuming and non-productive pitfall is to identify specific outcome variables in evaluation questions and focus data collection around them. Miller (1988, p. 387) for example, after a multisite evaluation on an adolescent parents project, cautions: "it is very difficult to investigate a wide range of variables effectively in a developing program. One must be very specific about the expected impacts of an intervention and direct the focus of the evaluation to those issues."

Qualitative Data Analysis Approaches

Qualitative data analysis is a systematic examination of all narrative data to generate categories of meaning which inform the evaluation questions. There are a variety of approaches to data analysis from which qualitative evaluators can select.

Phenomenological Analysis

Phenomenological analysis (Hycner, 1985) is an approach to analyzing narrative data, particularly interview data, which focuses on understanding the phenomenon or program in its own right and not from the perspective of the evaluator. The evaluator brackets or suspends her/his own meanings and interpretations as much as possible and allows meaning to emerge from the data. The evaluator delineates units of meaning in participant data relevant to the evaluation questions and establishes relations among units generated in different data sources and across data collection methods.

Qualitative Content Analysis

Content analysis is a well-known method for analyzing documents and written communication. Documents are frequently produced at a program site without guidance from the evaluator and often for reasons other than evaluation. Documents can be a good source of information about program implementation and interpretation by participants. Content analysis is defined by Holsti (1969, p. 14) as "any technique for making inferences by objectively and systematically identifying specified characteristics of messages." While content analysis is traditionally associated with frequency counts of words or phrases in documents, Guba and Lincoln (1981) make a case for qualitative content analysis, explaining that frequency counts are not necessarily associated with the importance of assertions in documents. Qualitative content analysis includes generation of categories from the data which are relevant to the purposes of the evaluation. Evaluator-generated rules for categorization, demonstration of representativeness of categories, relations among categories, and definitions of categories from participant perspectives are important outcomes of qualitative content analysis.

Constant Comparative Analysis

Constant comparative analysis (Glaser & Strauss, 1967; Strauss, 1987) is an approach to analysis that results in grounded theory. Analysis is ongoing throughout data collection. As data are displayed and reduced into categories of meaning, and relations among categories are identified, hypotheses are proposed to account for social meaning and interaction that are represented in the data. Through theoretical sampling, the evaluator is guided in the focus of data collection, identification of data sources, and selection of appropriate data collection methods. A process of writing theoretical and methodological memos, or notes about ongoing insights, informs the interrelated data collection and analysis process. The final grounded theory is written and also represented in visual schemas.

Rigor in Qualitative Data Analysis

There are strategies to enhance rigor in qualitative data analysis. The first relates simply to careful and organized methods of categorizing narrative data for understanding. Categories and their definitions should emerge from the data, all data should be categorized, data should be coded as the evaluation proceeds so that gaps in data can be filled while the program is being implemented, and relations among categories should be established early so that emerging substantive level hypotheses can be tested. The second strategy is to use a documentation structure in participant observation data collection (Becker & Geer, 1960) which allows you to interpret data relative to contextual variables such as whether other persons are present when information is shared, whether information is volunteered, whether actions are observed by the evaluator alone or with others present, and other similar situational events which might affect validity or representativeness of data. Another strategy is the inquiry audit (Guba & Lincoln, 1989), which is a documentation of the process of transformation of data to interpreted findings so that others can trace back through the steps to the raw data to determine whether there is evidence for the findings. The audit relates to the concern about the privatization of qualitative analysis (Constas, 1992). Constas (1992) proposed a structured method for documenting the analysis process which culminates in a table including origin of categories, category development, and source of category labels that can be included in research or evaluation reports.

Mixed-Methods Analysis

The demand in evaluation for "hard data" (quantitatively analyzed numerical data in tables and charts used to test hypotheses) has diminished somewhat to allow for qualitative and mixed-method designs (qualitative and quantitative methods to evaluate the same phenomenon). In mixed-method evaluation designs, qualitative methods are generally used to examine program processes and quantitative methods used to assess program outcomes. Evaluation scholars (Caracelli & Greene, 1993; Patton, 1990) detail a variety of approaches to triangulating qualitative and quantitative methods and analyses in evaluation designs. Other evaluators (Guba & Lincoln, 1989) argue that choice of philosophical paradigm precludes mixing methods. Caracelli & Greene (1993) suggest four analytic strategies for integrating qualitative and quantitative data to allow for statistical or thematic analysis of both data types together. As they reflect on their own suggestions for merged analysis in mixed designs, they provide important considerations for keeping analyses separate to maintain the potential power of a triangulation design and diverse ways of knowing. It is important to consider the initial purpose in selecting a mixed-method design before deciding whether to merge analyses (Caracelli & Greene, 1993).

WRITING THE EVALUATION REPORT

The final task in qualitative evaluation is writing the report. This communication of results is a critical stage in the evaluation. In formative evaluation, it is common to write multiple reports at natural reflection points so that program changes can be tested as the evaluation continues. The structure of interim reports should be the same as that of final reports. Basic elements of the final report include evaluation design, evaluation process description, sampling process, description of the sample, presentation of findings relative to evaluation questions, representative raw data (the "voice" of program participants and observational notes) to support findings, and evaluative conclusions about the worth of the program.

There is some controversy about the appropriateness of evaluator-generated recommendations for changes (Payne, 1994). Prior to beginning the evaluation, the evaluator and sponsor should discuss whether recommendations should be included in the report. I believe that the best strategy for communicating recommendations and enhancing evaluation utilization is for the evaluator to meet with stakeholders and discuss alternative recommendations or changes which mesh understandings from evaluation findings and stakeholders' knowledge of project and setting.

CONCLUSION

Carefully designed and conducted qualitative evaluation is a powerful source of understanding about social interaction, construction of social meaning, and educational processes in early childhood settings. It is a labor-intensive enterprise exacting careful and ongoing alignment between the evaluator, participants, stakeholders, contexts, and data. There are many points in a qualitative evaluation at which the evaluator must make critical decisions and act on them. There is no easy formula to guide development of qualitative evaluation designs in early childhood settings. The most important characteristic of the design is evaluator-stakeholder agreement to allow for structured flexibility which facilitates changes in the original evaluation design when suggested by ongoing interpretation of analyzed data.

REFERENCES

Allerton, M. (1993). Am I asking the right questions? What teachers ask of children. *International Journal of Early Childhood, 25* (1), 42–48.

Becker, H. S., & Greer, B. (1960). Participant observation: The analysis of qualitative field data. In R. Adams & J. Preiss (Eds.), *Human organization research: Field relations and techniques.* Homewood, Ill.: Dorsey Press.

Beer, V., & Bloomer, A. C. (1986). Levels of evaluation. *Educational Evaluation and Policy Analysis, 8* (4), 335–345.

Bloom, J. (1992). *Parenting our schools: A hands-on guide to education reform.* Boston: Little, Brown and Co.

Bowman, B. (1993). Early childhood education. In L. Darling-Hammond (Ed.), *Review of research in education* (pp. 101–134). Washington, D.C.: American Educational Research Association.

Brown, M. J. M. (1991, November). *Kids and parents at school: Parents' views of their involvement in preschool and their child's education.* Paper presented at the 90th Annual American Anthropological Association Meeting. Chicago.

Brown, M. J. M. (1992, April). *The school bus as a learning environment.* Paper presented at the American Educational Research Association Annual Meeting. San Francisco.

Brown, M. J. M. (1993). Massaging soft data, or making the skeptical more supple. In D. M. Fetterman (Ed.), *Speaking the language of power: Communication, collaboration and advocacy* (pp. 93–104). Washington, D.C.: Falmer Press.

Brown, M. J. M. (1994). Qualitative and ethnographic evaluation. In D. A. Payne (Ed.), *Designing educational project and program evaluations* (pp. 121–142). Norwell, Mass.: Kluwer Academic Publishers.

Brown, M. J. M., & Dukes, M. (1993, November). *Using preschool student and parent curriculum as a means to culture change: A preschool experiment for at-risk children.* Paper presented at the 92nd Annual American Anthropological Association Meeting, Washington, D.C.

Bruner, E. M. (Ed.). (1984). *Text, play and story: The construction and reconstruction of self and society.* Prospect Heights, Ill.: Waveland.

Caldwell, B. M., & Bradley, R. H. (1984). *Home Observation for the Measurement of the Environment.* Little Rock, Ark.: Authors, University of Arkansas at Little Rock, 33rd and University, 72204.

Caracelli, V. J., & Greene, J. C. (1993). Data analysis strategies for mixed-method evaluation designs. *Educational Evaluation and Policy Analysis, 15* (2), 195–207.

Chafel, J. A. (1990). "I'm doing much better than I did before!": Are young children capable of verbalizing temporal comparisons about the self? *Early Child Development and Care, 62,* 71–86.

Constas, M. A. (1992). Qualitative analysis as a public event: The documentation of category development procedures. *American Educational Research Journal, 29* (2), 253–266.

Cooke, B. (1992). *Changing times, changing families: Minnesota Early Childhood Family Education outcome interview study.* St. Paul: Minnesota State Department of Education. (ERIC Document Reproduction Service No. ED346994)

Denzin, N. K. (1989). *The research act* (3rd ed.). Englewood Cliffs, N.J.: Prentice Hall.

Eisner, E. W. (1985). *The art of educational evaluation: A personal view.* London: Falmer Press.

Erickson, F. (1984). What makes school ethnography "ethnographic"? *Anthropology & Education Quarterly, 15,* 51–66.

Erickson, F. (1986). Qualitative methods in research on teaching. In M. C. Wittrock (Ed.), *Handbook of research on teaching* (3rd ed.) (pp. 119–161). New York: Macmillan.

Geertz, C. (1973). *The interpretation of cultures.* New York: Basic Books.

Geertz, C. (1983). From the native's point of view: On the nature of anthropological understanding. In C. Geertz, *Local knowledge: Further essays in interpretive anthropology.* New York: Basic Books.

Glaser, B., & Strauss, A. L. (1967). *The discovery of grounded theory.* Chicago: Aldine.

Gold, R. (1958). Roles in sociological field observation. *Social Forces, 36,* 217–223.

Graue, M. E. (1993). *Ready for what? Constructing meanings of readiness for kindergarten.* New York: SUNY Press.

Greene, J. C. (1994). Qualitative program evaluation: Practice and Promise. In

N. K. Denzin & Y. S. Lincoln, (Eds.), *Handbook of qualitative research* (pp. 530–544). Thousand Oaks, Calif.: Sage.

Guba, E. G. (1978). *Toward a methodology of naturalistic inquiry in educational evaluation.* Los Angeles: University of California Press.

Guba, E. G. (1987). What have we learned about naturalistic evaluation? *Evaluation Practice, 8* (1), 23–43.

Guba, E. G., & Lincoln, Y. S. (1981). *Effective evaluation: Improving the usefulness of evaluation results through responsive and naturalistic approaches.* San Francisco: Jossey-Bass.

Guba, E. G., & Lincoln, Y. S. (1989). *Fourth generation evaluation.* Newbury Park, Calif.: Sage.

Harding, M. E. (1991). *Early childhood family education. K-3 expansion demonstration projects: A report to the Minnesota Department of Education on ten pilot sites.* St. Paul, Minn.: Harding, Ringhofer & Associates. (ERIC Document Reproduction Service No. ED352195)

Herman, J. L., Morris, L. L., & Fitz-Gibbon, C. T. (1987). *Evaluator's handbook.* Newbury Park, Calif.: Sage.

Holsti, O. R. (1969). *Content analysis for the social sciences and humanities.* Reading, Mass.: Addison-Wesley.

Howe, K. R. (1988). Against the quantitative-qualitative incompatibility thesis, or dogmas die hard. *Educational Researcher, 17* (8), 10–16.

Hycner, R. H. (1985). Some guidelines for the phenomenological analysis of interview data. *Human Studies, 8,* 279–303.

Kroeber, A. L., & Kluckhohn, C. (1952). *Culture: A critical review of concepts and definitions.* New York: Vintage.

Martin, R. P. (1988). *Assessment of personality and behavior problems: Infancy through adolescence.* New York: Guilford Press.

Mathison, S. (1988). Why triangulate? *Educational Researcher, 17* (2), 13–17.

Mehan, H. (1980). The competent student. *Anthropology and Education Quarterly, 11* (3), 71–77.

Miller, S. H. (1988). The Child Welfare League of America's Adolescent Parents Project. In H. B. Weiss & F. H. Jacobs (Eds.), *Evaluating family programs* (pp. 371–388). New York: Aldine de Gruyter.

Morgan, D. L. (1988). *Focus groups as qualitative research.* Newbury Park, Calif.: Sage.

Patton, M. Q. (1986). *Utilization-focused evaluation* (2nd ed.). Newbury Park, Calif.: Sage.

Patton, M. Q. (1990). *Qualitative evaluation and research methods* (2nd ed.). Newbury Park, Calif.: Sage.

Payne, D. A. (Ed.) (1994). *Designing educational project and program evaluations.* Norwell, Mass.: Kluwer Academic Publishers.

Pietrzak, J., Ramler, M., Renner, T., Ford, L., & Gilbert, N. (1990). *Practical program evaluation: Examples from child abuse prevention.* Newbury Park, Calif.: Sage.

Pitman, M. A., & Maxwell, J. A. (1992). Qualitative approaches to evaluation: Models and methods. In M. D. LeCompte, W. L. Millroy, & J. Preissle (Eds.), *The handbook of qualitative research in education.* New York: Academic Press.

Powell, D. R. (Ed.). (1988). *Parent education as early childhood intervention: Emerging directions in theory, research and practice.* Norwood, N.J.: Ablex.

Powell, D. R. (1991). Parents and programs: Early childhood as a pioneer in parent involvement and support. In S. L. Kagan (Ed.), *The care and education of America's young children: Obstacles and opportunities.* Ninetieth Yearbook of the National Society for the Study of Education. Chicago: University of Chicago Press.

Reichardt, C., & Cook, T. (1979). Beyond qualitative versus quantitative methods. In T. Cook & C. Reichardt (Eds.), *Qualitative and quantitative methods in evaluation research* (pp. 7–32). Beverly Hills, Calif.: Sage.

Rogoff, B. *Apprenticeship in thinking.* New York: Oxford University Press.

Sameroff, A. J., & Chandler, M. J. (1975). Reproductive risk and the continuum of care taking casualty. In F. D. Horowitz, M. Hetherington, S. Scarr-Salapapek, & G. Siegel (Eds.), *Review of child development research* (vol. 4, pp. 187–244). Chicago: University of Chicago Press.

Scriven, M. (1967). The methodology of evaluation. In R. E. Stake (Ed.), *Curriculum evaluation.* AERA Monograph Series in Evaluation (vol. 1, pp. 39–43). Chicago: Rand McNally.

Scriven, M. (1973). Goal-free evaluation. In E. R. House (Ed.), *School evaluation: The politics and process* (pp. 319–328). Berkeley, Calif.: McCutchan.

Scriven, M. (1993, November). *General evaluation methodology.* Paper presented at the American Evaluation Association Meeting, Dallas.

Smith, J. K., & Heshusius, L. (1986). Closing down the conversation: The end of the quantitative-qualitative debate among educational researchers. *Educational Researcher, 15* (1), 4–12.

Spindler, G. (Ed.). (1982). *Doing the ethnography of schooling: Educational anthropology in action.* New York: Holt, Rinehart and Winston.

Spindler, G. (Ed.). (1987). *Education and cultural process: Anthropological approaches* (2nd ed.). Prospect Heights, Ill.: Waveland Press.

Stake, R. E. (1975). *Evaluating the arts in education: A responsive approach.* Columbus, Ohio: Merrill.

Strauss, A. L. (1987). *Qualitative analysis for social scientists.* New York: Cambridge.

Trueba, H. T. (1991). Notes on cultural acquisition and transmission. *Anthropology and Education Quarterly, 22* (3), 279–280.

Trueba, H. T., & Delgado-Gaitan, C. (Eds.). (1988). *School and society: Learning content through culture.* New York: Praeger.

Walberg, H. J., & Niemiec, R. P. (1993). Validating exemplary programs: Methods and criteria. *Educational Evaluation and Policy Analysis, 15* (4), 429–436.

Walsh, D. J., Smith, M. E., Alexander, M., & Ellwein, M. C. (1993). The curriculum as mysterious and constraining: Teachers' negotiations of the first year of a pilot programme for at-risk 4-year-olds. *Journal of Curriculum Studies, 25* (4), 317–332.

Webb, R. B., & Sherman, R. R. (1989). *Schooling and society* (2nd ed.). New York: Macmillan.

Weiss, W. B., & Jacobs, F. H. (Eds.). (1988). *Evaluating family programs*. New York: Aldine de Gruyter.

Zimiles, H. (1993). The adoration of "hard data." Fetishism in the evaluation of infant day care. *Early Childhood Research Quarterly, 8* (3), 369–385.

Chapter 12

Ethical Conflicts in Classroom Research: Examples from a Study of Peer Stigmatization in Kindergarten

J. Amos Hatch

In this chapter, I describe ethical conflicts connected with a participant observation and interview study done in a kindergarten classroom. In the study, a boy I called Lester emerged as a powerful example of one who was stigmatized as an outsider and treated as "less than normal" by his peer group. I frame my discussion around a confrontation that took place between me and an unknown classroom teacher during a presentation of my findings at a national research conference. Having listened to my description of the social construction of Lester's outsider status, the teacher from the audience asked why I had not intervened in support of Lester.

In this chapter, I detail my answer to the teacher, discussing my role as a "passive participant observer" trying to capture the natural social setting of the classroom. I note that at the time I was doing the fieldwork I did not know Lester was going to be the focus of the intensive analysis that evolved and that the teacher was a very competent, caring person who was aware of Lester's social difficulties. After this explanation, I tell why my answer is still not completely satisfying to me today. The teacher in the audience was right to ask the question; I was wrong not to ask it of myself sooner. I summarize with some thoughts on the ethics of qualitative research in early childhood classrooms.

AERA 1986

The American Educational Research Association (AERA) meetings were in San Francisco in 1986, but I was much too nervous to enjoy California. I was presenting three papers, and, although I had presented at AERA as a graduate student, I was still unable to sleep or eat because of my anxiety. The way I handle my nervousness is to imagine the worst scenario—the most scathing criticism, the most difficult question, the most damaging comment—and construct in my head a way to save face so I can leave the situation with some dignity intact. With three papers to present, I had three different sets of "worsts" to preoccupy me. Of course, my way of dealing with anxiety is not healthy, but worse, in the session in which I presented a paper entitled "Learning To Be an Outsider: Peer Stigmatization in Kindergarten," it did not work.

As is common at AERA, this paper was only loosely connected to others in my session. When it was my turn, I talked some about my study and read from the paper, including some excerpts from children's conversations among themselves that provided evidence that one child in the class (Lester) was being defined as an outsider by his peer group.

The session discussant was a substitute, and my memory was that her comments were mildly critical, not very threatening, and framed in a way that did not make me feel like I had to defend myself in order to leave with my head up. However, when the audience of about forty was invited to ask questions, a woman (I do not know if she identified herself as a teacher or if I just assumed she was) stood and asked me a question that never entered into any of my worst-case scenarios: "If you knew Lester was being stigmatized by his classmates, why didn't you do something to intervene on his behalf?"

As she was asking the question, I knew she had me. Even while my mind was racing to construct an answer that would satisfy the moment, my heart was sinking because I knew I had missed something important as a researcher, as an early childhood educator, and as a person. In all the hundreds of hours I had poured into the study, I had never asked this question of myself. Writing this essay gives me a chance to try to address this question and deal with the sinking feeling that has stuck with me since that afternoon in San Francisco.

THE STUDY

The study was the third classroom participant observation study I had undertaken to examine the social behavior of kindergarten students in child-to-child interactions. I spent most of the second half of a school year sitting in a half-day kindergarten, recording field notes, collecting classroom artifacts and other unobtrusive data, and interviewing teachers and students. As data were analyzed, the behavior of Lester and of other children in relation to Lester became a focus of the study. Later data collection and analysis were designed to reveal patterns of interaction within the peer group that, in effect, stigmatized Lester as "less than normal." The findings of the study are analytical descriptions of Lester's "rule breaking" behaviors and classroom peers' "group responses" to him (Hatch, 1988).

What seemed important about the study was its interactionist stance (Becker, 1963; Erickson, 1966; Goffman, 1963) that takes Lester's stigmatization to be constructed within the norms and expectations of his peer group, not merely as a consequence of Lester's personality, physical features, or actions. The group and Lester participated in the construction of his less than normal status.

Lester's rule breaking included "aggression" toward peers, "teasing," and "contact incompetence" (poorly developed strategies for making positive contact with peers). Group responses in the study included "exclusion" (denying entry to previously established groups) and "snubs" (individual negative responses to Lester as an interaction partner). The study, it seemed to me, had the potential to help teachers and researchers think in new ways about children having social difficulties, to focus attention on group processes and definitions rather than individual problems and apparent deficiencies.

The AERA paper and the article reporting the study are full of excerpts that offer evidence for the hypotheses of the findings. I include one extensive excerpt here to give a flavor of Lester's interactions with peers. I will also use this incident to discuss my researcher role later in this chapter.

Sam and Steve have a set of Lego blocks, and Lester comes to the place where Sam and Steve are playing and sits down on the edge of the group. He reaches across what they are building, picks up a piece from the box and adds it to their construction. Steve: "Don't." Sam: "You're breakin' it." (When Lester put the piece in, it separated another set of pieces). Frank comes and stands between Steve and Sam. Lester to Frank: "You can play." [We'll both join.] Frank looks at Sam to see if it's OK. [I don't see Sam's reaction, but I see Frank sit down.] After Frank sits down, Sam says to Lester: "Only three can play." Steve: "Yea, only three. You have to leave." Sam: "I'll decide. Frank, what does your name start with?" Frank: "F." Sam: "Steve, what does your name start with?" Steve: "S." Sam: "My name starts with S. OK, S's and F's can stay." Steve to Lester: "You gotta leave." Lester looks down but does not move. Steve repeats: "You gotta leave. Only three can play." Lester continues to look down and says nothing. Steve: "I'ma tell the teacher." Sam: "OK, I'll decide. Go to your seats and I'll call who can play." Steve stands up and starts to leave. He looks over his shoulder and sees that no one else is leaving and returns to a standing position next to the group. Sam to Frank: "Go to your seat so I can call you." Frank: "No." Steve repeats: "Only F's and S's can stay." Sam: "OK, only those with red on can stay." Each boy checks clothing and announces: "I got red." Lester: "I got red." Sam tries another color: "Who's got white?" Lester points to his undershirt and says: "I got white." Sam: "That doesn't count. You gotta be wearin' it." Lester continues to check and sees white in his plaid shirt and says: "I got white." Sam continues to go through the colors [in what appears to be an exercise in getting Lester out of the group]. Lester does not leave but stays on the outside of the group. Occasionally, he reaches across to keep pieces in play. At one point he says: "Let's build a big house." Steve responds: "We already are. You can't stay." Another attempt by Lester was to pick up a toy lawn mower and say: "I'll mow the yard." (He acts as if he is mowing the rug with the mower.) Steve's response: "You can't stay. I'ma tell the teacher." (Hatch, 1988, pp. 67–68)

MY ANSWER

I'm not sure how coherent my answer was. I was stunned and embarrassed by the teacher's question. I acknowledged the importance of the question, mumbled something about having to think carefully about the implications, then made my pass at responding. I noted the connections of my work to what Spradley (1980) calls "passive participant observation." It was my goal, I explained, to be present in the social contexts I study, but to do my best not to influence the natural flow of social interactions among kindergarten peers. If I was to capture children's naturally occurring social behavior, I could not intervene.

I emphasized that my fieldwork was not exclusively focused on Lester and interactions that involved him. I was still interested in larger social interaction patterns in the group and trying to maintain a broader perspective while paying close attention to settings in which Lester was involved. If I changed my passive role and tried to help Lester's situation, I argued, I would give up not only the naturalistic analysis of peer stigmatization, but an analysis of "secondary adjustments" that was emerging as well (see Hatch, 1989). In fact, given the way I defined my research role, to intervene would be to violate the basis for my claim to be recording and analyzing naturally occurring social behavior.

I also explained that the teacher of the studied classroom was an excellent teacher and a sensitive person who was aware of Lester's difficulties with peer relations. In both formal and informal interviews, the teacher described relations between Lester and peers in terms that paralleled my observations in the classroom; in fact, her interviews provided a powerful source of triangulation for my other data. My reasoning was that here was a fully competent, caring teacher who knew that Lester was having problems. What could I do that this expert teacher was not already doing?

As I was answering, I knew I was not just throwing up a smoke screen to cover my escape. My reasons made sense within the research framework I had learned and taken as my own. What this teacher's question ultimately has done is force me to critique that research framework. Not intervening was problematic, but what frightened me was that I had never even considered such an intervention. That my way of thinking about and doing research would lead me to such a position was a troubling realization.

VOYEURISM AND VALUES

Roman (1989) and Tobin and Davidson (1990) describe a voyeuristic dimension in participant observation research. As I have thought about my studies in early childhood classrooms, I have come to accept the uncomfortable notion that at some level I have acted as a voyeur. The long excerpt above, an interaction in which Lester was clearly excluded by his peers, offers an example of how voyeurism played out in the study under examination in this chapter. I have many memories of interactions in the classroom, but I remember the incident recorded above especially well; I remember it as a turning point of the study.

The boys were playing on the rug in the front of the room. I had stationed myself at the side of the Writing Center less than five feet from the center of the boys' activities. I could hear their conversation clearly and see the faces of all except one child facing directly away from me (Sam). I had been in the classroom for several weeks by this time, and I have no evidence that these boys did anything differently because I was so close to them.

I remember a distinct feeling of exhilaration as it became clear how the interaction was going. My heart was beating fast and I knew I was getting "good data." I even remember my mind saying, "You are having a strong emotional reaction to this interaction so you better be extra careful to record it accurately." I even felt a kind of smug pride that I had the presence of mind to remember an old article by Schwartz and Schwartz (1955) that warned researchers to bracket their emotional reactions when powerful data were being gathered.

So there I sat, writing as fast as I could, intently involved in accurately capturing the conversation before me, and feeling emotionally and intellectually stimulated. I knew this was a great example of a "Lester as outsider" thesis, and I knew for the first time that a close analysis of Lester's status in the classroom group would be an important part of the study. I felt lucky that I was in the room that day and lucky that the interaction was taking place so close to my observation station. I also felt a sense of power and satisfaction that I was getting such strong evidence. I wish I could say that some part of me felt what I feel now, sadness and anger for the way Lester was treated, but my memories are only of the thrill of the voyeur being in the right place at the right time.

The feelings I have now about my voyeurism are parallel to the feelings I have when I see human suffering captured in newspaper or magazine photographs or in television video records. When I see news reports of suffering children or adults, I wonder why the photographers and reporters are not trying to help instead of doing their best to capture the horror as vividly as possible. My guess is that these professionals experience the same kind of exhilaration I did as I was fulfilling my role as a researcher. They can feel it when the shot is powerful: their hearts beat fast, and they become especially intent on making an accurate record. I wonder if they ever consider intervention, spoiling the impact of their story, but perhaps helping a fellow human in distress.

AN ETHICAL PARADOX

Peshkin's analyses of a variety of social settings (e.g., 1978, 1986) have taught me the importance of paradox in understanding the construction of roles, norms, and values in any social group. In some ways, you can know groups best by the paradoxes they keep. Qualitative researchers (like photographers and journalists) have access to sensitive situations and information that others want to (and probably should) know about. The paradox comes from the tension between providing descriptions and analyses that have the potential to raise awareness and ultimately help victims, and significantly altering descriptions and analyses in order immediately to assist the victims being studied.

Labov (1972) described the "observer's paradox" as the dilemma of trying to capture naturally occurring behavior in the unnatural context created by the presence of a researcher. That paradox obviously holds here as well, but the ethical paradox I am describing is larger. It is not just a matter of influencing the behavior of those we are studying by our proximity and record making; it involves the issue of active intervention when we see that those we are studying are at risk. I think researchers should be struggling with this paradox. I am concerned that many researchers, like me in the Lester study, are not.

I cannot speak for others, but I can confess why I think I overlooked the tension that should have moved me to consider intervening on Lester's behalf. I see three related factors that kept me from confronting this ethical paradox sooner: my own selfishness, being caught up in the moment, and my view of the "superior" nature of the researcher role.

In terms of selfishness, I recall having a meeting with a school district administrator (who also happened to be a friend) as I was trying to arrange permission to do my dissertation study. As we talked, the administrator asked how my study would benefit the district. As part of my response, I joked: "Because it will make me famous." This was a different study, and it really was a joke—I have always known that the audience for my peer interaction work is small and highly specialized. Still, the pattern in my thinking, then and as I did the Lester study, was: "I want to be a researcher" (later, "I am a researcher"); "I need to be doing research"; "I need a site in which to do research." I defined part of my professional identity as a researcher interested in studying children's social relations. Another major part of that identity was (is) "tenured university professor." I internalized the value system of the research university and saw doing research as inherently good and my doing and publishing research as inherently necessary. If becoming a tenured, full professor at a university that valued research meant "famous," then I was doing research to make myself famous. These selfish ends helped prevent me from seeing myself as engaged in an ethical paradox. I was on the scene to do research, so questioning the value of that activity never came up.

As a doctoral candidate and as a new assistant professor, I was so intent on doing what I thought of as quality research that I rarely stepped back to reflect on what I was doing or what it meant. While I was doing the Lester study, I was teaching several classes (all of which were new preparations), I was advising a large number of undergraduate and graduate students, and I was serving on department and university committees. I was doing what most new assistant professors do at the same time I was completing a labor-intensive participant observation study. I did not have time (or make time) to contemplate the ethical implications of my work—I was too busy *doing* my work. I was a prisoner of the moment-to-moment preoccupations of doing the research and my other faculty work, placing myself in a position to be justly challenged by the teacher who confronted me at AERA.

A third "blinder" was my view of research as superior to other activities. Holding this view kept me from seeing the importance of consulting directly with the teacher about what might be best for Lester. The "integrity" of the research was more important than the ongoing activity of the classroom. I felt a kind of superior vantage point from which to "look down" on what was happening in the classroom. After all, I was generating knowledge that might offer some new understandings of the day-to-day life of children like Lester. That superiority helped keep me from seeing Lester as a person (ironically, one of the goals of the study). My objectification of him in the research process (see Foucault, 1977) blinded me to possibilities for making his immediate day-to-day conditions better.

The paradox is genuine: I see two sides to all of these issues. Research has something to contribute to our understandings of what goes on in the everyday worlds of children and adults. My embarrassment comes from admitting that until the teacher pinned me, I did not see any dilemma. My selfishness, my myopic concentration on the moment-to-moment dimensions of my professional life, and my inflated notions of the importance of research caused me to miss a meaningful understanding of the paradox before me.

What would I do differently if I were doing the Lester study today? I would start by bringing the teacher in as a partner in the research process. If she had been more actively involved in the study's design and implementation, she would have known what I knew about Lester and his peers. Having observed Lester's social difficulties, I would share my data and concerns with the teacher. If she agreed, together we would plan an intervention on Lester's behalf, bringing in others as appropriate. The nature of the study would obviously change, but conceivably it could become an examination of Lester and his peers' social relations within a context that includes the planned intervention. I could maintain some distance as "passive observer" (i.e., I would not have to initiate the intervention myself) while addressing Lester's difficult social situation. In the discussion below, I outline more general ethical considerations related to doing qualitative research in early childhood settings.

ETHICAL CONSIDERATIONS

This is a personal story, and the conclusions are personal to me in this situation. I realize that these self-revelations qualify as what Patai (1994) has called "nouveau solipsism." Nevertheless, I think there is more here than just the awareness that "scholarly works do not fall from heaven, but are written by human beings" (Patai, 1994, p. A52). I have learned from dealing with the uneasiness this story reveals to invest more anxiety on the front end of a study in order to reduce the chances of facing such discomfort when it becomes too late to do anything about it. In part, this means facing my motives for doing a study, attempting to come to grips with the reality of my own self-interests.

Again, there are two sides here—it is not enough, and probably dishonest, to say, "I have no selfish interests in my research." I believe Tripp's (1994) comments about biographical studies of teachers' lives apply to the broader spectrum of classroom studies: "For others to gain more professionally from teacher [research] than the teachers themselves in an appropriation I believe to be socially unjust" (Tripp, 1994, p. 75). I want to get my selfishness out on the table and balance it with the other forces surrounding the research, including especially the needs and expectations of those I am lucky enough to study.

I want to be more reflective as I do my work. I do not want to become so caught up in the doing of the work that I forget to stop and check my feelings, perceptions, and thoughts about the work. Again, I do not want to get to the end of a study, then discover that something vital was overlooked because I was so busy with the moment-to-moment press of doing qualitative research. Even keeping a research journal is not necessarily sufficient (I was trained to keep such journals). Unless some real distance from the research process is generated and some difficult issues are addressed, writing in a journal can be just a written version of focusing on the immediate.

I want to keep research and my role as researcher in a more balanced perspective. I want to trust the good judgment of participants in the settings I study rather than assuming that they cannot offer helpful insights into research processes and the findings of the study as they emerge. I want to develop research relationships that give participants the opportunity to be "actively engaged in the construction and validation of meaning" (Lather, 1986, p. 268). I want to move beyond the conventional model of social science research in which the researcher takes what he or she wants from the research site, then abruptly pulls out (see Reinharz, 1979). As I work with teachers on research projects, I want to include them as partners in the work, dividing the responsibilities and the benefits.

Finally, I want to find ways to get in closer touch with my feelings as studies progress, to trust those feelings, and to act accordingly. I have had a nagging sense of remorse since the confrontation with the teacher at AERA. As I have noted, the main source of my guilt is that I never recognized I was dealing with an ethically paradoxical situation. I want to be a fully human and caring individual as I do my research, not just a data-collecting instrument. I want to know my feelings and trust them to guide me to do what is right in relation to those I study. One way systematically to keep tabs on those feelings is to force myself to answer tough ethical questions about my work. Some questions that go beyond the ethical-legal issues usually covered in human subjects safeguards and codes of research ethics are:

Why am I doing this study?
Why am I doing it at this site?
What is my relationship to the participants?
What are participants' roles in the design, data collection, analysis, and authorship of the study?
Who owns the study?
Who benefits from this study?
How do I benefit?
How do the participants benefit?
Who benefits most?
Who may be at risk in the contexts I am studying?
Should I intervene on behalf of those at risk?

Researchers need not be paralyzed by ethical concerns. By asking ourselves questions like these at every stage of the research process, we can contribute important knowledge without appropriating participants' experiences, understandings, and even their miseries to serve our own ends.

REFERENCES

Becker, H. S. (1963). *Outsiders: Studies in the sociology of deviance*. New York: Free Press.

Erickson, K. T. (1966). *Wayward Puritans: A study of the sociology of deviance*. New York: Wiley.

Goffman, E. (1963). *Stigma*. Englewood Cliffs, N.J.: Prentice-Hall.

Foucault, M. (1977). *Discipline and punish: The birth of the prison*. (A. Sheraton, Trans.). Harmondsworth: Penguin.

Hatch, J. A. (1988). Learning to be an outsider: Peer stigmatization in kindergarten. *The Urban Review, 20*, 59–72.

Hatch, J. A. (1989). Alone in a crowd: Analysis of secondary adjustments in a kindergarten. *Early Child Development and Care, 44*, 39–49.

Labov, W. (1972). *Sociolinguistic patterns*. Philadelphia: University of Pennsylvania Press.

Lather, P. (1986). Research as praxis. *Harvard Educational Review, 56*, 257–277.

Lincoln, Y. S., & Guba, E. G. (1985). *Naturalistic inquiry*. Beverly Hills, Calif.: Sage.

Patai, D. (1994, February 23). Sick and tired of scholars' nouveau solipsism. *The Chronicle of Higher Education*, p. A52.

Peshkin, A. (1978). *Growing up American: Schooling and the survival of community*. Chicago: University of Chicago Press.

Peshkin, A. (1986). *God's choice: The total world of a fundamentalist Christian school*. Chicago: University of Chicago Press.

Reinharz, S. (1979). *On becoming a social scientist*. San Francisco: Jossey-Bass.

Roman, L. G. (1989). *Double exposure: The politics of feminist materialist ethnography*. Paper presented at the Annual Meeting of the American Educational Research Association, San Francisco.

Schwartz, M. S., & Schwartz, C. G. (1955). Problems in participant observation. *American Journal of Sociology, 60*, 343–353.

Spradley, J. P. (1980). *Participant observation*. New York: Holt, Rinehart and Winston.

Tobin, J., & Davidson, D. (1990). The ethics of polyvocal ethnography: Empowering vrs. textualizing children and teachers. *International Journal of Qualitative Studies in Education, 3*, 271–284.

Tripp, D. (1994). Teachers' lives, critical incidents, and professional practice. *International Journal of Qualitative Studies in Education, 7*, 65–76.

Chapter 13

Post-Structural Research in Early Childhood Education

JOSEPH TOBIN

PREFACE: SOME THOUGHTS ON UNIVERSITY TOPOGRAPHY

Our college of education is on the wrong side of University Avenue, separated from the rest of the campus by six lanes of traffic. My colleagues and I in the Department of Curriculum and Instruction work in a building that sits between the lab school and Burger King. Our spatial remove marks a deeper difference. In the topography of the university, education faculty, and early childhood education faculty in particular, are not just outside but also down. The field of early childhood education is beneath as well as peripheral to the social sciences and humanities. This is a difference of job conditions, of academic status, and of scholarly expectations. Our colleagues across campus in the humanities and social sciences and down the hall in educational foundations have more time for theory and more latitude to play the role of intellectuals. While they are immersed in theory, we early childhood educators are preparing teachers and writing about issues of policy and practice.

The practicality of our teaching and scholarship is a virtue that only becomes a deficit when it lacks an active engagement with theory. Practice is necessarily informed by theory. But too often the theory that informs our teaching and writing is theory we have carried with us more or less untouched, unexamined, and uncritiqued from our undergraduate social science courses and from our graduate seminars in educational psychology and social foundations. Our problem is not that we are on the periphery of the university (for things are rotten in the core) but that we are stuck in time, too often failing to engage with emerging theory in the humanities and social sciences.

. I am not suggesting that we early childhood educators should change our research agenda with each passing scholarly fad in the humanities and social sciences. But I believe that by failing to engage with the post-structural theories and methods that are enlivening debate in faculties across campus we are missing the chance to open important new lines of inquiry. Tied too tightly to structuralist theories and assumptions, our research is too safe, conventional, self-referential, and self-affirming. Meanwhile, disturbing, dangerous, unaskable questions hover at the edge of our intellectual consciousness. There are things we know about early childhood education but cannot or will not say aloud or put into print. Post-structuralism provides a language we can use to address our unspeakable concerns and to critique our unquestionable assumptions. Although post-structural theorists such as Michel Foucault, Mikhail Bakhtin, Frederic Jameson, Jacques Derrida, and Judith Butler have written little or nothing about young children, their theories beg to be applied to early childhood education.

POST-STRUCTURALISM ACROSS CAMPUS

Post-structuralism is an umbrella term for loosely allied writings that seek to destabilize the positivism, optimism, and systematicity of such structuralist/modernist movements as Sausserian linguistics, Marxist political economy, Freudian psychoanalysis, Levi-Straussian anthropology, Piagetian psychology, and Proppian literary criticism. As Jonathan Culler writes: "Structuralists are convinced that systematic knowledge is possible; post-structuralists claim to know only the impossibility of this knowledge" (1984, p. 22). No longer believing in the possibility of describing reality objectively, post-structural anthropologists and historians are viewing the texts they write as stories rather than as treatises. Rejecting their orthodox predecessors' reduction of all causation to material conditions, neo-Marxists are exploring the circulation of such non-material commodities as knowledge, power, and pleasure. Disillusioned with the structuralists' project of uncovering authentic underlying meanings, post-structural literary critics are arguing that the meanings of texts are multiple and fluctuating. Terry Eagleton refers to this movement as "a shift from seeing the poem or novel as a closed entity, equipped with definite meanings which it is the critic's task to decipher, to seeing it as irreducibly plural, an endless play . . . which can never be finally nailed down to a single, centre, essence, or meaning" (1983, pp. 139–140).

Post-structuralism's penetration of the academy is incomplete. In colleges of education, post-structuralism is for the most part contained within departments of educational foundations and doctoral programs in curriculum theory. Early childhood education remains largely unaffected. Child development courses generally get no closer to post-structuralism than Vygotsky (who is post-structural only in comparison to Piaget). On most campuses, doctoral students in early childhood education programs read little or no post-structural theory in their required courses. *Young Children, The Journal of Research in Childhood Education*, and *The Early Childhood Research Quarterly* publish little that is post-structural in theory or style. The names Foucault, Derrida, Bourdieu, Bakhtin, and Butler do not come up often at mainstream early childhood educational conferences.

An Explanation for This Absence

Although my aim is to arrange a marriage, I must admit from the start that post-structuralism and early childhood education make an unlikely match. To put the problem in caricature: post-structural academicians (like their post-modern cousins in the arts) are cool, ironic, detached, well-dressed, urbane, wealthy, elitist, insincere, and relentlessly intellectual (in a word, French). Early childhood educators are earnest, sincere, fashionless, underpaid, egalitarian, and relentlessly practical (we know how to make play-dough from scratch). Although early childhood education in the United States has been influenced over the years by continental theorists from Froebel, Montessori, and A. S. Neil to the currently popular Italian Reggio Emilia movement, it remains, at heart, a very American field.

Since its beginnings, scholarship in early childhood education has been characterized by a belief in the authenticity of firsthand experience and knowledge: to understand children we need only careful observation and common sense. If we listen and watch children sensitively, it will become clear what they need. The favorite studies in early childhood education are based on close readings of children: Paley on four-year-olds talking about super-heroes in the doll corner; Piaget on his cognitively developing daughters; Erikson's case studies of the gendered block play of boys and girls.

These authors are structuralists, as each seeks to uncover meanings that lie beneath the ordinariness of children's everyday speech and action. The structuralism of Piaget and Erikson is of a special type: developmentalism, the belief that maturation is the movement along an irreversibly sequenced set of stages (O'Loughlin, 1992). The stories they tell are travel narratives: tales of young children journeying along the road toward emotional and cognitive maturity, encountering challenges and setbacks, but nearly always arriving at their destination.

This preference for firsthand description and for developmental case studies has tended to make us more open than our colleagues in elementary and secondary education to qualitative research. But for the most part, qualitative studies published in early childhood educational journals have failed to throw off the positivism of the quantitative research paradigm. Most qualitative research in early childhood education reflects the belief that people mean pretty much what they say, that texts have stable meanings, and that the reality of a classroom can be captured by a careful ethnographer. Post-structural research, in contrast, is characterized by a suspicion of the meaning of words and actions, a lack of belief in the stability of textual meaning, and a cynicism about the claims of ethnography and other naturalistic research methods.

A MODEST PROPOSAL

Despite the many reasons that post-structural theory and early childhood education are unlikely to get along, I believe that research in early childhood education can be enriched by a turn to post-structuralism (and post-structuralism by an engagement with early childhood education). As the caricature above suggests, there are a number of things wrong with post-structuralism. It is too often elitist, disconnected from practice, and fatalistic about the possibility of change.[1] Yet, as I read post-structural texts I find myself thinking not just that these theories can be made to fit early childhood education, but that these theories cry out for such an application.

In the (name-dropping, playful, reckless) spirit of post-structuralism, I offer a series of half-written (half-baked?) speculations on what a post-structural research project for early childhood research might look like. What follows are a series of premature expositions, each of which pairs the writing of a particular post-structural theorist with a troubling issue in early childhood education. These are notes for research projects of my own, some recently begun, some already abandoned, some waiting to be started.

SIGHT-LINES AND CHILDHOOD SEXUALITY

There are many reasons to set up a child care center's physical space, staffing patterns, and curricular routines in ways that allow teachers to be able to monitor what each child is doing at all times. It is desirable, for example, to be able to tell at a glance if children are growing bored with a scheduled activity, or if two children are about to start a fight, or if someone is about to knock over a jar of paint. For these reasons and others, when we are caring for children, it is often desirable to have them in our sight. But it is fear of dangerous sexuality that transforms this desire to watch children into an imperative. Sight-lines and other technologies for making children visible have taken on a sense of urgency. This urgency is the result of the popular perception that young children in our care but out of our sight are vulnerable to sexual abuse. This perception has led child care providers to conclude that staff members who fail to keep children in their sight are laying themselves open to lawsuits.

In the late eighteenth century, the philosopher/social engineer Jeremy Bentham, in search of a humane alternative to the dungeon and the stockade, came up with a design for a modern penitentiary. He called his invention the Panopticon because it would allow a single guard, peering out from slotted windows in a central tower, to see all that occurs in a hundred or more small jail cells arranged in a grid before him. If this design sounds familiar, it is because it is the basic layout of Stateville and other well-known American prisons. In his book *Discipline and Punish*, Michel Foucault explains the power of the Panopticon:

The panoptic mechanism arranges spatial unities that make it possible to see constantly and to recognize immediately. In short, it reverses the principle of the dungeon; or rather of its three functions—to enclose, to deprive of light and to hide—it preserves only the first and eliminates the other two. Full lighting and the eye of a supervisor capture better than darkness, which ultimately protected. Visibility is a trap. (1979, p. 200)

At first glance, it seems ludicrous to compare preschools to prisons. But Foucault's project is to push us to make such counter-intuitive connections. *Discipline and Punish*, despite its subtitle, "The Birth of the Prison," has a much larger central concern than penology. As he uncovers the archaeology of punishment and discipline in the seventeenth and eighteenth centuries, Foucault is commenting on our present condition, suggesting that we are all imprisoned by our sense of being watched, of being guilty, and of being candidates for regimes of rehabilitation. For Foucault, the meaning of panopticism is both literal and metaphoric. Following Foucault, we can see in the everyday practices of the contemporary American preschool not just the play of such metaphorical panoptic mechanisms as self-scrutiny and psychological testing, but also of a literal panopticism obsessed with sight-lines and other techniques for making young children constantly visible.

Foucault's discussion of panopticism provides me with a theoretical basis for the study I am conducting on parents' and teachers' beliefs, attitudes, and practices toward preschool children's sexuality. This study grew out of my experiences in 1989 as the supervisor of preservice teachers of young children. I was surprised to find that the student teachers in my weekly seminar were struggling with how to respond to incidents of sexual play in young children, incidents that to me were innocent, natural, even inevitable: girls chasing and kissing boys; four-year-olds with their hands in their pants; playing doctor in the housekeeping corner. Why were my student teachers finding these ordinary childhood behaviors to be so problematic and even dangerous?

I had a hunch about the answer because during the late 1980s I, like other males in early childhood education, experienced firsthand the sudden development of suspicion of caretakers' motives and actions. Males (and more recently females) who work in early childhood education have been made to see themselves not only as caregivers and teachers but also, if not as potential pedophiles, as potential targets of accusations of sexually abusing children. Using stories I collected from my students, I designed a study that seeks to understand why as a society we suddenly are perceiving early childhood educational settings to be sexually dangerous and to explore the implications of this sense of danger on the lives of the young children and underpaid teachers who spend their days in preschools. This study, like Foucault's work, is dangerous because it may be read as an excuse or apology for not preventing the sexual abuse of children. In a climate where the conventional wisdom suggests that no price is too high to pay to prevent child abuse, it may be foolhardy to ask what is lost when teachers become afraid to touch or comfort children, when children lose the chance to be physically affectionate with each other and with adults, and when children's curiosity about their own bodies and the bodies of others is construed to be perilous and disgusting, or read as an indicator of past or potential abuse.

Foucault's post-structural project helps us ask these questions and to understand the historical development of these dynamics. Foucault's work teaches us that liberal discourses such as psychoanalysis, feminism, and child advocacy subscribed to by such well-meaning people as teachers, child care experts, and politicians can lead to repressive practices. Foucault advises us to ignore the conscious, stated intentions of do-gooders, and to concentrate instead on the effects of the practices they recommend. The explicit intention of those who lobby for fingerprinting teachers, for making toddlers wear swim suits over their pampers when they run through the sprinkler, for male care providers not changing diapers, and for children never to be out of adult sight is to prevent child abuse. The reality, which we know but choose to ignore, is that fingerprinting teachers, preventing male staff from changing diapers, and keeping children under constant surveillance will have virtually no impact on child abuse in our country. The ignoring of this reality is a special, active form of ignorance akin to the system of coded knowledge, open secrets, group amnesia, and unsayable truths that Eve Sedgwick describes in her book *The Epistemology of the Closet* (1990). We are unwilling or unable as a society to confront sexual abuse in homes, within families, where it is epidemic, and so we turn instead to imposing draconian measures in preschool settings, where proven cases of sexual abuse are exceedingly rare. The explicit intent of the new practices being instituted in preschools may be to prevent the sexual abuse of young children, but the result is to divert attention from the sexual abuse of children at home and to subject children and their caretakers to reduced freedom and spontaneity in their interactions.

The research method I am using for this study is to ask groups of preschool teachers, administrators, and parents to discuss eight case vignettes. Each of these vignettes is a short narrative that presents its readers with a situation in which a teacher or administrator must decide how to deal with an aspect of children's sexuality (or with what might appear to others to be a potentially sexually dangerous situation). For instance, one story describes a four-year-old girl who runs around the room kissing boys on the lips. Another describes a day care director walking by a classroom late in the day where a young male teacher's aide is holding a four-year-old girl on his lap. Another story tells of a teacher who catches two girls and a boy playing obstetrician in the housekeeping corner.

I have not yet fully analyzed the stories I gathered from parents and teachers, but my reading of Foucault helps me begin to make sense of statements such as these told to me in the last few years by preschool teachers:

A child center director: To catch that kind of problem before it gets started the secret is to set up the room so you can see at a glance right into the dress-up corner, and the quiet reading area, and everywhere else. We've totally reorganized our set-up here to give us improved sight-lines. Now, standing right here where we are sitting, if you stand up and turn around you can immediately see where everyone is and what they are doing.

A day care teacher: If I was the teacher in that story, I would be concerned. We've had to change our policies on closing the door in the bathroom and on kids going into the playhouse where they can't be seen.

A male university lab school teacher: I'm no longer allowed to change diapers or wipe the kids in the bathroom. I'm finding that I'm getting hesitant to even let kids sit on my lap anymore. It's not that I don't trust myself. But I have this awareness of how it might look to someone, how they might walk by and look at me with a girl in my lap and might draw the wrong conclusion.

A day care director: It's not that I don't trust my teachers, but I have to be realistic about things and enforce certain rules in order to protect the teachers and the school from being sued.

A female kindergarten teacher: When I was a kid, my Mom didn't work so I didn't go to nursery school everyday, and I must have been four or five and there were tons of kids on my block, and we'd gather in my garage. I remember being the doctor, and making some little boys from next door—they must have been younger than me, maybe three-years-old or so—I remember making them line up and I was the doctor and they were the patients and I'd call out, "Next patient." And when they came over to me I'd pretend to take their temperatures and give them a shot, but really the point of the game was to pull down their pants. Didn't everyone play games like that? My mother was probably in the house, cooking or watching TV. I guess she didn't feel like parents do now, that they have to be watching their children every second. I wonder if children these days ever get the chance to play doctor like we used to? I guess I'd like for kids to have the chance for that kind of sex play, because its part of growing up. But as a teacher, there is absolutely no way I can look the other way and let kids play doctor in my classroom. Do I sound hypocritical?

Where does this panopticism come from? Who orders it? Who benefits from it? Foucault teaches us to be aware of the diffuseness of power. There is no central authority enforcing panopticism in our preschool setting. Instead, the panopticism that rules the lives of preschool children and teachers is something we do to ourselves and to each other. Like the other repressive disciplinary practices Foucault describes, panopticism in early childhood education settings seems so necessary, prudent, inevitable, and logical that we do not ask where it came from or question what it costs.[2]

SELF-EXPRESSION AS POST-MODERN MALAISE

A post-modern critique of the curriculum of the American preschool would suggest that the self-expression taught in schools and practiced around dinner tables, in therapists' offices, and on talk shows is the quintessential empty discourse of the culture of late capitalism. If we were to give a name to this empty discourse, it would be the "hallmarkization of feeling." In the old days (when we were children), greeting cards offered conventional messages for conventional occasions, messages such as "Congratulations on Your 25th Anniversary!" or "Our feelings are with you during your time of bereavement." But now greeting cards are sold that contain such personal messages as "I hope last night was as special for you as it was for me." A store-bought card that purports to communicate a personal feeling is a paradigmatic product of a culture of late capitalism.

Frederic Jameson (1984) has defined the key features of late capitalism as superficiality, the dominance of the signifier over the signified, simulation, commodity reification, and the waning of affect. Each of these characteristics can be usefully applied to the discourses and practices of contemporary American early childhood education.[3]

The valorization of signifiers can be seen in early childhood education's logocentrism. The belief that signifiers (words) can adequately represent the signified (feelings) is essentially a modernist/structuralist belief (Derrida, 1976). In the contemporary American version of self-expression, we have moved further, beyond the modernist faith in meaningful communication through the spoken and written word, to the post-modern condition in which the word becomes more real and more important than that which is signified. In the post-modern early childhood educational world, statements about feeling ("I feel angry") replace expressions of feeling ("Give me the truck, you doo-doo head!"), which replace feelings (anger? competition? desire?).

In their 1989 paper, "Emotional Socialization in the Postmodern Era," Robin Leavitt and Martha Power offer a troubling exposition of what they see as the inauthenticity and superficiality of emotional expression in day care settings. Leavitt and Power paint a bleak portrait of day care settings in which childminders aggressively substitute their own interpretations of what children are feeling for children's authentic experiences of their bodies and emotions ("You aren't hungry. You just need a nap"). Leavitt and Power observe caregivers putting great emphasis on simulations— on children displaying desirable surface emotions at odds with their actual feelings:

Dwain and Gwen (both two years) were playing in a large gym with the rest of their day care class. . . . Dwain hit Gwen for no readily apparent reason. Gwen started to cry. A caregiver approached the two of them and said, "Dwain, that's not nice. You shouldn't hit your friends. Now give Gwen a hug and tell her you're sorry" (p. 38).

Other examples of the simulation and inauthenticity[4] of emotion can be seen in early childhood educational settings that have rules such as "We don't use mean words here," or "You are not allowed to tell someone 'I won't be your friend' " (Paley, 1992), or "You can come out of the time-out corner when you are ready to apologize."

Commodity reification is another characteristic of late capitalism that can be found in middle-class American preschools. Commodity reification in preschools is manifested by a conflation of things with value and by a consumer-oriented approach to the curriculum. Capitalism in its early stages is driven by production; late capitalism is driven by consumption. Late capitalism thus requires the endless manufacture of consumer need. As Jean Baudrillard (1988) argues in his essay on "consummativity," needs are not authentic, innate, spontaneous cravings but functions produced by the demands of the decaying capitalist system. Late capitalism requires consumers who have an insatiable need for new toys, gadgets, trendy clothes, decorative objects, and leisure activities. In late capitalism, the ideal man or woman is not self-made but self-consumed.

Consumer desire is reproduced by the material reality of our pre-schools. The variety of things and choices offered by middle-class preschools is overwhelming to many children. We create cluttered, ov-erstimulating environments modeled on the excess of the shopping mall and the amusement park and then we complain that children are hyper-active and unable to focus on what they are doing. We have become so used to the hyper-materiality of our early childhood care settings that we become oblivious to the clutter. Hyper-materiality has become so natural to us that settings that provide more structure and are less distracting seem stark or bleak. Many parents select a preschool the way they settle on an amusement park, shopping mall, or resort: by counting the variety of choices available.

In such a commodified world, a successful, well-adjusted preschooler is one who is an adroit consumer, able to cruise the aisles of the learning centers and know a good value when she sees it. A key characteristic of consumer society is the notion of scarcity amidst abundance. Although an excess of materials is available, consumers must believe that if they do not act quickly and impulsively, the opportunity will pass them by ("Only three left on the lot . . . " "The first two callers . . . "). Learning centers mirror this sense of consumer frenzy. For example, most preschools put limits on how many children (customers) can be in a learning center at any one time. To avoid a land-rush approach to deciding who will get access to the most desirable learning centers, many preschools use an auction system, which functions like the Home Shoppers Network. At the end of circle time, the teacher presents to the children a set of icons, each representing one of the learning centers that will be available for the next period. In one hand she holds up a firemen's hat, representing the dramatic play area, and with her other hand she puts up four fingers, representing the number of children the center can accommodate. The auction begins. Each time a child puts in a bid for the dramatic play area, another one of the teacher's fingers goes down. Excited, anxious children frantically attempt to assess the value of this option. The hat looks good, and the dramatic play area is certainly desirable, but is it more desirable than the other learning centers coming up later in the auction? As higher and lower status children make their bids, the value of the dramatic play area rises and falls like a commodity in the pit.

A personal note: When our son Isaac was three we enrolled him in a progressive children's center. The first hour of each day was free choice. Isaac would arrive at school, and the teachers would say, "Choose some-thing you want to do, Isaac." But Isaac did not know how to choose. He did not want to choose. He needed an adult to choose for him, to give him direction. At the time, we and his teachers viewed this inability or unwillingness to choose a play activity as a cognitive or emotional deficit of Isaac's that needed remediation. We and his teachers spent all year trying to get him to make choices and stick to them. But why should children have to have strong preferences about what to do and what to play with? Because we associate choice with democratic values (i.e., the sanctity of the ballot box) and with human rights (i.e., pro-choice) rather than with shopping, we fail to see how our choice-driven early childhood educational curriculum functions as an education in commodity reification and consumer desire.

DECONSTRUCTING CHILDREN'S TALK

Deconstruction is a school of literary studies in which texts are shown to have no fixed, stable, coherent meaning. Where formalist critics explicate and celebrate the genius of the author, and structuralists uncover a work's deep unity, deconstructionists such as Jacques Derrida search texts for internal inconsistencies, instabilities, and aporia (gaps). Madan Sarup summarizes Derrida's approach:

> He suggests that we should fasten upon a small but tell-tale moment in the text which harbours the author's sleight of hand and which cannot be dismissed simply as contradiction. We should examine that passage where we can provisionally locate the moment when the text transgresses the laws it apparently sets up for itself, and thus unravel—deconstruct—the very text. (1993, p. 43)

To be clear, texts do not deconstruct because they are poorly written. They deconstruct because their unity and coherence are an illusion. Texts can have no unified meaning or unambiguous message because the words (signifiers) that make up the text have no fixed or stable relationship to the things and concepts they are meant to signify. The meanings of words can only be described by using more words. Thus, Derrida argues, meaning is endlessly deferred.

What does this have to do with early childhood education? If, as deconstructive critics show us, great works such as *Hamlet* have no fixed meaning, what then of children's talk? Cognitive psychologists, clinicians, and classroom observers of young children have taught us to find meaning in the apparent meaninglessness of children's play and conversation. From Piaget we have learned that what appears to be an absence of reasoning in children's answers to our questions is in fact the presence of pre-operational stages of thought. From Erikson we have learned that what looks like random play and bizarre symptomology can be read as the playing out of predictable stages of psychosocial dynamics. From Paley (1984) we have learned to hear in children's doll corner conversations complex negotiations of gender roles.

There is something aesthetically pleasing in readings such as these which transform children's talk into orderly, meaningful, coherent narratives. But are these readings uncovering meaning that was already there, or imposing adult meanings onto children's conversation? I believe that the field of early childhood education could use some unreadings, some deconstructing of what have come to be conventional ways of reading children's conversations.

Consider the case of children and the media. Most educators are convinced that watching violent, sexist, and racist movies has a deleterious effect on young children. But how do we know this? My colleague Donna Grace and I are in the midst of a study of elementary students' critical understanding of television and movies. This study has turned into a deconstructive venture, an uncovering of what we do not and perhaps cannot know about the meanings children make out of the television shows and movies they watch.

To study young children's reactions to popular media, we show elementary students scenes from movies, television shows, and advertisements, then videotape the discussions that follow. For example, to get at children's reactions to violence, sexism, and racism, we showed lower-elementary students in a public school in Hawaii an action scene from the Disney movie, *Swiss Family Robinson*. In this scene, an army of Asian and Polynesian pirates attempts to dislodge the Robinson family from their hilltop fortress. The pirates are repulsed by coconut bombs and an avalanche of logs the inventive Robinsons drop on them. Here is an edited segment from the transcript of a focus group interview session with six eight-year-old girls (four of whom are Asian-American, two of whom are part-Hawaiian). The first set of comments are made while watching the scene, the second just after I turned off the VCR.

(*During watching*)

Joanna (in a silly sing-song): Aha, aha, good for you.

Summer (to Joe): Did you ever watch *Snowy River*?

Tina: Right on his head!

Summer: One guy got trump, tramp, tramped to death.

Summer (commenting on the action on the screen): Japanese against Americans.

Joanna (to Joe): How long does it take?

Joe: About one more minute. Are you bored?

Summer: No.

Joanna: I'm getting hungry. I want to eat Cheerios now.

Summer: They're, they're wasting wood. You should use it as paper.

Ritchel: Use it as paper?

(after watching the segment)

Joe: How can you tell who were the good guys in that movie and who were the bad ones?

Ritchel: Because they were attacking.

Summer: No, because they look more bad and more good.

Joe: What makes the bad ones look bad? I don't know what you mean.

Summer (pulling on her eyelids): Like Chinese eyes, and . . .

Kuuipa: And they have knives, that's why.

Joe: What made the good guys look good?

Ritchel: They had clothes on that aren't like junk.

Of the forty focus group discussions we conducted on *Swiss Family Robinson*, this one immediately drew our attention because it seemed to contain perfect answers to the central questions of our research. We began with the concern that children were vulnerable to racism, sexism, imperialism, and violence in the media. We selected the *Swiss Family Robinson* segment as an interview stimulus because it contained these themes. The children's answers seemed to bear out our concerns. They laughed as the Swiss family threw coconut bombs and logs on the pirates. They did not question the sexism of the young boy in the family being a more capable fighter than his older sister or his mother, whose involvement is limited to reloading rifles. And they accepted the imperialist depiction of the legitimacy of the white family's claim to the tropical island and the racist depiction of the white family's moral and cognitive superiority to the ragtag collection of people of color who fought them.

The moment in this group interview that is most disturbing is when Summer says you can identify the bad guys by their "Chinese eyes." Summer, who is Japanese-American, tugged on the corners of her eyelids as she made her comment. Her words and action are chilling. A young Asian-American girl identifies with the Caucasian protagonists and locates villainy in the bad guys' Oriental features. What clearer evidence of the vulnerability of young viewers to racist images could we hope to find?

The problem is that each time we play the videotape of this focus group, we become less clear about the meaning of Summer's words. Gradually, after our twentieth or thirtieth time through the videotape and the transcript, a new reading began to emerge. Summer's "Chinese eyes" comment could mean not that she believes that Asians are less good than whites but that her viewing experiences have taught her that Hollywood often represents evil with knives, tattered clothing, buffoonish behavior, and non-white physical features. Instead of seeing Summer as a media victim, we began to see her as a media expert. I asked her how you tell the good guys from the bad guys and Summer answered with a semiotic analysis of the representation of evil in Disney films.

What internal evidence is there in the text (the transcript of the focus group interview) for this reading of "Chinese eyes"? Summer's first comment to me is "Did you ever see *Snowy River*?" I didn't understand this question at the time, but have since concluded that Summer, immediately intuiting the point of our project, decided to play the role of the model student who would give me, the teacher and researcher, the answers I needed. Surmising, correctly, that I was looking for evidence of the effects of violent and racist movies on children, as the *Swiss Family Robinson* segment began to roll, Summer asked me if I had seen *Snowy River* and if I were aware that it, also, contains a scene of people being "tramped" to death. *Snowy River* is an Australian children's movie, an Australian equivalent to a Disney action film. I believe Summer was saying to me, "Oh, I get it. You are interested in our reactions to movies that contain scenes of violence. You must have had a hard time deciding which film segments to use in this research. Perhaps you should consider using the stampede scene from *Snowy River*."

Joanna, who throughout the session played the disruptive, bad girl role to Summer's good girl role, also seemed to know from the start what we were up to. Joanna quickly saw that I was showing them movie clips and television commercials for my research needs rather than for their pleasure. She resisted first by encouraging the other girls to be active, silly viewers ("Aha, aha, good for you . . . ") and then by telling me she was bored and hungry ("I want to eat Cheerios"). Why Cheerios? Because just before showing the *Swiss Family Robinson* segment, we showed the children a Cheerios commercial to gather information about their susceptibility to advertisements. Joanna resisted by teasing me about my project. I read her comment as: "You are asking us if we are affected by what we watch? You know we are. If you didn't want us to get hungry, you shouldn't have shown us a food commercial! You are responsible for my hunger, and thus for my inability to pay attention to your questions."

These readings of Summer's and Joanna's comments are more structural than post-structural. There is nothing yet deconstructive or unconventional in my reading, nothing that suggests the impossibility of getting to the bottom of things. Where is Derrida's "aporia"? Where are the fissure, the gap, the moment where the text transgresses its laws and begins to unravel? Joanna's and Summer's comments have a hint of the uncanny, a feeling that the meaning of their words is simultaneously more and less than what they seem. Their comments are answers to my questions about the effect of media on children, but they are also performance pieces which comment, parodically, on our project. In the discussion, are Summer and Joanna reacting to a Disney movie, or playing the parts of children reacting to an adult/researcher/teacher watching them react to a Disney movie?

I now believe that there is something too good to be true in the starkness of Summer's "Chinese eyes" comment. Part of this feeling comes from my sense that her words are uncannily like the words I would have scripted for her to write if I had made up the research instead of actually conducting it. Or perhaps, were I making it up, I would hesitate to put the words "Chinese eyes" in the mouth of a young Asian-American girl because the meaning is so clear and shocking that it threatens to overwhelm us and lose its effect.

There is another point in the interview where the internal consistency of the text deconstructs, where it turns inward on itself, and exclaims its incoherence. This point is Summer's comment: "They're wasting wood. You should use it for paper." Summer made this comment at the moment that John Mills, playing the father, chops through a rope with his ax, unleashing a stack of logs he had arranged as a booby trap for the pirates. One reading of this unlikely comment is that Summer, the politically correct good girl who has intuited the central concerns of our project, is throwing in an ecological perspective. It is as if she is thinking, "He's interested in violence and sexism and imperialism in movies—what about the media's depiction of the wasting of natural resources?"

This was my working, structuralist interpretation of the line "they're wasting wood" until recently, when I presented my research to the graduate students in my qualitative research methods class. One student commented "there is something weird about that line. You aren't supposed to save trees to use them for paper. You are supposed to use less paper in order to save trees. Doesn't she have things backwards?"

Backwardness, upsidedownness, illogic, and other inversions cry out to us for deconstruction. "They're wasting wood. You should use it for paper" is inverted on several levels. It is an inversion of the usual hierarchy of humane concern: shouldn't we be more concerned (at least for the moment) for the men who are being crushed by the avalanche of logs than for the trees that are doing the crushing? It is an inversion of student and teacher roles: even before the current era of ecological consciousness, teachers have been justifying their control of the school's supply of paper by accusing students who fail to draw on the backs and edges of their paper of being wasteful; students never get to lob this accusation of wastefulness at teachers who daily distribute piles of mimeographed worksheets. And it is most significantly an inversion of commonsense logic and everyday language, an inversion akin to a Freudian slip (for deconstruction owes much to psychoanalysis), that alerts us that something here, and in the text as a whole, is not what it seems.

The more I struggle to understand statements like "Chinese eyes" and "they're wasting trees," the less clear I am about what they mean. Summer's "Chinese eyes" comment could mean that we should be disturbed by this evidence that children are hurt by racist media images. On the other hand, Summer's comments can be interpreted to suggest that young viewers understand much more than we give them credit for about the semiotics of children's movies. Or the comments of Summer and the other children in the focus group can be viewed as a performance, as a parody of adults' fears and fantasies about children's media watching. Children are adept at answering teachers' and researchers' questions in ways that make them simultaneously transparent and opaque (Bucking-ham, 1990). What it means for us is that two years into our media education project, we know less than we did at the start about the sense that children make out of movies and television. Or rather, we now know a lot more about what we do *not* know and *cannot* know about children and the media.[5] I find this all encouraging, rather than depressing, for an appreciation of our ignorance is the beginning of understanding. As Peggy Phelan writes: "Perhaps the best possibility for 'understanding' racial, sexual, and ethnic difference lies in the *active* acceptance of the inevitability of misunderstanding" (1993, p. 174).

CARNIVAL AND BODILY LOWER STRATUM

The lot of the child care worker is to toil in an infantile, grotesque world of spilled milk, dirty diapers, silly talk, naughty words, and doo-doo jokes. The central goal of early childhood education typically is construed as helping children rise up out of their lowly state: to move from actions to words, from the body to the mind (from sensory-motor thinking to concrete operations), from the polymorphous perversity of oral, anal, and genital preoccupation to the earnest task-centeredness of the latency stage. Structuralist, topographical understandings of the world locate the words and actions of young children beneath and below, down with the primitive, the developmentally delayed, and the lower classes. According to this spatial/temporal mapping, early childhood, like the neanderthal period and feudalism, is something to transcend. Mikhail Bakhtin's (1984) writings on the carnivalesque provide us with a much more fluid view of high and low culture, of the upper and lower classes, of the mind and the body, and thus, by extension, of the humor and interests of adults and children. Instead of seeing grotesqueries, scatology, and the humor of the "bodily lower stratum" as something to loathe and transcend, Bakhtin sees in the carnivalesque humor of the peasantry in the Middle Ages the affirmation of life and society. Bakhtin writes of the carnival:

We find here a characteristic logic, the peculiar logic of the "inside out," of the "turnabout," of a continual shifting from top to bottom, from front to rear, of numerous parodies and travesties, humiliations, profanations, comic crownings and uncrownings. A second life, a second world of folk culture is thus constructed; it is to a certain extent a parody of the extracarnival life, a "world inside out" (p. 11).

A hallmark of the humor of carnival is grotesque realism: "The essential principle of grotesque realism is degradation; that is, the lowering of all that is high, spiritual, ideal, abstract; it is a transfer to the material level, to the sphere of earth and body in their indissoluble unity" (pp. 19–20).

Although preschool and lower-elementary teachers are well aware of the grotesque realism of the play of young children, early childhood educational research has shied away from studying children's bodily pleasures. A prissy hesitancy to write in other than clinical terms about children's interest in the bodily lower stratum contributes to a bowdlerized curriculum that fails to live up to its claim to begin "where children are at."

Donna Grace and I have learned something about where children are at in our video education project at Waiau Elementary School in Hawaii.[6] Our plan was to give children video cameras and let them make movies about things that interest them. We anticipated, naively and optimistically, that students would choose to make movies based on classics of children's literature such as *Where the Wild Things Are*, *Charlotte's Web*, and *The Magic School Bus*. Neither we nor the teachers were prepared for the scripts that emerged in classroom after classroom: remakes of *The Three Ninjas*, *The Simpsons* ("Fart Simpson"), and *The Little Mermaid*, and a series of original screenplays in the genre of grotesque realism.

Example One: A group of third graders wrote a screenplay for a parody of the television show "America's Funniest People." Scenes written for "Waiau's Funniest Kids" include a boy with a cold who repeatedly wipes his snot-drenched hands on his classmates' shirts; a blind girl who bumps into walls; a stuttering singer who can't get through the school song; and hula dancing girls whose grass skirts fall off. Example Two: The first grade teacher told her class to write stories on the theme of "adventures in space." A group of her students decided to make one of these student-authored stories, "Chase Master Monster," into a movie. The script is simple. There is a planet that is so hot that the kid-monsters who live there have to wear ice-cube shoes when they go out to play. One day they get so caught up in their chasing game that their shoes melt. Too hot to stay on their feet, they drop onto their butts, which quickly start smoldering. They then run home, fanning their butts and screaming. At home, they drop their butts into buckets of ice water. The expression on their faces is pure pleasure. One actor sighs, "Man, that feels good!"

This second video fits Bakhtin's celebration of the bodily lower stratum. The first, which is also full of grotesque realism, follows the parodic humor of the carnival which comments sarcastically and irreverently, but not angrily, on the social order. Why the jokes about handicapped students and hula dancers? Because these are important social issues at Waiau. Waiau School stresses full inclusion of special needs students, and Waiau is one of the four elementary shools in Hawaii that houses a Hawaiian Language Immersion program.

Donna Grace and I have found reading Bakhtin useful for understanding and responding to student projects. Bakhtin's praise of the pro-social spirit of carnival undercuts our tendency to tell the students that scripts about snotty hands and hot butts do not belong in school.[7] Peter Stallybrass and Allon White build on Bakhtin's work to argue in *The Politics and Poetics of Transgression* (1986) that the grotesque humor, irreverent parodies, masquerades, and inversions that entertained European peasants on market days and at carnivals strengthened the fabric of society. In the pre-modern era, merchants, clergy, and the ruling classes joined in the revelry, rather than attempting to stamp it out. As the figure of the court jester suggests, kings not only tolerated but encouraged transgressive humor. Bakhtin argues that rulers in the Enlightenment era became threatened by transgression. Those in power, from government leaders to school teachers, cut themselves off from the synthetic joy of the communal body and the carnivalesque spirit of inversion. A lesson we early childhood educators can learn from Bakhtin is that class clowns are to be treasured rather than reformed and that bodily humor and parody can bind a classroom together as a community.

QUEERING UP OUR RESEARCH, THEORY, AND PRACTICE

A problem in attempting to outline an avant garde research agenda for early childhood education is that by the time I write it and you read it, it is already old. My goal has been to suggest some daring directions for research, but I fear that my discussion has been entirely too safe and too conventional. What is needed, in this paper and in our research, is to "queer things up".[8] Queering up means not only paying attention to gay and lesbian perspectives in our research on young children but more generally calling into question "the regime of the normal." As David Warner writes in *Fear of a Queer Planet*:

Can we not hear in the resonances of queer protest an objection to the normalization of behavior . . . and to the cultural phenomenon of societalization? If queers, incessantly told to alter their "behavior," can be understood as protesting not just the normal behavior of the social but the *idea* of a normal behavior, they will bring skepticism to the methodologies founded on that idea (1993, p. xxvii).

The emerging fields of queer theory, post-colonialism, gender studies, and performance studies are challenging us to move beyond the safety of our conventional notions of identity, ethnicity, gender, and pleasure (Sedgwick, 1990; Butler, 1990, 1993). And what better place to see identity, culture, gender, and the formation of pleasure at play than in preschools? Carnivalesque hyper-masculinity and hyper-femininity (Irigaray, 1985; Butler, 1990) are on full display everyday in the dress-up corners and housekeeping centers of our preschools and kindergartens. The polymorphous perverse desire and scatological aesthetics that performance critics like Peggy Phelan (1993) celebrate in Robert Mapplethorpe's infamous photos of naked gay men and Mira Shorr's paintings of dismembered body parts are on permanent display in our children's centers. The gender-bending, power-playing mimesis and hybridity that post-colonial scholars debate in their essays on films such as *The Crying Game*, *Paris Is Burning*, and *M. Butterfly* (Butler, 1993; Phelan, 1993; Kondo, 1993) are familiar scripts in the block corners and sandbox societies of early childhood education. The exhibitionism and performativity that queer theorists locate in New York vamping and San Francisco camp are always on display in our preschools, where children are continually calling out to us, "Watch this!" and "Look at me!"

Early childhood educational research should be at the cutting edge of the emerging fields of gender studies, queer studies, post-colonialism, and cultural studies. Suddenly the most avant garde of theorists are enthralled with the raw gender and power issues that are the everyday stuff of our work with young children. Shouldn't we be joining in the exploration of these issues?

NOTES

1. Since the form of this essay is an appeal for a post-structural research agenda in early childhood education, I shall isolate my critiques of post-structural theories to these notes, where they are unlikely to do my argument much harm.

2. A problem with Foucault's argument is that it does not acknowledge the possibility of resistance. I believe that the good news about the Panopticon is that in practice, unlike in theory, it does not work all that well. Preschool teachers and children, like prisoners, find ways to resist and avoid the panoptic gaze.

3. Jameson, Baudrillard, and other post-modern theorists of late capitalism see the materialism, inauthenticity, and affectlessness of contemporary society as being a unique historical development. Critics respond that life in the era of late capitalism is not all that different from life one hundred years ago and that the material conditions and class interests described by Marx and Engels still apply.

4. Post-structural deconstructions of the inauthenticity of day care centers and other sites of late capitalism run the danger of repeating modernism's romantic (humanist) fallacy. To suggest that the contemporary early childhood educational discourse on the emotions is inauthentic may seem to imply that in some earlier era or under some conditions feelings could be expressed authentically. When they are not careful, post-structural critics ensnare themselves in the same Rous-

seauian trap as those natural learning and whole language theorists who suggest that if adults would only get out of the way and not impose rules on discourse, children's authentic voices will come through. If all forms of self-expression are culturally constructed, are they not all equally (in)authentic?

5. Critics point out that in problematizing all forms of interpretation, deconstruction undermines emancipatory political action and thereby supports the status quo. This critique can be applied to my deconstructive reading of Summer's "Chinese eyes" comment. I hope that my suggestion that we do not know what meanings Summer makes out of Disney's racist semiotics will not be read as an apology for Hollywood's racism or as an argument for being sanguine about the effects of the media on children.

6. Donna Grace, who is my colleague in studying video in schools, has recently completed a dissertation on "Butt Jokes and Gummy Worms: Pleasure and Popular Culture in the Elementary School Curriculum."

7. Our telling children that they could make movies about anything they wanted to may have been confusing, for surely we did not really mean that *anything* they made we and their teachers would find acceptable. David Buckingham (1990) raises the point that there is a danger that our invitations to children to bring their interest in popular culture into the classroom may serve to colonize one of the last outposts of children's pleasure by making it a topic for our curricular machinations. We share this concern, but we find reassurance in Peggy Phelan's (1993) argument that the unmarked (the unsocialized realm of identity and pleasure) is not a finite land.

8. A danger in using the term "queer" is that seeing it in print may serve to further marginalize gays and lesbians. But queer theorists and activists argue that in a profoundly homophobic society, homosexuals are "abjects" (rather than subjects) whether they are called homosexuals, gays, lesbians, or queers, and that it is useful to call attention to this abjection.

REFERENCES

Bakhtin, M. (1984) *Rabelais and his world*. Bloomington: Indiana University Press.

Baudrillard, J. (1988). *Selected writings*. Stanford, Calif: Stanford University Press.

Buckingham, D. (1990) *Watching media learning: Making sense of media education*. London: Falmer Press.

Butler, J. (1990). *Gender matters*. London: Routledge.

Butler, J. (1993). *Bodies that matter*. London: Routledge.

Culler, J. (1984). *On deconstruction: Theory and criticism after structuralism*. Ithaca, N.Y.: Cornell University Press.

Derrida, J. (1976). *Of grammatology*. Baltimore: Johns Hopkins University Press.

Eagleton, T. (1983). *Literary theory: An introduction*. London: Redwood Burn Ltd.

Foucault, M. (1979). *Discipline and punish: The birth of the prison*. New York: Vintage Books.

Irigaray, L. (1985). *Speculum of the other woman*. Ithaca: Cornell University Press.

Jameson, F. (1984). *Postmodernism: Or, the cultural logic of late capitalism*. Durham, N.C.: Duke University Press.

Kondo, D. (1993). "Orientalism, gender, and a critique of essentialist identity. *Cultural Critique, 5,* 5–29.

Leavitt, R., & Power, M. (1989). Emotional socialization in the postmodern era: Children in daycare. *Social Psychological Quarterly, 52* (1), 35–43.

O'Loughlin, M. (1992). Rethinking science education: Beyond Piagetian constructivism toward a sociocultural model of teaching and learning. *Journal of Research in Science Teaching, 29,* 791–820.

Paley, V. (1984). *Boys and girls: Superheroes in the doll corner.* Chicago: University of Chicago Press.

Paley, V. (1992). *You can't say you won't be my friend.* Cambridge, Mass.: Harvard University Press.

Phelan, P. (1993). *The unmarked: The politics of performance.* London: Routledge.

Sarup, M. (1993). *An introductory guide to post-structuralism and postmodernism.* Athens, Ga.: Georgia University Press.

Sedgwick, E. (1990). *Epistemology of the closet.* Berkeley: University of California Press.

Stallybrass, P., & White, A. (1986). *The politics and poetics of transgression.* Ithaca: Cornell University Press.

Warner, M. (Ed.). (1993). *Fear of a queer planet: Queer politics and social theory.* Minneapolis: University of Minnesota Press.

Index

About the Contributors

JO AGNEW is Assistant Professor and Chair of Early Intervention and Elementary Interrelated Special Education at Washburn University in Topeka, Kansas. Her experiences in education include Montessori teacher, early interventionist, special education teacher, special education consultant and director, and four years as an assistant professor in special education. Her current research interests center on issues related to early childhood equity.

PAMELA C. BROWNING is Assistant Professor of Education at Lee College where she teaches early childhood methods courses and children's literature. She is a doctoral candidate at the University of Tennessee and is currently conducting dissertation research related to literacy instruction in kindergarten classrooms.

DAVID E. FERNIE is Associate Professor of Early and Middle Childhood Education at Ohio State University. His research interests include children's play and social development, social processes in early childhood classrooms, educational ethnography, and the influence of media on children's lives.

M. ELIZABETH GRAUE is Assistant Professor in the Department of Curriculum & Instruction at the University of Wisconsin, Madison, where she teaches courses in early childhood education and qualitative research methods. She is interested in early childhood policy, assessment practice, and research methodologies. She is the author of *Ready for What? Constructing Meanings of Readiness for Kindergarten* and has published articles in *Early Childhood Research Quarterly, Early Education and Development, Educational Policy*, and *Qualitative Studies in Education*.

J. AMOS HATCH is Associate Professor of Inclusive Early Childhood Education at the University of Tennessee at Knoxville. He has published widely in the areas of children's social behavior, qualitative methods, and educators' perspectives on early childhood theory and practice. He is currently involved with four teachers in a collaborative narrative inquiry into the appropriateness of "Developmentally Appropriate Practice" for inner-city early education settings. He is editor (with Richard Wisniewski) of the *International Journal of Qualitative Studies in Education*.

MARY E. HAUSER is Assistant Professor of Education at Carroll College in Waukesha, Wisconsin. Her research and teaching interests are based in the social context of education and focus primarily on issues related to young children. Her publications include contributions to two current volumes: *Pathways to Cultural Awareness*, edited by George and Louise Spindler; and *Children and Families "At Promise": Reconstructing the Discourse of Risk*, edited by Beth Swadener and Sally Lubeck.

REBECCA KANTOR is Associate Professor of Family Relations and Human Development at Ohio State University where she is also Director of the A. Sophie Rogers Lab School. Her research interests include language, literacy, and social processes in early childhood classrooms; young children's friendships and peer culture; and classroom ethnography.

ROBIN L. LEAVITT, in addition to her experience as a university instructor and researcher, has worked as a caregiver, director, and consultant in day care programs serving infants and toddlers. Her research interests include the daily experiences of children in child care programs, the relationships between families and child care programs, and caregivers' perspectives on their daily work. She is author of *Power and Emotion in Infant-Toddler Day Care* and *Toddler Day Care: A Guide to Responsive Caregiving*. She is currently a postdoctoral research associate in early intervention with the Department of Special Education at the University of Illinois.

SALLY LUBECK is Assistant Professor in the School of Education at the University of Michigan. She teaches courses in early childhood education, the anthropology of education, and qualitative research methods. She has been a Bush Fellow and a Spencer Fellow. Her book, *Sandbox Society: Early Education in Black and White*, received Choice Magazine's Outstanding Academic Book Award in 1987. A new book, *Children and Fam-*

ilies "At Promise": Reconstructing the Discourse of Risk, edited with Beth Swadener, will be published in January, 1995.

MONICA MILLER MARSH has taught preschool, kindergarten, and a fifth-grade, gifted class. She has authored and co-authored several papers and chapters on her collaborative study of antibias education in her kindergarten classroom. She has presented papers at the Ethnography in Education Research Forum, American Educational Research Association, Reconceptualizing Early Childhood Education Conferences, and at two Collaborative Early Childhood Seminars in Nairobi, Kenya.

MARY JO McGEE-BROWN is Assistant Professor in the Department of Educational Psychology at the University of Georgia and teaches qualitative research methods, advanced qualitative data analysis, and research design. She has written chapters in three books on educational evaluation and conducted numerous qualitative evaluations of state-funded innovative educational projects. She is conducting an ongoing ethnography of a National Science Education Reform, Project 2061. Most recently she has written a manual on teacher interpretive inquiry and facilitated teacher research workshops for teachers at the six Project 2061 sites.

MARGARET K. NELSON is Professor of Sociology at Middlebury College. She is author of Negotiated Care: The Experience of Family Day Care Providers. She has also edited (with Emily K. Abel) Circles of Care: Work and Identity in Women's Lives.

MAIKE PHILIPSEN was born and raised in the Federal Republic of Germany. She is Assistant Professor in Foundations of Education at Virginia Commonwealth University. Her areas of specialization are sociology and anthropology of education; race, class, and gender in education; issues of equity; school reform; global education; and qualitative research.

BETH BLUE SWADENER is Associate Professor of Early Childhood Education at Kent State University. Her teaching and research focus on social policy, antibias and inclusive early education, qualitative research, and pre-primary education in African nations. Previous publications include Reconceptualizing the Early Childhood Curriculum: Beginning the Dialogue (edited with Shirley Kessler) and Children and Families "At Promise": Reconstructing the Discourse of Risk (edited with Sally Lubeck). She is also active in anti-oppression work and collaborative research with teachers in urban schools. She was recently awarded a Fullbright African Regional Research Grant to study family involvement in early childhood education in Kenya, Tanzania, and Uganda.

JOSEPH TOBIN is Associate Professor in the University of Hawaii's College of Education and Center for Youth Research. Among his publications are Preschool in Three Cultures: Japan, China, and the United States

(1989) and several papers on early childhood education in Japan and qualitative research issues. He is currently studying children's understanding of media and adult beliefs about early childhood sexuality.

DANIEL J. WALSH is Associate Professor of Early Childhood Education in the Department of Curriculum and Instruction at the University of Illinois at Urbana-Champaign. He teaches courses in child development, qualitative research on children, and advanced qualitative inquiry. He has published in various journals and edited volumes including *Reading Research Quarterly, Early Childhood Research Quarterly, Journal of Curriculum Studies, Teachers College Record, Educational Evaluation and Policy Analysis, Handbook of Research on the Education of Young Children*, and *Psychological Bulletin*.

KIMBERLEE L. WHALEY is Assistant Professor in Family Relations and Human Development at Ohio State University. She is also Coordinator of the A. Sophie Rogers Infant-Toddler Lab School. Her research interests and publications address the social development of infants and toddlers, particularly those in group care settings. Her most recent work examines the social relationships formed among peers in these settings.

ISBN 0-275-94921-4

9 780275 949211

HARDCOVER BAR CODE